LITERATURE AND THE POLITICS OF POST-VICTORIAN DECADENCE

In *Literature and the Politics of Post-Victorian Decadence*, Kristin Mahoney argues that the specters of the fin de siècle exercised a remarkable draw on the British cultural imagination well into the twentieth century. These authors and artists refused to assimilate to the aesthetic and political ethos of the era, representing themselves instead as time travelers from the previous century for whom twentieth-century modernity was both baffling and disappointing. However, they did not turn entirely from the modern moment but rather relied on Decadent strategies to participate in conversations concerning the most highly vexed issues of the period, including war, the rise of the Labour Party, the question of women's sexual freedom, and changing conceptions of sexual and gender identities.

KRISTIN MAHONEY is associate professor of English at Western Washington University. She is the editor of a scholarly edition of Baron Corvo's *Hubert's Arthur*, and her articles have appeared in such journals as *Victorian Studies*, *Criticism*, *English Literature in Transition*, and *Victorian Periodicals Review*.

LITERATURE AND THE POLITICS OF POST-VICTORIAN DECADENCE

KRISTIN MAHONEY

Western Washington University

CAMBRIDGE
UNIVERSITY PRESS

CAMBRIDGE
UNIVERSITY PRESS

32 Avenue of the Americas, New York, NY 10013-2473, USA

Cambridge University Press is part of the University of Cambridge.

It furthers the University's mission by disseminating knowledge in the pursuit of education, learning, and research at the highest international levels of excellence.

www.cambridge.org
Information on this title: www.cambridge.org/9781107109742

First published 2015

Printed in Great Britain by Clays Ltd, St Ives plc

A catalog record for this publication is available from the British Library.

Library of Congress Cataloging in Publication Data
Mahoney, Kristin.
Literature and the Politics of Post-Victorian Decadence / Kristin Mahoney, Western Washington University.
pages cm
Includes bibliographical references and index.
ISBN 978-1-107-10974-2 (hardback)
1. English literature – 20th century – History and criticism. 2. Decadence (Literary movement) – Great Britain. 3. Modernism (Aesthetics) – Great Britain. 4. Modernism (Literature) – Great Britain. 5. Politics and literature – Great Britain – History – 20th century. I. Title.
PR478.D43M34 2015
820.9'0091–dc23 2015003343

ISBN 978-1-107-10974-2 Hardback

Contents

List of Illustrations

Acknowledgments

This book is a product of the tremendous generosity of the people within the field of Victorian aestheticism and Decadence. It emerges from the thinking I began to do as a graduate student at the University of Notre Dame, and the conversations I have been having with my dissertation director, Kathy Psomiades, for the past fifteen years are present on almost every page of this manuscript. Richard Dellamora took an interest in the project at an early stage, and the thought-provoking discussions I have been having with him for the past decade have consistently led my thinking in new directions. My argument took shape at a National Endowment for the Humanities seminar at the William Andrews Clark Memorial Library organized by Joseph Bristow, and his insights and the community that he fostered at this seminar truly formed the foundation for this project. Every participant in the seminar has informed my thinking in some way, but I am particularly indebted to Diana Maltz, whose thoughtful feedback and friendship have been absolutely invaluable to me; Brooke Cameron, who has similarly provided unflagging enthusiasm and support; and Emily Harrington, Simon Joyce, and So Young Park. Through the seminar, I met Mark Samuels Lasner, whose knowledge informs so much of what I have written. I have also benefited in countless ways from the warmth and kindness of the broader community of scholars interested in aestheticism and Decadence, including Ellen Crowell, Dennis Denisoff, Neil Hultgren, Alex Murray, Andrea Wolk Rager, and Vincent Sherry, and from the wider community of Victorian studies scholars, including Tanya Agathocleous, Genie Babb, Julie Codell, Kristen Guest, Nathan Hensley, Mary Elizabeth Leighton, Sara Maurer, Anne Stiles, Lisa Surridge, Chris Vanden Bossche, and Athena Vrettos. Anna Jones was one of my most challenging and helpful readers. I am also grateful for the feedback I received while presenting chapters from this project at conferences organized by the North American Victorian Studies Association, the Victorian Interdisciplinary Studies

Association of the Western United States, and the Victorian Studies Association of Western Canada.

I would like to thank Ray Ryan and the editorial team at Cambridge University Press, who were patient, efficient, and helpful during every step of the process. Margaret Stetz and an anonymous reader for Cambridge University Press provided incredibly insightful and helpful feedback on the manuscript.

It would have been impossible to do this work without the financial support that I received from the Office of the Dean of the College of Humanities and Social Sciences and the Office of Research and Sponsored Programs at my home institution, Western Washington University, and Marc Geisler was instrumental in helping me to secure this funding. The project was also supported by a research grant from the Paul Mellon Centre for Studies of British Art and by a Pre-Raphaelite Studies Fellowship from the University of Delaware and the Delaware Art Museum. I completed the final revisions to the manuscript while being supported by an Andrew W. Mellon Foundation Research Fellowship at the Harry Ransom Center at the University of Texas.

Adrian Woodhouse was kind enough to grant me access to his private collection of materials related to Beresford Egan. His guidance influenced my thinking about Egan in countless ways. I am also grateful to Julia Walworth and the Warden and Fellows of Merton College Oxford; Alyson Price at the British Institute of Florence; and the librarians and staff at the University of Delaware Special Collections, the Mark Samuels Lasner Collection, the Delaware Art Museum, UCLA's William Andrews Clark Memorial Library, the University of Reading Special Collections, the Shakespeare Centre Library and Archive, the National Library of Ireland, Columbia University's Rare Book and Manuscript Library, Pennsylvania State University's Eberly Family Special Collections Library, and the BBC Written Archive.

Chapter 2 previously appeared in *English Literature in Transition* 56, no. 3 (2013): 313–32 and is reprinted with permission. For permission to reproduce artworks, I would like to acknowledge the Estate of Max Beerbohm, the Estate of Beresford Egan, and the Estate of Vanessa Bell. For permission to quote lines of poetry, I would like to thank the Estate of Beresford Egan and the Estate of P. R. Stephensen. For permission to quote unpublished copyrighted material, I would like to thank the Estate of Max Beerbohm and the Estate of Augustus Edwin John/Bridgeman Images. BBC copyrighted material is reproduced courtesy of the British Broadcasting Corporation. All rights reserved. I would also like to thank the National Library of Ireland and Pennsylvania State University's Eberly Family Special Collections Library for permission to quote from archival materials.

I am so thankful for the support I have received from everyone in the English Department at Western Washington University. Bill Smith has been at once the kindest and most incisive reader. Brenda Miller and Lysa Rivera have been supportive colleagues and wonderful friends. I am grateful to my new colleague Christopher Loar for providing feedback at the eleventh hour. Finally, I would like to thank the wide network of friends and family who gave me the energy to complete this project. My parents and siblings modeled tough and funny responses to difficulty. Brian Whitener modeled an endless inquisitiveness about culture. Niki Bhattacharya, Lee and Ed Gulyas, Tara Samat, Gabe Viles, Marcus Aurin, Max Harless, Allison Whitney, Jessica Spivey, Rich Brown, and Kendall Dodd have been my community. Most of all, this work is about the time I have spent thinking and talking with Kaveh Askari. I thank him for his comradeship and his curiosity.

Introduction
The Fighting Nineties: The Age of the Critical Function

In December 1928, the Leicester Galleries hosted an exhibition of the works of Max Beerbohm titled "Ghosts." The exhibition included caricatures of Oscar Wilde, Lord Queensberry, John Lane, Walter Pater, Henry Harland, and Aubrey Beardsley. In the exhibition catalog, Beerbohm characteristically apologizes for his own anachronism, feigning embarrassment at the irrelevance of his work to the modern moment. He lives in Italy now, he notes, and it's very hard to keep up: "So very many people with faces and figures unknown to me have meanwhile become famous that I have abandoned all hope of being 'topical.'"[1] Nevertheless, he suggests that perhaps the visitors to the gallery won't mind "looking at some people who flourished in past days."[2] He first addresses his fellow specters from the Victorian era: "Those of you who are as old as – or almost (and even that is saying much) as old as I – will perhaps like to have the chords of memory struck by the drawings on these walls."[3] But he continues to suggest that "even the young . . . may conceivably feel a slight thrill" while contemplating the "ghosts" in the gallery.[4] "I have noticed," he writes, "that the young in this era have what those in my own era hadn't: a not unfriendly interest in the more or less immediate past."[5]

This "not unfriendly interest" in the late-Victorian period had been on the rise since the publication of Holbrook Jackson's well-received *The Eighteen-Nineties* in 1913. In fact, Beerbohm's caricature of a few years earlier, his well-known *Some Persons of "the Nineties,"* speaks directly to this revival of interest in the literary figures of the fin de siècle (Figure I.1). While we often turn to this image now out of interest in the figures represented, the topic of this work is not the 1890s per se but the attraction they held for the critics of the 1910s and 1920s. The full caption reads, "Some Persons of 'the Nineties' Little imagining, despite their Proper Pride and their Ornamental Aspect, how much they will interest Mr. Holbrook Jackson and Mr. Osbert Burdett."[6] Burdett's *The Beardsley*

Figure I.1. Max Beerbohm, *Some Persons of "the Nineties,"* from *Observations*, 1925. Left to right: Richard Le Gallienne, Walter Sickert, Arthur Symons, George Moore, Henry Harland, John Davidson, Charles Conder, Oscar Wilde, Will Rothenstein, Max Beerbohm, W. B. Yeats, Aubrey Beardsley, and Enoch Soames. © Estate of Max Beerbohm. Reproduced courtesy of the Harry Ransom Center, University of Texas at Austin.

Period, which appeared in 1925, and Jackson's *The Eighteen-Nineties* presumably stand in here for a whole host of critical texts on the fin de siècle that appeared in the 1910s and 1920s, such as W. G. Blaikie-Murdock's *The Renaissance of the Nineties* (1911), Arthur Ransome's *Oscar Wilde: A Critical Study* (1913), Elizabeth Pennell's *Nights: Rome and Venice in the Aesthetic Eighties, London and Paris in the Fighting Nineties* (1916), Bernard Muddiman's *The Men of the Nineties* (1920), Bohun Lynch's *Max Beerbohm in Perspective* (1921), Joseph Pennell's *Aubrey Beardsley and the Other Men of the Nineties* (1924), and Richard Le Gallienne's *The Romantic Nineties* (1925), to name a few. Even the excessively proud dandies of the fin de siècle might have been surprised, Beerbohm suggests, by the alacrity with which future generations set about canonizing their set.

As the title of Beerbohm's exhibition suggests, the specter of the 1890s truly haunted the early twentieth century. In this book, I investigate what it was about the fin de siècle that seemed so appealing and so useful during the early twentieth century, and I focus in particular on the turn to late-Victorian Decadence in the literature and art of the period. In his *Men of the Nineties*, Bernard Muddiman refers to the decade as the "age of the critical function."[7] Many of the authors and artists on whom I focus were drawn to the "critical function" of Decadence. The rebellious spirit of critique associated with this movement operated as a model of enthusiasm that remained at the same time skeptical and apart, which, in its immunity to unthinking loyalties or allegiances, retained the capacity for clear perception. Practicing Decadence at a historical distance compounded its detachment and its capacity for critique. For many practitioners of post-Victorian Decadence, reinvigorating a past aesthetic operated as a method for subtly communicating distaste for the methods and values of the present. During the early decades of the twentieth century, surviving members of the late-Victorian Decadent Movement highlighted their connections to the fin de siècle, and younger men and women revived late-Victorian aesthetic practices or organized communities around the appreciation of late-Victorian figures. Affiliating themselves with the fin de siècle seemed to promise refined insight into the politics and problems besetting the initial decades of the twentieth century. Meditating on the late-Victorian period, bringing the period's practices to bear on the present, yielded insulation from the modern moment, an illuminating point of comparison, and critical detachment from the contemporary. The critical function of Decadence was, it seems, multiplied and reinforced in the twentieth century.

Attending to the presence of post-Victorian Decadence in what we consider to be the modernist period allows us to see yesterday's avant-garde in the process of becoming an old guard, an aesthetic in its twilight coming to an understanding of the peculiar kinds of cultural critique that this temporally marginal position enables. The authors and artists on whom this study focuses posited themselves as out of place and of the past, as marginal or outsider figures for whom twentieth-century modernity was tremendously disappointing. However, they did not turn entirely from the present. They relied on aestheticist and Decadent strategies to respond to the political problems of the period. Post-Victorian Decadents wrote, thought, and drew alongside the modernists, but they carefully positioned themselves as separate from the energies and appetites of the twentieth century. They stubbornly insisted on their own disconnectedness from the era, representing themselves as late-Victorian time travelers, while continuing to play a vital and important role in the intellectual and political culture of the 1910s, 1920s, 1930s, and 1940s.

Although I have chosen to use the term *Decadent* to describe the set of authors and artists with whom I am dealing, I do so with an acute sense of the limitations associated with that term. Early-twentieth-century critics interested in the 1890s were extremely hesitant to use the term because of its negative connotations, and the majority of the figures under discussion here are slippery, skeptical individuals who would have hesitated to identify themselves with any one movement in particular. In addition, the term *Decadence* has proven itself notoriously difficult to define. The "fuzziness" of the term, as Jonathan Freedman has argued, "exceeds that of even 'aestheticism' itself."[8] As Matthew Potolsky notes, Decadence "never adumbrated a single, unified doctrine," and the figures and practices we have come to identify with Decadence are incredibly diverse.[9] This project, in fact, foregrounds the political and aesthetic diversity of Decadence, acknowledging that it offered progressive models of cosmopolitanism and sexual dissidence while at the same time often reinforcing an aristocratic ethos or disseminating troubling ideas about self-sacrifice. Furthermore, as I emphasize, Decadence could look very different when practiced with an Irish inflection or at a South African remove. It would perhaps be more appropriate to refer to Decadence as a loosely connected set of aesthetic practices and political postures rather than as a wholly unified or clearly demarcated movement.

Nevertheless, I have chosen to deploy the term to designate the later phase of aestheticism, the aestheticism of the 1890s, and the individuals and practices associated with that later phase of aestheticism, such as Max Beerbohm, Vernon Lee, Oscar Wilde, Baron Corvo, the Yeats of the fin de siècle, Aubrey Beardsley, the Yellow Book circle, dandyism, camp aesthetics, and detachment. I find the term useful to describe figures who were linked in the cultural imagination to the fin de siècle and who, moreover, advertised and reinforced that sense of association between themselves and the aestheticism of the Yellow Nineties. Their work extended beyond the boundaries of the late-Victorian period while constantly recalling and referencing their connections with that period. I am using the term strategically to unite a set of figures associated with a particular, late-nineteenth-century moment in the history of aestheticism while at the same time calling attention to the fact that these figures continued to play a prominent role in the cultural landscape of the early twentieth century. My reliance on the term to reference a distinct period in the history of aestheticism might in that sense seem contradictory. However, I wish to make the point that the aestheticism of the 1890s performed a specific set of functions in the 1910s, 1920s, and 1930s. It was the aestheticism of the fin de siècle, what we might refer to as "Decadent aestheticism," that seemed at once exotic and within reach during the early twentieth century, close enough that it might still be contacted or that its spirits might still walk the earth. With this in mind, I use the term to at once make note of and undo Decadence's association with a specific moment in time, and, while I deploy the term, I do so with an awareness of its murkiness and with the desire to further diversify the range of practices and figures we might refer to as Decadent.

Post-Victorian writers and painters often turned to Decadence in the hopes of finding an antidote to the chauvinism of wartime and the despair of the interwar period. Decadent satire and cosmopolitan aestheticism presented artists with appealing alternatives to jingoistic enthusiasms, enthusiasms lacking the critical function altogether. Many post-Victorian Decadents foregrounded their connections to the previous century to signal their dissatisfaction with the escalating militarism and aggression of the period, and they used anachronistic, "outmoded" late-Victorian aesthetic strategies to fashion a peculiar political voice that was at once highly engaged and purposefully marginal. Vernon Lee's Paterian critique of jingoistic biosociology in the years following World War I and Max Beerbohm's dandyish radio broadcasts during World War II relied on a sense of connectedness to the late-Victorian past to theorize a way out of early-twentieth-century violence. However, although post-Victorian Decadence was certainly useful in revising conceptions of international conflict and national identity, this was only one of the many ways in which late-Victorian aesthetics and ideas were implemented during the early twentieth century. The revival of the 1890s facilitated responses to most of the highly vexed issues of the period, allowing authors and artists to intervene in debates about war, jingoism, and pacifism as well as conversations concerning the rise of Labour, the question of women's sexual freedom, and changing conceptions of sexual and gender identities. Post-Victorian Decadents brought to these debates a uniquely anachronistic yet distinctly modern perspective, drawing on the thinking of their fin-de-siècle peers and precursors to craft a peculiarly late-Victorian set of responses to a distinctly non-Victorian set of historical conditions.

I. The Boom in Yellow: The Fin de Siècle at the Debut de Siècle

Conventional visions of periodization along with modernist dismissals of the fin de siècle have obscured from view the persistence of Decadence in the twentieth century. By 1914, Wyndham Lewis was insisting that Decadence had been *BLAST*ed into the past and rendered passé by the emergence of new avant-gardes. Archival evidence tells a different story, revealing that Decadence remained vibrant and visible throughout the modernist moment. The specters of the Yellow Nineties haunted the theaters, the galleries, the bookstalls, the cinemas, and the airwaves, operating as a divergent strain of modernism that exercised a remarkable draw on the twentieth-century cultural imagination.

Wilde in particular seemed like he might reappear at any second. The *Los Angeles Times* devoted a full page to sightings of Wilde on the West Coast in 1908, and in 1913, Arthur Cravan, Wilde's nephew, published a posthumous interview with his uncle in his Surrealist magazine *Maintenant*.[10] In 1913, a *New York Times* correspondent investigated the rumors that Wilde was still alive and determined that "no one is now in Paris who saw Wilde dead."[11] In 1918, the "Cult of the Clitoris" trial demonstrated clearly Wilde's continuing capacity to cause a stir from beyond the grave. The dancer Maud Allan had contracted to appear in private performances of *Salome* (1891) at J. T. Grein's Independent Theatre, and news of the performances attracted the ire of the conservative politician Noel Pemberton Billing. Billing believed that Germans, wishing to "[exterminate] the race" by introducing homosexual practices, were blackmailing forty-seven thousand "British perverts" and exerting dangerous influence over England in wartime. He accused Allan of being an associate of the conspirators and a member of the "Cult of the Clitoris," "implying that she was a lesbian and that her performance in Wilde's play would promote sexual perversion among its vulnerable wartime audience, thereby opening 'fruitful fields for espionage.'"[12] Allan in turn sued Billing for libel. The case attracted a great deal of publicity and even drew Lord Alfred Douglas to the stand to testify in support of Billing. Jodie Medd refers to the case as "perhaps the most sensational scandal in Britain during World War I."[13] One of the period's most alarming and salacious scandals centered around a play from the fin de siècle, a piece of Decadent drama that seemed capable of endangering national security, demonstrating how much Wilde maintained his ability to disrupt and scandalize in the early twentieth century.

While in the eyes of Billing, Wilde's ghost posed a threat to national security, he was also a source of cultural capital for the burgeoning film industry. Numerous prestige productions of Wilde's work appeared in the 1910s as part of the film industry's efforts to legitimize cinema by linking it to literature and theatre. Philips Smalley's 1913 production of *The Picture of Dorian Gray* (1891), for example, was written by Lois Weber, a woman film pioneer who went on to play a significant role in Universal's prestige productions. The "aesthetic" qualities of Wilde's work could apparently endow the emergent realm of cinema with high-art aura. More high-profile and heavily marketed adaptations of Wilde's plays premiered in the 1920s. Ernst Lubitsch's 1925 adaptation of *Lady Windermere's Fan* (1893) was greeted with tremendous enthusiasm. This reception was certainly a reflection of Lubitsch's bankable reputation, as indicated by the *New York Sun*'s description of the work as a "directorial triumph."[14] However, Wilde's reputation also played a significant role in the warm reception of the film. The *New York American* described the film as "brilliant with little darting shafts of wit, almost as piercing as the words of Oscar Wilde."[15] A review in the *Los Angeles Times* noted that Wilde's "epigrams have retained their magnetic sparkle even today, though the plays were written before the close of the Victorian era."[16] This is not to say that Hollywood disregarded Wilde's sexual dissidence and his capacity to generate scandal. Nazimova's production of *Salomé* with its Beardsleyesque costumes and set design appeared in 1923, and United Artists marketed the film as "an orgy of sex and sin," while *Photoplay* warned audiences that the movie was "bizarre."[17] Wilde's recently rehabilitated reputation as a significant literary figure made his work attractive to a medium in pursuit of legitimacy, but his capacity to shock had just as much to do with his appeal to Hollywood directors and producers.

It was not only Wilde's ghost that continued to walk the earth. In addition to Max Beerbohm's series of well-received exhibits at the Leicester Galleries in the 1920s, which either satisfied or provoked the escalating desire for late Victoriana, and Vernon Lee's persistent presence in public intellectual discourse into the 1930s, Ada Leverson continued to publish novels populated with male and female dandies and peppered with Wildean aphorisms during the 1900s and 1910s. Leverson had first made a name for herself in the 1890s publishing short fiction, sketches, and parodies of aestheticism in periodicals such as *Punch* and the *Yellow Book*.[18] She was close friends with Beerbohm and was a particularly loyal friend to Wilde, and the work that brought her recognition during the late nineteenth century is very much in conversation with theirs. However, while Leverson's aesthetic is definitively fin de siècle, she reached the height of her popularity with a series of novels that appeared in the early twentieth century. Leverson's novels advertise themselves clearly as poised between two periods, inflected by Decadent style while well aware of more recent aesthetic developments. The characters themselves seem to hover between the Victorian and the modern. Edith Ottley, who appears in *Love's Shadow* (1908), *Tenterhooks* (1912), and *Love at Second Sight* (1916), is said by some people to be "like a Sargent, others called her a post-impressionist type."[19] While Edith's close friend Vincy Wenham Vincy is clearly a dandy or "what used to be called an exquisite," he has "in art an extraordinary taste for brutality and violence, and his rooms were covered with pictures by Futurists and Cubists, wild studies by wild men from Tahiti and a curious collection of savage ornaments and weapons."[20] Vincy was inspired by a close friend of Wilde's and Leverson's, Reggie Turner, and he reads as a remnant of the 1890s, yet he greets the coming of the modern with enthusiasm, lending Edith copies of *Rhythm* to "convert her to Post-Impressionism."[21] Leverson's novels reveal Decadent figures thriving in the post-Victorian period, able and willing to engage with modernism, while at the same time exhibiting a continued preference for the refinement and wit of the previous age. In discussing the Futurists, Aylmer Ross, Edith's beloved, notes, "I prefer the pose of depression and pessimism to that of bullying and high spirits. When the affected young poet pretended to be used up and worn out, one knew there was vitality under it all. But when I see a cheerful young man shrieking about how full of life he is, banging on a drum, and blowing on a tin trumpet, and speaking of his good spirits, it depresses me."[22] He concludes that "the modern poseurs aren't so good as the old ones. Odle is not so clever as Beardsley."[23] Leverson's novels as well as the characters within them take pains to indicate their awareness of contemporary artistic trends while continuing to pay tribute to the recent, fin-de-siècle past. Her works of the early twentieth century reveal a world in which Decadence and modernism thrive simultaneously as equally vital and viable aesthetic choices.

The artist and book designer Charles Ricketts, who had illustrated Wilde's works in the 1890s, similarly kept Decadence before the twentieth-century public eye in his designs for the stage. Although Kenneth Clark referred to him as the "quintessence of the nineties," and he considered himself a "post-Raphaelite," Ricketts had a vibrant and successful career as a stage designer for three decades after the century turned.[24] Ricketts's costume designs, with their exaggerated silhouettes and intricate patterns, resemble Beardsley illustrations decorated with a Decadent palette of rich and highly symbolic color. In 1906, the Literary Theatre Society staged

Wilde's *Salome* along with *A Florentine Tragedy*, and the synopsis of dresses Ricketts designed for *Salome* reads like a piece of Decadent verse:

Salome, dressed in a mist rising by moonlight, with a train of blue and black moths.
Herodias, in a peacock train of Dahlias and a horned tiara.
Herod, is robed in silver and blue lined with flame decorated with griffons, sphinxes and angels.
The scene is all blue on blue.[25]

Roger Fry's response to the production indicates that Ricketts's designs spoke successfully across the Victorian/modern divide: "C. Ricketts did the staging with ideas of colour that surpassed belief. I've never seen anything so beautiful on the stage."[26] Into the 1910s and 1920s, Ricketts continued to inflect his costume and set designs with Decadent imagery, peacock feathers and jewels, exposed flesh and elaborate headdresses, and he worked with some of the most innovative twentieth-century playwrights, designing for Yeats and Synge and Shaw, bringing to his productions of the "new" drama of the twentieth century an opulent, fin-de-siècle sensibility.

Figures such as Leverson and Ricketts ensured that Decadence remained a vital part of the cultural conversation in the early twentieth century, but for those who could no longer speak for themselves, a new generation of post-Victorian dandies operated as advocates and representatives, reanimating the aesthetic of the Yellow Nineties for the 1920s. Harold Acton and Brian Howard drew on the Decadence of the fin de siècle as they developed their own modernist mode of dandyism, first at Eton, and then at Oxford. At Eton, they established the Cremorne Club and drew up a manifesto stating, "Life is an Art, and is to be encountered with a buttonhole of flowers. Members of the Cremorne Club must believe in the interpretation and appreciation of life as evolved in 1890."[27] Honorary members of the club included Beardsley, Wilde, Symons, and Beerbohm. Although, as Martin Green notes, Acton and Howard often made scornful remarks about the dandies of the fin de siècle, whom they felt had been defeated, they also "knew that they were the children of the 90s."[28] Their very public performances of dandyism and Decadence at Oxford, at events organized by the Sitwells, and in the pages of the new "little magazines" ensured that the 1890s remained a part of avant-garde conversation during the 1920s.

Of all the post-Victorian dandies, however, Ronald Firbank was the most excessive in his performance of a Decadent persona. As Martin Green notes,

Osbert Sitwell first began to notice Firbank in 1912 at ballets, concerts, and exhibits, "a very odd-looking man . . . who giggled and hid his painted face behind his hand, talked in a high-pitched voice, and tripped along as if hoping to disappear."[29] Like Acton and Howard, Firbank announced and advertised his affiliation with the Yellow Nineties at Oxford and at the Sitwells' parties, and he sought out surviving remnants of the 1890s, corresponding with Lord Alfred Douglas, befriending Wilde's son Vyvyan Holland at Oxford, and requesting from Holland in turn an introduction to Ada Leverson. (This first engagement did not go well. Leverson did not answer the doorbell when they arrived for the appointment, and Firbank decided she must have seen through the window and disliked the mauve pants he put on for her. He consequently cut the pants into pieces and threw them into the fire.[30]) His fascination with the fin de siècle registers clearly in the unique and challenging style of his works, in which modernist obscurity and innovation are integrated with the purple prose of aestheticism. As Brigid Brophy states, "Firbank's writings are studded with images from Wilde's: frequent wayside shrines, at which Firbank's genuflections in passing continually placed him again under the protection of his literary saint."[31] This practice of returning to, rethinking, and revising Wilde is evident, as Brophy argues, in one of his earliest, posthumously published works, *The Artificial Princess* (1934), which reworks the Salome theme; in the title of *Inclinations* (1916), which mischievously modifies the title of Wilde's *Intentions*; and, as Joseph Bristow has asserted, in the Wildean figure of Reggie Quintus in *The Princess Zoubaroff* (1926).[32] The echo of Wilde's voice is heard in the weary aphorisms articulated by the jaded women who inhabit his novels and, as Richard Canning notes, in Charlie Mouth's declaration of butterflies, much as Wilde had declared only his genius, on passing through customs in *Sorrow in Sunlight* (1924).[33] E. M. Forster characterized Firbank's backward-glancing aesthetic as a form of "literary conservatism," arguing that "there is nothing up-to-date in him. He is *fin de siècle*, as it used to be called; he belongs to the 'nineties and the *Yellow Book*; his mind inherits the furniture and his prose the cadences of Aubrey Beardsley's *Under the Hill*."[34] However, rather than simply operating as a retreat from the modern moment, Decadence is so exaggerated and amplified in Firbank's novels that it becomes a type of modernism. He also exaggerated the sexual dissidence of the 1890s, as Bristow argues, "modernizing Wilde, making works such as *Salomé* much queerer than they had ever been before."[35] Firbank's works throw all notions of stable gender identities, normative desire, and conventional domesticity into chaos. Marriages are quickly and easily dissolved, infants are sent away to school, women are absorbed into queer religious communities, priests pursue young boys, and torture is discussed with frank enthusiasm. What is suggested at in Wilde and Beardsley becomes explicit and farcical in Firbank, and the resultant works are avant-garde in terms of their content as much as their form. Firbank's novels represent a strain of modernist practice that kept the fin de siècle alive, well, and central to contemporary aesthetic discourse in the early decades of the twentieth century.[36]

Post-Victorian dandyism and the renewed interest in the styles and postures of the fin de siècle were not confined to England. As Kirsten MacLeod has recently argued, figures like Carl Van Vechten transmitted this enthusiasm for the Yellow Nineties across the Atlantic, developing a "Decadence for the jazz age," which, in Van Vechten's eyes, compounded the strangeness of the original movement: "To be 1890 in 1890 might be considered almost normal. To be 1890 in 1922 might be considered almost queer. There is a difference, however. The colour is magenta. Oscar's hue was green. The fun is warmer; the vice is more léger."[37] Alex Murray's recent work demonstrates that a lengthy and complicated refashioning of Decadence took place in Manhattan over a forty-year period and was expressed most clearly in landscape writing that centered on industrial lighting, skyscrapers, and motorcars and positioned itself at the tension between new and old, generating a Decadence that was simultaneously nostalgic and future oriented.[38] David Weir's work on Decadent culture in the United States reveals that the *Yellow Book* aesthetic had a rich afterlife in North America during the 1910s and 1920s and was intimately bound up with the concept of new or "modern" culture.[39] Post-Victorian Decadence was a truly transnational affair.

Post-Victorian dandies on both sides of the Atlantic curated collections and events that allowed for continued contact with the immediate past. The American book publishers Albert Boni and Horace Liveright, for example, "relied almost exclusively on fin-de-siècle authors" for the first year of business of their Modern Library imprint (1917).[40] Across the Atlantic, A. J. A. Symons published *An Anthology of Nineties Verse* (1928) with Elkin Mathews, a volume resembling a copy of the *Yellow Book* with a Beardsley design on its striking yellow cover. Symons resurrected the outrageous periodical and, like Boni and Liveright, brought an aesthetic only recently deceased back to life. In his introduction to the collection, he acknowledges the peculiarity of his shortsighted taste for the past, stating that the poetry of the period resembles "elderly furniture that has not yet attained the prestige of antiquity."[41] However, he celebrates those readers capable of appreciating the elderly as opposed to the antique, readers whose vision focuses on the middle distance, at a moment only recently past: "To those whose reading does not end with Wordsworth or begin with Joyce, who retain what Pater called a 'sweet depravity of ear,' the poetry of the 'nineties, within its self-imposed and unstrained limits, offers many and varied savours and essences."[42] The following year, Symons further cultivated this taste for the middle distance by founding the Corvine Society, which celebrated the "strangest artificial orchid of the Nineties," Baron Corvo, with a pair of elaborate banquets, the second of which was attended by Wyndham Lewis, one of the most vociferous detractors of the Yellow Nineties aesthetic.[43]

The presence of figures such as Lewis at events like the Corvine Society banquets suggests that the modernists' professed distaste for or disinterest in the fin de siècle must have been little more than a pose. Or perhaps it was a rebuttal, an anxious response to the ongoing touting of that period's power and allure. In any case, while speaking so aggressively of their desire to make things new, many modernists actively pursued contact with things slightly old, with the figures who had survived the 1890s and the literary remains of those who had not. Lewis sat at a table with Oscar Wilde's son Vyvyan Holland to pay tribute to the most Decadent of Decadent writers.[44] Max Beerbohm's visitors' book indicates that he received Ezra Pound, T. S. Eliot, and Ernest Hemingway at his home in Rapallo.[45] Though the Yellow Nineties awaited them at every turn, on the screen, on the stage, at exhibitions, on the pages of the little magazines, the most avowedly modern of the moderns seem to have purposefully sought out further knowledge of their immediate precursors, begrudgingly paying homage to an aesthetic that refused to fade into the past.

The immense amount of criticism on the literature and art of the 1890s produced during the early twentieth century illuminates the nature of the attraction that the period held for authors and artists in the 1910s, 1920s, and 1930s. The Yellow Nineties were celebrated by twentieth-century critics as a moment of rebellion, critique, and rebirth. Elizabeth Pennell, an American writer who lived in London during the 1890s and frequently hosted salons attended by Wilde, Beerbohm, and Beardsley, referred to the period as the "Fighting Nineties," for, she argues, "people . . . were much more awake in the Nineties, much more alive, much more keen about everything, even a fight, or above all a fight." It was a period "of insurrection, of vigorous warfare," when "the incident, or work, or publication that roused any interest at all was the signal of the clash of arms, for the row and the rush."[46] Critics in the early twentieth century turned to the Decadent "critical function" as a font of rebirth and hope, expressing sincere admiration for the Decadents' oppositional stance, their antagonism and critical capacity, their earnest desire to remake the world and experience. The Decadent poet Richard Le Gallienne, looking back to *The Romantic Nineties* in 1925, refers to the final years of the nineteenth century as "romantic" "because their representative writers and artists emphasized the modern determination to escape from the deadening thralldom of materialism and outworn conventions, and to live life significantly keenly and beautifully, personally and, if need be, daringly; to win from it its fullest satisfactions, its deepest and richest and most exhilarating experiences. The will to romance: that, in a phrase, was the motive philosophy of the '90s."[47] The Decadents' will to romance must, according to Le Gallienne, be understood in relationship to their critical spirit, their oppositional relationship to their own present. In *The Beardsley Period*, the literary critic Osbert Burdett celebrates the emphasis on perception in the works of the 1890s, for, he argues, it is the "blunting of [modern] faculties" that facilitates acquiescence to brutality and commercialism. Were modern Europeans alive at every moment to the world around them, forever "courting new impressions" in the manner endorsed by Pater, they would perceive injustice, and their capacity for protest and revolt would be vitalized.[48] He speaks longingly of the "disillusion" he associates with the 1890s, an attitude that for him "implies a conscience that is still sensitive," but disillusion, he argues, is "out of date" and "has been replaced by indifference."[49] In celebrating disillusion, Burdett foregrounds the apartness and aloofness that is so central to the Decadent stance, and he makes the political significance of this apartness explicit in the opening of *The Beardsley Period* when he describes the scene of the 1890s as "not local or patriotic but cosmopolitan."[50]

In the eyes of many critics who were drawn to the fin de siècle during the interwar period, the Yellow Nineties represented a promising model of cosmopolitan detachment.[51] While Amanda Anderson has demonstrated that throughout the nineteenth century, British authors tested the "progressive potentiality" of distancing oneself from one's community, from one's nation, or from objects of study, she also argues that this ideal was radicalized at the end of the century by Oscar Wilde: "Wilde seeks to protect the process of thinking that he associates with self-consciousness or criticism from any constraint, limit, determination. . . . In being so freed, thought is also released from the limitations of any given viewpoint and ascends to the realm of disinterestedness, which is also, paradoxically, the realm of unfettered self-realization, or individuality."[52] This constitutes a radicalization of Arnold's ideal critical stance, according to Anderson, because Wilde has conflated disinterestedness with radical freedom and the conditions for the fullest possible self-expression. In a sense, however, Pater himself radicalized Arnold's ideal of disinterestedness, celebrating personal pleasure and subjective response while simultaneously endorsing a hyperkinetic detachment from any philosophy, school of thought, or creed that might delimit the subject's perception. "How," Pater asks, "may we see in [every pulse of our experience] all that is to be seen in them by the finest senses? How shall we pass most swiftly from point to point, and be present always at the focus where the greatest number of vital forces unite in their purest energy?"[53] We must, according to Pater, avoid forming habits, reject facile orthodoxies, and eschew any belief system that might limit our capacity for perception. Detachment almost paradoxically enables the finest and most thorough absorption, the ability to immerse oneself fully in refined and unfettered perception. This hyperkinetic detachment became a central element of late-Victorian Decadence, contributing to the development of the "critical function" in the work of the men of the Beardsley period, and it was this sense of detachment that Beerbohm celebrated in his obituary for Beardsley, in a passage that Lawrence Danson insists must be understood as somewhat self-referential. According to Beerbohm, Beardsley had always remained "rather remote, rather detached from ordinary conditions, a kind of independent spectator. . . . This kind of aloofness has been noted in all great artists. . . . It is because they stand at a little distance that they can see so much."[54] Exhausted and exasperated critics writing during the interwar period often turned to the Yellow Nineties because of their interest in this specific element of the Decadent aesthetic, the emphasis on a form of radical aloofness that engenders clarified perception. They fostered connections with Decadent detachment in order to establish a similar apartness from nation as an antidote to the aggressive energies of the interwar period.

Interwar critics writing on the 1890s, however, understood the Decadent ethos as a hostage, as opposed to a casualty, of the modern moment. If considered carefully enough, if attended to properly, perhaps the spirit of the fin de siècle could be reinvigorated and brought to bear on the wounded present. While critical works composed in the 1910s, 1920s, and 1930s expressed disparate visions of the Yellow Nineties, they shared a belief that the ethos of the period could be retrieved, for the peculiar type of revolt the period represented was much needed in the years following one war and preceding another. If new kinds of violence seemed possible, an older model of critical detachment, drawn from the work of the more or less immediate past, seemed increasingly necessary.

II. The Long 1890s: The Persistence of Decadence in the Twentieth Century

The early-twentieth-century desire for contact with the immediate past was satisfied in part by the proliferation of criticism on the period, but other options existed for those who wished to connect with the middle distance and its ethos. Surviving members of the Decadent Movement, such as Max Beerbohm and Vernon Lee, continued to practice a defiantly anachronistic style drawn from the late-Victorian past. Communities of appreciation organized themselves around specters of the 1890s, such as Baron Corvo and Althea Gyles. Post-Victorian dandies, such as Beresford Egan, revived the practices of the fin de siècle, channeling Wilde and mimicking Beardsley. *Literature and the Politics of Post-Victorian Decadence* focuses on these figures and the manner in which they allowed yesterday's avant-garde to persist and thrive during the modernist period.

Attending to these figures certainly complicates our understanding of the Victorian/modern divide. In this sense, this book is part of a larger conversation that is working toward a more nuanced vision of that divide. Vincent Sherry's illuminating *Modernism and the Reinvention of Decadence* (2014), for example, has allowed us to see that Decadence and modernism, far from operating as two distinct movements or periods, should, owing to their shared temporal sensibility, their similar aching sense of lateness and lost time, be understood as "one sensibility developing in two of its acutest registers."[55] Recent scholarship on the Victorian/modern divide has also given us a much richer sense of the turn of the century by bringing to our attention figures who blur that divide as well as modernism's Victorian genealogy.[56] My work is in every way informed by these arguments, but my focus is somewhat different. I am looking at authors and artists who aggressively reinscribed the Victorian/modern divide, figures who purposefully and defiantly practiced an aesthetic of the recent past, refusing to assimilate to a modern moment that they found fundamentally wanting, and insisted on a fundamental difference between their own practices and the aesthetic and political values of the present.

Acknowledging that Decadent practices persisted well beyond the end of the nineteenth century allows for a reperiodization of the Decadent Movement. It also allows for a repopulation of the early twentieth century by foregrounding figures who remain invisible when the period is read as a purely modernist moment. Consequently, while this project is very much about extending the timeline of the Victorian period, it might also be understood as emerging from recent work in the field of "new modernist studies."[57] As new modernist studies has demonstrated, if we perceive the early twentieth century through something other than a high modernist lens, a much richer and more complex vision of the period emerges. We are able to see the diverse range of figures and movements that spoke to one another during this period, the manner in which high spoke to low, traditional spoke to radical, past spoke to present, and so on. We may also perceive that late-Victorian voices did more than persist during this period. They were valued and respected. Decadence continued to perform vital political functions in the 1910s, 1920s, and 1930s, remaining in play as a viable aesthetic alternative to high modernism and other more properly twentieth-century forms. Recognizing that late-Victorian figures and concepts remained a part of the conversation following the turn of the century engenders a fuller and more complete understanding of the cultural terrain. For example, whereas Virginia Woolf's dismissive treatment of Victorian realist fiction is well known, what is less recognized is her admiration for Max Beerbohm. Likewise, even as Wyndham Lewis *BLAST*ed the "Britannic Aesthete," he was engaging enthusiastically with practitioners of post-Victorian Decadence, such as A. J. A. Symons.

By examining the political uses to which post-Victorian Decadence was put during the early twentieth century, I am also able to intervene in the ongoing debate concerning the politics of aestheticism and Decadence.[58] Although for many years the aestheticist credo "art for art's sake" was accepted at face value, recent work in Victorian studies has cast the conventional vision of the aesthetes as apolitical into question. Much of this recent scholarship, however, focuses on the manner in which aestheticism is implemented in other political projects, such as socialism or philanthropy.[59] The focus here is on Decadence itself as a specific mode of participation in the political realm. Decadent strategies, such as detachment, camp, parody, and perversity, which seem to shirk the political, actually allow post-Victorian Decadents to forge a very powerful and effective mode of political intervention.

Detachment emerges as a central focus in my treatment of the politics of post-Victorian Decadence. The very characteristics of Decadence that have led critics to so frequently characterize the movement as apolitical, its coolness and apartness, reveal themselves as particularly useful in the contestation of national politics and jingoism during the First and Second

World Wars. Authors and artists wishing to resist the pull of militaristic nationalism in the early twentieth century find the dandy's immunity to heated enthusiasms an appealing model of composure during a decidedly discomposed time. Pater's call to "never [acquiesce]" in "facile [orthodoxies]," Wilde's wit and disdain, and Beardsley's knowing smirk serve as antidotes to the violent passions of the period.[60] Joseph Bristow has made the point that "there is something distinctly unEnglish about camp," perhaps because "it acts derisively on the commensensical outlook that one readily associates with philistine Englishness."[61] Post-Victorian dandies turned this cosmopolitan, withering, camp humor on the overexcited, patriotic English public, refusing to be drawn into their violent wartime enthusiasms. Firbank, for example, was so derisive in his treatment of empire and so thoroughly refused to be bound up in English identity that he is often described as Anglophobic.[62] Georges Letissier has explicitly linked Firbank's Decadent detachment with pacifism, arguing that Firbank defiantly "[eschews] the characteristic tropes of wartime writing." In his novels, "the reality of wartime England is transposed into a neo-pastoral landscape in which characters pursue their separate pleasures, away from the pressures of institutional drives towards hetero-normativity and patriotic commitments. They are literally out-of-the way, that is: away from it all and shamelessly so, by shirking their duties, to embrace erotically-charged pacifism."[63] Figures like Lee and Beerbohm implement this cosmopolitan detachment, which operates as a form of implicit pacifism in works by figures like Firbank, in a more clearly political fashion in their wartime works.

It is worth noting that the majority of the figures under discussion here occupied a nationally hybrid or expatriate position for much of their careers, their cosmopolitanism arguably compounding their Decadent detachment.[64] Lee, Beerbohm, and Corvo spent many years living in Italy. Althea Gyles left her home country of Ireland and never returned. Egan, though born in London, was raised in South Africa, and then returned to London in his twenties. These are mobile figures for whom a single national characterization does not apply. In the cases of Beerbohm, Lee, and Egan in particular, the detached critical perspective born of a feeling of separateness from nation merges with the aloofness derived from the Decadent aesthetic. These are individuals who felt in some way separate from their nations of origin as well as from their historical moments and who believed that temporal and geopolitical homelessness contributed to a sharpened perception. Their disinterestedness and hyperkinetic detachment allowed them to see the political present with a greater degree of clarity, unfettered by national enthusiasms or the kind of rootedness in the present that might render one vulnerable to jingoistic fears and passions.

This book begins by considering the politically progressive uses to which post-Victorian Decadence was put in the early twentieth century. The first and second chapters focus on two of the most canonical and well-known practitioners of late-Victorian Decadence, Max Beerbohm and Vernon Lee. Beerbohm and Lee offered twentieth-century audiences contact with the wit and aloofness of the fin de siècle, serving as representatives of what Shaw referred to as "the old guard of Victorian cosmopolitan intellectualism."[65] In addition, while operating themselves as appealing specters from the Yellow Nineties, they channeled to their readers earlier forms of Victorian aestheticism, bringing a traumatized British public into contact with the Pre-Raphaelites and Walter Pater. Foregrounding the lineage of fin-de-siècle Decadence, its own indebtedness to a series of aestheticist precursors, they allowed their readership to engage in a compounded form of aesthetic time travel that shuttled them back to the 1890s and then even further back to Rossetti's 1850s and 1860s and the Aesthetic 1870s and 1880s. In doing so, they demonstrated the murky boundary between aestheticism and Decadence. By linking themselves to Rossetti and Pater, they undid the lines of demarcation between Decadence and first-wave aestheticism, and by bringing their vision of Rossetti and Pater to twentieth-century audiences, they wrote across the line that divides the Victorian and modernist moments. In this sense, they can be seen as working on multiple fronts to generate contact between movements and literary historical periods.

In Chapter 1, "'Queer Indifference': Max Beerbohm, Post-Victorian Decadence, and Camp Nostalgia," I consider Max Beerbohm's reliance on links with the Victorian past, with Pre-Raphaelitism and fin-de-siècle dandyism, in his expression of distaste for violence and jingoism during and between the world wars. From the earliest moments of his career, Beerbohm insisted on his own anachronism, stating in 1896 that he could have no part in modern life, and his performance of temporal outsiderism became even more pronounced as Britain moved into the twentieth century. He cast himself as a ghost from the Victorian past, a bemused and perplexed dandy forced into a series of bafflingly vulgar situations. His civility and wit served as an implicit rebuttal to the increasing incivility of the period. In the years following the First World War, Beerbohm's performative anachronism, his caricatures of Rossetti and his circle, and his stories of time travel and temporal inversion allowed a traumatized public contact with a more aesthetically pleasing past. However, his use of a camp form of ironized nostalgia allowed these works to operate as something more than a simple withdrawal from the political realities of the present. He invoked nostalgia's power to signal the failings of the modern moment while at the same time highlighting the impossibility of fully indulging in a retreat from contemporary problems. He continued this work in his BBC broadcasts during World War II, talks that to Rebecca West emanated from the mouth of the "last civilized man on earth."[66] Transporting his listeners to Pre-Raphaelite salons and 1890s London, Beerbohm engaged in a purposeful refusal of modern brutality, facilitating a keener perception of the failings of modernity by allowing audiences a moment of detachment from the present.

In Chapter 2, "Pacifism and Post-Victorian Decadence: Vernon Lee at the Margins of the Twentieth Century," I examine a slightly less humorous appeal to the powers of post-Victorian aestheticism and Decadence. An avowed pacifist and through-and-through cosmopolitan, Lee was appalled by the onset of the First World War. She was troubled in particular by the manner in which early-twentieth-century theories of the subject generated by scientists and social scientists posited violence as inevitable and argued that aggressive impulses ran central to human nature. Countering this brutal vision, Lee generated an alternative theory of the subject founded on the principles of late-Victorian aestheticism, locating the desire for beauty at the core of human behavior. Pater in particular played a crucial role in Lee's efforts to construct an alternative theory of the subject that associated the aesthetic impulse with ethical behavior. As a representative from the Yellow Nineties, she operated as a bridge between the Paterian past and the modernist moment, allowing the Aesthetic Movement of the 1870s to infiltrate and inform the World War I era. To trace the evolution of Lee's post-Victorian Decadent vision of the subject, I pay close attention to the marginalia in the copies of the social scientific treatises that she digested and discarded in the early twentieth century, and I foreground the manner in which she, like Beerbohm, highlighted her detachment from the modern moment, her marginal role in a present that she found fundamentally disappointing.

In Chapters 3 and 4, I move on to consider case studies that represent political counterpoints to the more progressive or positive models of post-Victorian Decadence discussed in Chapters 1 and 2. While many critics in the early twentieth century celebrated Decadence's capacity for facilitating cosmopolitan pacifism, radical economic critique, and political regeneration, post-Victorian Decadence did at times function in far more conservative or destructive ways. First I discuss the role that a radically simplified vision of Decadent class politics played in the cultivation of an elitist posture in the 1920s and 1930s. I then move on to acknowledge that post-Victorian Decadence was not always linked to detachment and irony. Certain strands of post-Victorian Decadence, in fact, fostered far more earnest ideas about self-sacrifice and inspired self-destructive behavior on the part of their adherents.

In the third chapter, "'Towards Aristocracy': Baron Corvo and the Corvine Society," I consider the manner in which a post-Victorian Decadent reception community put a particular vision of Decadence to highly conservative use during the interwar period. In the late 1920s, the post-Victorian dandy A. J. A. Symons founded the Corvine Society, an elite club that centered on the appreciation of the Decadent writer Baron Corvo (Frederick Rolfe, 1860–1913). As I argue in this chapter, the manner in which this group of connoisseurs and conservative men chose to understand Corvo says more about their own embattled status during a period of economic crisis and shifting political realities than about Corvo himself. Corvo lived in poverty for most of his life, but his books are filled with shrill declarations concerning the appeal of aristocracy and the thrill of enacting power on others. Rather than turning to socialism as a potential solution to the problems of inequality that so dramatically impacted his own life, Corvo retreated into fantasies of absolute power, imagining himself as pope or as the sadistic master of a group of poor young boys. His interest in aristocracy emerged directly from his extensive experiences of degradation. The more poignant and pathetic elements of Corvo's vision, however, were neglected by the members of the Corvine Society. They chose to accept his excessive and ridiculous declarations concerning class hierarchy at face value and generate an influential and highly reductive reading of Corvo as archconservative that continues to inform current scholarship on his writing. This chapter disinters the political complexities of Corvo's work to illuminate what was neglected by the Corvines and places that neglect in historical and political context, showcasing how rallying around a simplified vision of Corvo's politics might have insulated this group of elite dandies and connoisseurs from troubling realities such as the economic crash and the rise of Labour.

Chapter 4, "Irish Decadence, Occultism, and Sacrificial Myth: The Martyrdom of Althea Gyles," focuses on another less pleasing legacy of late-Victorian Decadence. The two most prominent Irish Decadents, Yeats and Wilde, had a tremendous influence on the life and work of the Irish book designer and writer Althea Gyles. Gyles garnered from her contact with Yeats's brand of Celtic occultism and Wilde's tragedy in 1895 a highly romanticized vision of suffering and a belief that self-sacrifice might initiate a new age. Her investment in sacrificial ideals contributed to her vision of herself as a martyr for the cause of women's sexual freedom. She entered into a very public and scandalous affair that resulted in her abandonment by the Decadent circles that had facilitated her success, and she suffered an emotional breakdown, after which she never drew again. She lived, however, for another forty-nine years, operating as a material reminder of the extent to which the utopian promise of the 1890s had not been fulfilled. Gyles survived to signal to the women of the twentieth century how little progress had been made on the front of women's liberation. In the final sections of this chapter, I examine the poignant representation of Gyles in the works of Eleanor Farjeon and Faith Compton Mackenzie. Engaging with this specter from the late-Victorian past allowed two twentieth-century women writers to care for one of the casualties of the ongoing struggle for women's equality. The two strands of Irish Decadence that impacted Gyles, Yeats's Celtic occultism of the 1890s and Wilde's sexual dissidence, are highly disparate in their aims, but they share a romanticized vision of martyrdom. Gyles's strange career highlights the dangerous post-Victorian legacy of Irish Decadent sacrificial ideals, and Farjeon's and Mackenzie's representations of her demonstrate how those dangers were parsed by twentieth-century women writers.

While these initial chapters foreground the manner in which Victorian aestheticism and Decadence persisted in the practices of post-Victorian writers and reception communities of the early twentieth century, in Chapter 5, "Crusading Decadent: Beresford Egan, Global Dandyism, and Post-Victorian Decadent Feminism," I turn to a figure who represented himself as a reincarnation of Victorian Decadence. Egan was born after the century's end, and he grew up in South Africa, where Decadence appeared to him like "a cry in the wilderness of muscular christianity," allowing him to play with alternative models of gender identity.[67] The draw of British bohemianism eventually lured Egan back to the metropole, where he spent the remainder of his career implementing a globally inflected form of post-Victorian Decadence in the satire and critique of British sexual and gender politics. His cosmopolitan sensibility and his dandyism allowed him to remain detached from nationalist politics and to perceive the cruelty of purity campaigns conducted in the name of national security in the years following World War I. He celebrated "sexual inversion" at a moment when sexual dissidence was often cast as a form of political dissidence with much wider and more dangerous ramifications. Practicing a pastiche of Beardsley's style, Egan illustrated pamphlets satirizing the reactionary sexual and gender politics of the 1920s and 1930s and the suppression of "obscene" works such as Radclyffe Hall's *The Well of Loneliness* (1928). Collaborating with his wife, Caterina Bower Alcock, he generated a nuanced form of post-Victorian Decadent feminism, and, in his illustrated novels of the 1930s, he celebrated the figure of the female dandy, a feminist Decadent figure who surpasses her precursors in the works of Wilde and Beardsley and triumphs over cultural restrictions as well as every male dandy to cross her path. Attending to Egan's revision of Beardsley's aesthetic allows for insight into the global circulation of Decadence, and his interwar works allow us to see how Decadence continued to function in progressive political projects in the hands of Beardsley's and Wilde's successors. Egan's anachronism, his turn to the late-Victorian past, and his transnational sensibility facilitated his detached and contemptuous treatment of early-twentieth-century sexual and gender ideologies and allowed him to engender a radical form of feminist dandyism.

Concluding with Egan allows me to return to the more liberatory and appealing potentialities of post-Victorian Decadence, to acknowledge the extent to which the aesthetic of the "Fighting Nineties" retained its critical function during the early twentieth century. The disillusionment and detachment that modern critics found so alluring could, it seems, be reanimated and put into play in the interwar cultural scene. New post-Victorian Decadent dandies emerged to taunt, provoke, and critique, occupying a stance of perpetual protest akin to that of their 1890s precursors.

III. The Political Uses of the Past: Post-Victorian Decadence

This is, then, a project about time and history and the uses of the past. While the work of post-Victorian Decadence is connected to nostalgia, it is my hope that the term *post-Victorian* will highlight the peculiar form of political engagement and liminal temporal positioning that distinguishes this aesthetic from more properly escapist forms, forms that constitute a decisive retreat from modernity.[68] Historical tension is central to the post-Victorian aesthetic. Rather than fully inhabiting the modern present, these figures dwelt partially out of time, their feet in two periods. They persisted beyond the boundaries of a period, and they continued to practice an aesthetic associated with that period. However, their interest in past forms did not always constitute a conservative retreat from the politics of the modern moment. The critical detachment their temporal liminality engendered allowed for a particularly clear and aloof form of political perception, and they turned in their work to a previous period to engage in critical thinking concerning the present that they occupied. Even when putting post-Victorian Decadence to conservative use, as the Corvines did in response to the rise of Labour, this aesthetic mode cannot be read as a simple and straightforward rejection of the present. Implementing the post-Victorian aesthetic allowed these figures to negotiate the realities of modernity.

The term *post-Victorian* is useful because it evokes the term *postmodern*, an aesthetic with which post-Victorian Decadence has much in common. Like postmodernism, which often relies on pastiche, parody, and a return to traditional forms, the post-Victorian aesthetic expresses its critique of modernity through the recasting and revision of previous avant-garde strategies. Post-Victorian Decadence also shares postmodernism's playfulness, humor, and sense of ironic detachment. Beerbohm's camp mode of ironized nostalgia, for example, or the Beardsleyesque satires of Beresford Egan are sly and arch in a manner that resembles comic postmodernism. In her discussion of postmodernism, Linda Hutcheon argues that postmodern work is "not a nostalgic return; it is a critical revisiting, an ironic dialogue with the past of both art and society."[69] Post-Victorian Decadents, like many postmodernists, often engaged in indirect forms of political intervention through the implementation of past techniques and styles, at once invoking and ironizing that past aesthetic and its ethos.

The term *post-Victorian* also gestures toward the element of critique implicit to so much post-Victorian Decadent practice. The present remains unmentioned. It is the modern that has been found wanting, and the modern that is not named. Nevertheless, unlike the term *postmodern*, which has at times been criticized because of its excessive reliance on a spirit of negation, a foregrounding of that which it is not, the term *post-Victorian* highlights the desire for continuity that is so much a part of the post-Victorian aesthetic. A sense of longing and warmth permeates the term. The term articulates an affirmation, even if that which is affirmed lies beyond reach. It speaks to the possibility of extending a beloved past moment even as it acknowledges that moment as over.

Owing to its focus on the persistence or reinvigoration of Victorian aesthetic practices, this book also offers a prehistory of Neo-Victorianism.[70] Focusing on the earliest of Victorian afterlives, the coterie of survivors of the 1890s and the young men and women who established modes of understanding them in the 1910s and 1920s, allows us to see that, in Rohan McWilliam's words, "the Victorians never went away."[71] The post-Victorian must, of course, be understood as distinct from the Neo-Victorian based on its proximity to the late-Victorian past. This project focuses on the persistence of Decadence in the decades immediately following the Victorian period as opposed to the reinvigoration or refashioning of Victorian aesthetics in post-1960s culture. The figures under discussion in *Literature and the Politics of Post-Victorian Decadence* are authors and artists who are continuing to practice an aesthetic that has only recently fallen out of fashion rather than retrieving an archaic style and engaging in a pastiche that references the forms and content of a long-bygone era. The contact Beerbohm and Lee had with the Victorian past was immediate and intimate, and thus their methods for dealing with that past are of a different quality than what we see in the self-conscious reflections on the appropriation of antiquated styles in the works of postmodern novelists. Nevertheless, the excavation of post-Victorian Decadence provides a backstory for Neo-Victorianism and the postmodern turn to the Victorian period and its aesthetic practices. Post-Victorian Decadence shares with Neo-Victorianism an interest in the manner in which the aesthetic modes of the Victorian period may foster effective negotiations with the present. By turning to the earliest examples of this practice, we are able to see how the traumas of twentieth-century modernity almost seemed to demand the resurrection of Victorian practices, and recent work in the field of Neo-Victorian studies demonstrates that this perceived need for rethinking the Victorian period has only increased in the twenty-first century. As Mark Llewellyn notes, "even as we move further away from the Victorian, the ideas of the period come to haunt us more deeply."[72] As scholars continue to be interested in contemporary refashionings of Victorian aesthetics, attending to the ideas about the utility of Victorian aesthetics that began to be generated the moment the nineteenth century ended may serve as a useful foundation for understanding how that practice was revised by postmodern writers in the 1960s and beyond.

The practitioners of post-Victorian Decadence occupy an incredibly complex web of political and temporal positions during the early twentieth century. Their anachronism, their affection for the past, and their revision and reinvigoration of past aesthetic practices facilitated a unique form of political engagement. In the chapters that follow, I trace the divergent political directions this practice took in the early decades of the twentieth century, its implementation in programs of pacifism, cosmopolitanism, conservative elitism, and progressive sexual and gender politics. In each case, it is in dwelling with "a not unfriendly interest" on "the more or less immediate past" that these authors and artists were able to come to a new understanding of the problems besetting their vexed and often disappointing present.

CHAPTER I

"Queer Indifference"
Max Beerbohm, Post-Victorian Decadence, and Camp Nostalgia

In 1922, Max Beerbohm published a collection of caricatures entitled *Rossetti and His Circle*, an affectionate series of images in which Beerbohm transported himself into the Pre-Raphaelite world of the 1850s and 1860s and adopted an exaggerated version of Rossetti's style. The collection opens with an image that might be understood as a key to the collection as a whole and to Beerbohm's peculiar political positioning during both the First and Second World Wars. The caricature depicts Dante Gabriel Rossetti as a small child hiding beneath a table sketching, while the men in the room around him gesticulate wildly and shout with great enthusiasm. The caption describes Rossetti "precociously manifesting, among the exiled patriots who frequented his father's house on Charlotte Street, that queer indifference to politics which marked him in his prime and his decline" (Figure 1.1).[1] Rossetti's detachment, his cool demeanor in the midst of heated political debate, his "queer indifference," is foregrounded immediately. Beerbohm's Rossetti is arch and skeptical, critical and apart. He does not get swept up in the enthusiasms that encircle him. Rossetti's imagined capacity for separating himself must be understood in relationship to the fact that the images in *Rossetti and His Circle* were created during World War I. As Beerbohm watched the world gesticulate wildly and shout with enthusiasm, he chose, like Rossetti, to remain detached, to hold himself separate from violence and jingoism. To do so, he traveled into the not-so-distant past, extricating himself from an incomprehensible and distasteful present, turning to an even earlier instantiation of aestheticism for a model of supreme Decadent detachment. Imaginatively occupying Rossetti's world and practicing a pastiche of Rossetti's style allowed him to remain in close proximity to a man who represented to him the height of cosmopolitan aloofness.

During the world wars, Beerbohm insisted on his own anachronism, his connections with the Victorian past, and his distance from the modern moment. Rossetti operated as an important model in this respect as well, for

Figure 1.1. Max Beerbohm, *Rossetti in Childhood*, frontispiece for *Rossetti and His Circle*, 1922. © Estate of Max Beerbohm. Reproduced courtesy of Mark Samuels Lasner.

he similarly posited himself as an import from another period and another place. In the introductory note to *Rossetti and His Circle*, Beerbohm asserts that though Rossetti technically "belonged" to the Victorian Era, "for Him the eighteen-fifties-and-sixties had no romance at all."[2] He seemed to have "been born outside his proper place," and it was this that made him remarkable.[3] "In the Qauttrocento and by the Arno," he might not have been as noteworthy, "but in London, in the great days of a deep, smug, thick, rich, drab, industrial complacency, Rossetti shone, for the men and women who knew him, with the ambiguous light of a red torch somewhere in a dense fog."[4] Like Beerbohm, Rossetti adopted an anachronistic posture to signal his dissatisfaction with the present, and, like Beerbohm, he was a practitioner of pastiche whose adoption of prior aesthetic modes allowed for a way out of a troubling modernity.

This chapter investigates the politics of Beerbohm's peculiar mode of camp nostalgia and the cultural role that he played in the British cultural imagination during the first half of the twentieth century. Beerbohm consistently represented himself as outmoded and baffled by the twentieth-century present. He had, of course, been insisting that his era had ended from the moment it first began. As early as 1896, he stated, "Surely I could have no part in modern life. . . . I belong to the Beardsley period," but he did not pass away until sixty years later, and he thus spent the majority of his life in a century to which he insisted he did not belong.[5] Though he had departed for Italy in 1910, he remained a highly visible presence in England during the period in which he was most frequently absent and, according to his own assessment, most irrelevant, producing many of his most important works and performing a crucial role for an English public that turned to him as an antidote to the barbarism of the early twentieth century. In the 1910s, he wrote "Enoch Soames" (1919), the story of an 1890s poet who travels into the future; *Rossetti and His Circle*; and the ambitious but never completed text *The Mirror of the Past*, an illustrated tale of a mirror that allows the narrator to see into the Victorian past. During the First World War, Beerbohm returned repeatedly to nostalgic images and tales of temporal inversion. Fond visions of Rossetti's coterie and fin-de-siècle bohemia insulated the dandy under assault from the ugliness of the present. In the 1930s and 1940s, Beerbohm continued to look to the past, delivering a series of BBC radio broadcasts designed to improve morale that transported listeners to the Victorian period, to prewar London, its great men and its music halls. In addressing the BBC's listeners, Beerbohm frequently cast himself as a post-Victorian Decadent medium. In his 1936 broadcast "A Small Boy Seeing Giants," for example, he described himself as "what the writers of obituary notices call an interesting link with the past."[6] His twentieth-century works, the fiction, the Rossetti caricatures, and the broadcasts, are linked by a shared refusal of modern brutality and wistfulness for past civility, and they offered twentieth-century audiences a much-needed corrective to the incivility of the period.

Beerbohm's temporal outsiderism was central to the cultural work that he performed in the twentieth century. As one of the best-known members of the *Yellow Book* circle, he offered twentieth-century audiences a link with Decadence and the fin de siècle, and, by operating as a conduit to a slightly more remote period, the era of Rossetti and his circle, he promised a traumatized public contact with an even rosier and more romantic moment. He served as a comforting old guard representative of England's previous avant-gardes. However, he did not simply engage in or facilitate retreat from the present. He might have wished to insist that he belonged to the Victorian period, that he had no part in modern life, but he was valued by the British public for bringing a Victorian mode of critique to bear on the modern world. When he was first invited by Moray McLaren to speak on the BBC, McLaren stressed to Beerbohm that he wished his talk to be "partly reminiscent and partly observant."[7] This recipe captures nicely the nature of Beerbohm's work with the past, which cannot be cast as entirely escapist. His reminiscences were meant to facilitate observation of and engagement with the troubles of the present.

The term *post-Victorian* is particularly appropriate for describing the tension in Beerbohm's temporal situation because it calls to mind the postmodern and the debates concerning the political significance of postmodernism's interest in the past, described by Linda Hutcheon in 1998 in the following manner: "Was this postmodern recalling of the past an example of a conservative – and therefore nostalgic – escape to an idealized, simpler era of 'real' community values? Or did it express, but through its ironic distance, a 'genuine and legitimate dissatisfaction with modernity and the unquestioned belief in . . . perpetual modernization'?"[8] Beerbohm's twentieth-century works raise a similar set of questions. While listeners spoke in glowing terms of the manner in which Beerbohm transported them from the ugliness of the present, his radio broadcasts quiver with quiet anger concerning the commercialism, vulgarity, and violence of that present. He explicitly acknowledges the critical valence of his nostalgia in a 1936 talk, arguing that "the love of by-gone things is a quite recent growth – due mainly to the fact that we have fallen on evil times. If we could all of us follow Mr. H. G. Wells's example, dismiss the present from our minds, and fix our eyes steadfastly on the future, then we would share his wholesome contempt for the past. But we can't. We are morbid."[9] An earlier draft of the preface to *Mainly on the Air*, the collection of Beerbohm's BBC talks published in 1946, included the somewhat biting question, "What civilized person in these days . . . isn't nostalgic?"[10] Who, Beerbohm seems to ask, could encounter the modernity of the twentieth century and not wish himself elsewhere? A similarly sharp and biting tone of nostalgia registers in Rebecca West's response to the broadcasts: "I felt . . . that I was listening to the voice of the last civilized man on earth."[11] Beerbhom's performatively anachronistic late-Victorian dandyism was not meant to be read and, at least in West's case, did not read as quaint. His excessive civility threw the barbarity of the period into sharp relief. As he writes in the manuscript of *The Mirror of the Past*, "every decent man hates his own time in proportion to his decency."[12] However, as much as Beerbohm condemned the present, he never turned entirely from it. He relied on past aesthetic modes to express an engaged critique of modernity.

Beerbohm's treatment of history is particularly Decadent in its playfulness and ironic detachment. Dennis Denisoff has described Beerbohm's manner of dealing with the late-Victorian past as camp, an aesthetic with intimate ties to Decadence. As Gary McMahon notes, camp and

Decadence are often "conflated."[13] In her foundational essay "Notes on Camp" (1964), which is dedicated to Oscar Wilde, Susan Sontag certainly seems to conflate the two, referring to camp as a "mode of aestheticism" and placing Beerbohm's *Zuleika Dobson* (1911) on the top of her list of examples of the "canon of camp."[14] Camp figures prominently in Beerbohm's peculiar mode of nostalgia. According to Denisoff, "[Beerbohm] used camp to sustain a transhistorical community, extending sympathy backward while also poking fun at the very people from whom, he was well aware, his own writing and values developed."[15] As much as Beerbohm's nostalgia must be understood as critically engaged with the present from which it seems to be retreating, his treatment of the Victorian past was also often at once critical and sympathetic, derisive and loving, in a manner that only the term *camp* properly encapsulates. He practiced nostalgia in quotation marks.[16] His post-Victorian Decadent form of camp nostalgia is at once critically detached from and engaged with both the past *and* the present and neither simple, sweet, nor escapist. His relationship to the past has much in common with postmodern architecture's manner of dealing with history as described by Hutcheon. Postmodern architecture, Hutcheon states, "does indeed recall the past, but always with the kind of ironic double vision that acknowledges the final impossibility of indulging in nostalgia, even as it consciously evokes nostalgia's affective power. In the postmodern, in other words, (and here is the source of the tension) nostalgia itself gets both called up, exploited, and ironized. This is a complicated (and postmodernly paradoxical) move that is both an ironizing of nostalgia itself, of the very urge to look backward for authenticity, and, at the same moment, a sometimes shameless invoking of the visceral power that attends the fulfillment of that urge."[17] Beerbohm's post-Victorian Decadent camp nostalgia is similarly knowing, similarly wistful, and similarly detached and double-voiced in its use of the past.

I. The Dandy with a Dagger: 1890–1913

Beerbohm began to cultivate his distinctively detached persona from the earliest moments of his career, when he simultaneously practiced and satirized late-Victorian Decadence. As Lawrence Danson notes, he "[satirized] the movement from an insider's point of view."[18] His "Defence of Cosmetics" (1894), for example, exhibits a camp sensibility, lauding and lampooning the Decadent craze for artifice, rejoicing that "the day of *sancta simplicitas* is quite ended" and "the era of rouge is upon us."[19] The essay, which appeared in the first issue of the *Yellow Book*, was read by many as an earnest endorsement of the ethos with which it played, and it managed, according to Beerbohm, to "provoke ungovernable fury" and caused "the mob [to lose] its head."[20] Beerbohm's follow-up "Letter to the Editor" (1894) in the next issue of the *Yellow Book* expresses dismay that the public did not see that the work was a hoax. Nevertheless, Beerbohm concludes the letter by taunting readers with threats that English literature may "fall at length into the hands of the decadents," that Artifice may be at the gates, and, in fact, "by the time this letter appears, it *may* be too late."[21] He playfully practices a Decadent style, indulging in the Decadent mode of outraging the public while at the same time sending up the excessiveness of the affectedly sinister movement.

Beerbohm's relationship to Oscar Wilde was similarly complex. Wilde had an enormous influence on the development of Beerbohm's style in the 1890s. As N. John Hall notes, "it's hard to imagine what Max's early essays would have been like had it not been for Wilde's influence."[22] He took up Wilde's "formula of aestheticism and comedy and put the emphasis on the comic."[23] He expressed great sadness at Wilde's imprisonment, and he attended the second trial and reported that "Oscar has been quite superb. His speech about the Love that dares not tell his name was simply wonderful."[24] While Wilde was in prison, Beerbohm published *The Happy Hypocrite* (1897), which bears an unmistakably Wildean mark. In a letter to Beerbohm following his release, Wilde states that "the implied and accepted recognition of 'Dorian Gray'" in the story "[charmed]" him.[25] Yet Beerbohm oscillated between reverence and satire in his treatment of the writer. In 1894, he composed an essay titled "A Peep into the Past" that mocks Wilde's feminine home decor and "the constant succession of page-boys" whose visits "so [startle] the neighborhood."[26] His caricatures of Wilde from this period border on cruelty. However, while he was at all times ready to laugh at Decadence and to make sport of Wilde, the two continued to inform his thinking. He moved with ease between parody and admiration in his relationship to both the movement and the man who facilitated the development of the Beerbohmian mask in the 1890s. He was at once of and apart from *The Yellow Book* and its circle, a dandy with what Wilde referred to as a "style like a silver dagger" that might be turned upon the very ethos that endowed it with power.[27]

The potential value this style might have in terms of facilitating political perception became much clearer as the century turned and the Boer War escalated. As David Cecil notes, the Boer War represented to Beerbohm the "aggressive, hustling, ungentlemanlike" "new middle-class imperialist Toryism," which was "all that Max detested most."[28] In 1901, in response to the Boer War, he exhibited a series of cartoons titled *The Second Childhood of John Bull.* These cartoons take the dandy's cool dagger to the heated political mood of the period. Exhibiting a queer indifference to national affiliations, Beerbohm ridicules an England filled with a smug sense of superiority and a perceived right to take from the world whatever might be desired. John Bull is represented in these cartoons as boastful and vulgar, ready to "teach them Colonists a lesson," fawning on the nations from which he needs assistance (such as the United States) and neglecting pleas for assistance from the countries he has weakened (such as Ireland).[29] He is often drunk and blustering. His understanding of art is severely limited. He cautions the Theatre not to "get *Ideas* into [her] 'ead."[30] He expresses keen admiration for the work of Rudyard Kipling, sharing a pint with him while effusing, "Yes, I've took a fancy to you, young feller. 'Taint often I cottons to a Pote, neither.... Most of 'em is... *not wholesome*, and can't keep a civil tongue i' their 'eads. You're different, you are: don't give yourself no 'aughty airs, and though you're rough (with your swear-words and your what-nots), I will say as 'ow you've always bin very civil an' respec'ful to myself. You're one o' the right sort, you are."[31]

It was during the Boer War that Rudyard Kipling truly began to operate for Beerbohm as a representative of all that he reviled. In his jingoistic imperialism, his enthusiasm for violence and brutality, Kipling was the exact inverse of the cosmopolitan detachment and civility that Beerbohm so valued. As Danson argues, he was in Beerbohm's eyes "a hyperactive little monster of uncontrollable enthusiasm.... What Beerbohm hated in Kipling was Kipling's hatred, his fierceness of feeling that only made itself more dangerous when it appeared in the service of chauvinism or sentimentality."[32] In a letter to Holbrook Jackson concerning *The Eighteen Nineties* (1913), Beerbohm expressed this hatred in the following terms: "To me... the sort of person that Kipling is, and the sort of thing that Kipling does, cannot strongly appeal – quite the contrary. I carefully guard myself by granting you that Kipling is a genius. Indeed, even *I* can't help *knowing* him to be that. The *schoolboy*, the *bounder*, and the *brute* – these three types have surely never found a more brilliant expression of themselves than in R. K.... But as a poet and a seer R. K. seems to me not to exist, except for the purpose of contempt."[33] Kipling was for Beerbohm politically suspect as well aesthetically vile. In an "improved" copy of one of Kipling's works, Beerbohm wrote, "By R. K. the Apocalyptic Bounder who can do such fine things but mostly prefers to stand on tip-toe and stridently for all that is cheap and nasty."[34] To be strident and to like cheap and nasty things ran exactly contrary to Beerbohm's mode of dandyism.

Beerbohm constructed his own detached persona in direct opposition to the brutishness and bounderishness Kipling represented, and, as he further developed this persona in the early twentieth century, Kipling continued to serve for him as both an object of contempt and a rich source of inspiration. In *The Poets' Corner* (1904), Kipling appears dancing foolishly beside Brittania, and in "P.C., X, 36," the parody of Kipling that appeared in *A Christmas Garland* (1912), Kipling celebrates the beating of Santa Claus on the grounds that he is a foreigner. As the story begins, K*pl*ng follows a loutish constable on his rounds, and the two then encounter a man "with a hoary white beard, a red ulster with the hood up, and what looked like a sack over his shoulder" "emerging from a chimney-pot."[35] The constable calls him down and immediately begins pummeling him. "I'm S-Santa Claus, Sir," he cries, "P-please, Sir, let me g-go."[36] But K*pl*ng shouts, "Hold him. . . . He's a German. . . . Frog's march him!"[37] The parody has been described by N. John Hall as "the cruelest thing Max ever wrote."[38] It is certainly hard on Kipling, but it expresses most clearly the horror Beerbohm felt at the shrieking brutality and bloodlust that Kipling represented to him. This type of jingoistic incivility would soon be on much wider display and would require on Beerbohm's part the continued implementation of a distinctively 1890s sensibility of dandyish detachment.

II. The Pacifist Satirist as Swordsman: 1914–1935

Less than a year after World War I began, Beerbohm and his wife, Florence, returned to England from Italy so as not to be, as Beerbohm put it, "away from England during the *whole* of England's hour of need."[39] David Cecil has argued that "all his latent patriotism flooded forth" as the war began, but the term *patriotism* does not properly capture the extent to which Beerbohm kept his head in the teens.[40] His affection for the concept of England does seem to have intensified during the war, but the war itself truly appalled him.[41] In a letter to Reggie Turner, he bemoaned the escalation of violence: "What a world! What a period we have been born into! It is very epical and all that; but the horror and sadness and absurdity of it! The horror duly horrifies me, and the sadness saddens, whereas by the absurdity 'we are,' like Queen Victoria, 'not amused.'"[42] He refused to become absorbed in vengeful nationalist fantasies or romanticized conceptions of heroism. In the same letter to Turner, he referred to the war as a "poison" that would only create "more hatred and bitterness": "It is all very well to talk about beating Germany to her knees, freeing Europe from the dread of an insolent hegemony, and so forth. But not the most bloodthirsty person proposes that Germany shall be altogether crushed out of existence; and I am sure that whatever is left of her will have even more recuperative power than France had after 1870, and a more urgent spirit; so that either she will have to be crushed all over again . . . which wouldn't be a very pretty thing to do, nor an epical thing; or we shall in the not very remote future have the epical business all over again."[43] He certainly wished for England to emerge victorious, but his fastidiousness and dandyish detachment made him all too aware that violence is distasteful, that it begets more violence, and that the proceedings to which he was witness were only the beginning of an ongoing degeneration of civility in the twentieth century.

The violence does, however, seem to have inspired in Beerbohm a more sharply honed thoughtfulness and to have necessitated his development of the modes of pastiche, parody, and camp nostalgia for which he would become so well known. As much as he deplored the war, this was, as Cecil notes, "the most productive period of his life," and it was the period during which he produced his most beloved works.[44] In a 1947 letter to Louis Kronenberger, Christopher Morley advances the claim that it was during this moment, during this war, that Beerbohm truly became Beerbohmian, stating that "it's an odd thing that it really took a world convulsion to bring this '*petit maître*' to his largest creativeness and more generous ardor. . . . Max's beginnings, however witty and charming, were on the coterie and smarty side of things; it was only later that he became the completely judging and accomplishing satirist, the critic as swordsman."[45] Morley's reference to Beerbohm's stylistic swordsmanship echoes Wilde's earlier statement that he possessed a "style like a silver dagger" as well as Bohun Lynch's claim that "Max fights, not with a blunted sabre (for he is seldom rude), but with a foil – from the point of which he has, now and again, snicked off the button."[46] Each writer works to articulate the sense that Beerbohm's weapons are precise rather than destructive, that he is incisive, not aggressive. As Lynch argues, "there is nothing assertive or pushing about Max, even when he is most egoistic. He is quiet always, and delicate."[47] It is this delicacy that was the foundation of his appeal in the twentieth century and that dictated the nature of his unique approach to conflict. In "Dandies and Dandies" (1896), Beerbohm argues that "all delicate spirits . . . assume an oblique attitude towards life."[48] As an extremely delicate spirit, his approach to the war had to be extremely oblique, and because the war seemed to heighten his delicacy, his approach became all the more indirect. The works he composed in response to the war never refer explicitly to the conflict. They implement camp nostalgia to express, through an exaggerated performance of longing for the past, a critique of a fundamentally disappointing and disturbing present. The precise sword or dagger or foil he wielded at this time came at its object in a roundabout fashion, striking at the heart of the present by way of wistful reminiscence.

The *Rossetti and His Circle* caricatures are perhaps the most well known works of this period, and they enact an oblique form of post-Victorian camp critique by pining for the "eighteen-fifties-and-sixties."[49] The composition of the pictures in the volume allowed Beerbohm to aesthetically inhabit that period. He temporarily transformed himself into a Pre-Raphaelite by adopting the visual rhetoric of Rossetti, mimicking his style, surrounding the caricatured figures with Pre-Raphaelite furniture and paintings of Jane Morris, reproducing the works for which the Brotherhood was most well known. The cartoons in the collection are saturated with images of the famous Rossetti stunners. He imitates Rossetti's method of representing Elizabeth Siddal, the long neck, the hair pulled back loosely, the drooping eyelids, the vivid red hair. He echoes the tendencies of Rossetti's treatments of Jane Morris, the serpentine neck, the thick nest of hair, the enlarged lips and eyes (Figure 1.2). These women loom in the backgrounds and emerge into the foregrounds of each page, and, in each case, these are caricatures not simply of Rossetti's circle but of Rossetti's style, a Pre-Raphaelite camp pastiche that allowed Beerbohm to momentarily occupy a beloved past moment and to affectionately mimic the forms of that period.

Beerbohm also crafts in this collection a unique and peculiar vision of Rossetti that was not shared by his peers in the early twentieth century. The Pre-Raphaelites were a bit out of fashion in the 1910s and 1920s, but those critics who did make a case for Rossetti based their argument for his appeal on his passion. A discussion of his watercolors in the *Bulletin of the Metropolitan Museum of Art* refers to the "intensity and strangeness" of the "power and the force" in his early works.[50] A 1916 essay in the *Christian Science Monitor* argues that his "pictures have poetic fervor."[51] Writing for the *Burlington* in 1916, Roger Fry argues that "passionate desire was the central point of [Rossetti's] world."[52] The myth of Rossetti that circulated in the popular imagination of the period was of a man moody and a bit deranged, liable to be taken by fits of rage or desire. Beerbohm, conversely, seems to revel in the idea of a Rossetti who was rather cool and detached. As Danson argues, "the Rossetti of Max's caricatures is a silent still point in the world of human and animal specimens that surrounds him."[53] Danson notes, in an image of Rossetti and his circle socializing in the yard, the artist's "[indifference] to the circle of admirers – Burne-Jones and Pater, Swinburne kneeling in reverence, Morris expansively introducing him to a

Figure 1.2. Max Beerbohm, *Mr. Morley of Blackburn, on an Afternoon in the Spring of '69, Introduces Mr. John Stuart Mill*, from *Rossetti and His Circle*, 1922. © Estate of Max Beerbohm. Reproduced courtesy of Mark Samuels Lasner.

kangaroo."[54] In *A Man from Hymettus*, Rossetti is so indifferent to Frederic Leighton's entreaties to join the Royal Academy that he can't even be asked to fully enter the frame (Figure 1.3). Only his feet make an appearance as the rest of his body pulls itself further from Leighton's earnest calls to "Come over and help us!"[55] Leighton insists he understands the appeal of Rossetti's "life recluded," that he envies the other's "ivory tower," but he still must insist that Rossetti allow him to "put [his] name down in our Candidates' Book."[56] The viewer is left to imagine, or perhaps even enact, Rossetti's expression of skepticism and disdain.

Beerbohm's Rossetti is also distinctly cosmopolitan. He inhabits a transnational milieu and exhibits an Italian sensibility. Beerbohm foregrounds Rossetti's connections to foreign lands in the caricature *British Stock and Alien Inspiration*.[57] Two Tory MPs alongside Millais and Holman Hunt express their misgivings about Disraeli and Rossetti: "Very clever, no doubt – Full of wonderful ideas but – Not to be trusted for one moment."[58] Rossetti is marked as not fully English, and in this again the two artists are linked. Beerbohm's expatriate status and his connections with places abroad are highlighted in the advertising pamphlet for the collection, which pictures Beerbohm emerging from a map of Italy and scribbling his insights onto a pad of paper (Figure 1.4).[59] In a 1948 review of *Mainly on the Air*, Edmund Wilson suggests that Max possessed "a mixture of foreign with English blood, . . . an element unassimilated by England that inevitably gravitated away from her."[60] While "there had always been present in his work an alien whose instincts and fancies were not amenable to English standards[,] this alien side of Max Beerbohm makes its fullest and frankest statement in the album of drawings called 'Rossetti and His Circle.'"[61] In theorizing the role Rossetti's transnationalism played in his cultivation of a detached persona, he, according to Wilson, revealed much about his own cosmopolitanism. "The alien element" in Beerbohm, Wilson argues, "is at least as exotic as Rossetti."[62] He possessed "the dandiacal aberration of the foreigner."[63] While he might have loved England and returned to England to be at her side when the war began, his dandiacal foreignness, the "alien element" in him, remained unassimilated by the jingoistic energies of the period, and here, too, Rossetti operated as an important model.

The images in *Rossetti and His Circle* are related to a larger and never completed project, one that speaks even more clearly to Beerbohm's desire to be transported from the 1910s. *The Mirror of the Past* has been described by Lawrence Danson as "quintessential Beerbohm," and the work is certainly the height of post-Victorian camp nostalgia in its treatment of the

Figure 1.3. Max Beerbohm, *A Man from Hymettus*, from *Rossetti and His Circle*, 1922. © Estate of Max Beerbohm. Reproduced courtesy of Mark Samuels Lasner.

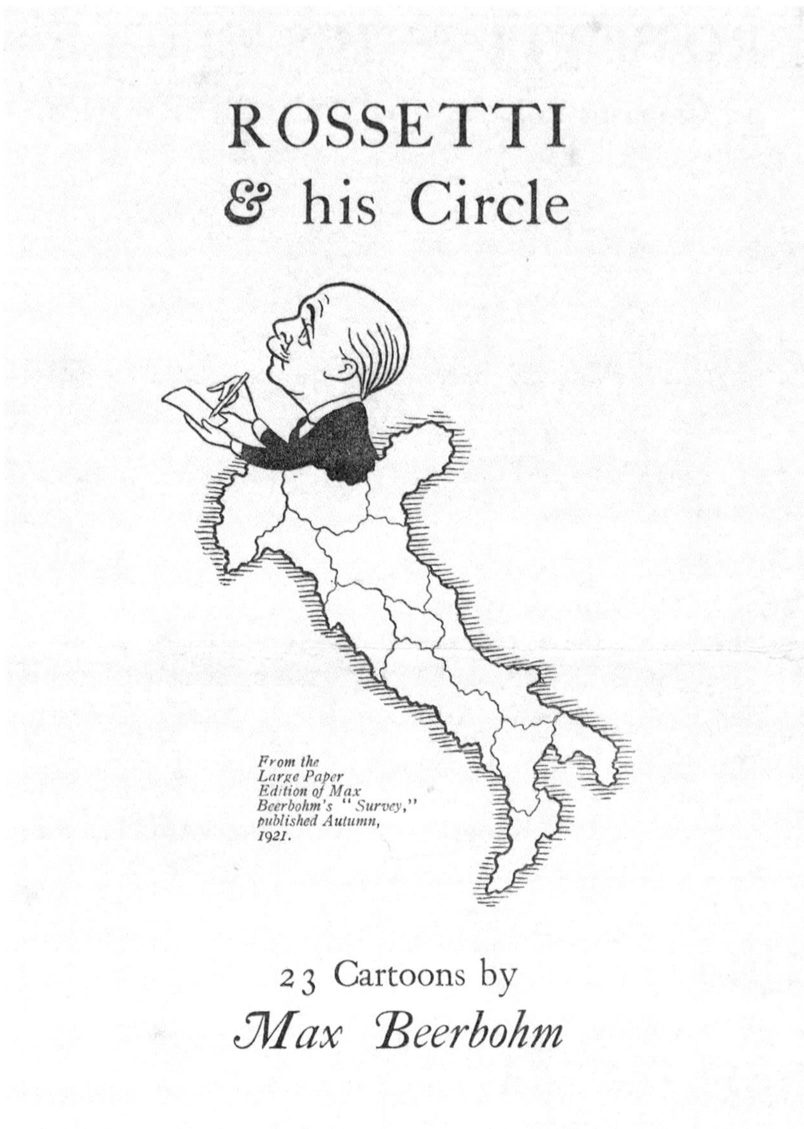

Figure 1.4. Advertising pamphlet for *Rossetti and His Circle* (Mark Samuels Lasner Collection, on loan to the University of Delaware). © Estate of Max Beerbohm. Reproduced courtesy of Mark Samuels Lasner.

fantastic possibility of traveling back into a gently lampooned nineteenth century.[64] It is the story of a mirror in the possession of an amateur scientist named Sylvester Herringham, who was once a host to what were referred to as "Herringham's Mondays," events at which the great cultural celebrities of the 1860s and 1870s mingled in his home. While visiting Herringham one day, Tennyson remarked that the mirror on his wall had certainly seen a great deal of things, inspiring Herringham to begin experimenting with the mirror, altering it so it begins to reflect the past. As time moves forward, the images in the mirror move regressively further back in time, reflecting remoter moments each day. By the time the narrator encounters the mirror, it is reflecting the 1870s, and as time progresses, he is granted access to all the great men and women who moved through Herringham's home in the latter half of the nineteenth century, including Rossetti, Morris, and Swinburne. The narrative enacts the same sort of fantasy time travel in which the *Rossetti and His Circle* caricatures engage but in far more explicit terms. The stories the mirror tells allow the audience to at once laugh about and long for the past it reflects. The Victorian subjects are gently mocked as Beerbohm works to balance the opportunities such a plot provided for sentimentality "with the opportunities it provided for parody, satire, and caricature."[65] He seems to be carefully restraining himself from the overwhelming pleasure that the nostalgic retreat of the mirror promises, implementing humor as an antidote to mawkishness, peering into the mirror with that "ironic double vision that acknowledges the final impossibility of indulging in nostalgia, even as it consciously evokes nostalgia's affective power."

Conceiving the story necessitated an extended and complex consideration of temporality on Beerbohm's part. The plot's complicated movements required charts and outlines, calendars and chronologies that are in the manuscript crossed out, revised, and reworked. Beerbohm was at this time becoming increasingly interested in the political uses of the past, and the practical elements of constructing a narrative about time travel allowed him to meditate extensively on the movements of history and the connections between the present and the past. The scenario he generated in *The Mirror of the Past*, however, eventually began to fold in onto itself, bending under the pressure of an excessively convoluted treatment of temporality. The manuscript that survives is, as Danson has discussed in his edition of the work, a mess. It seems at a certain point to have grown beyond Beerbohm's control and at this point to have been abandoned. He told S. N. Behrman many years later that "it became too involved, you know, too complicated. I couldn't understand it myself."[66] The project itself speaks poignantly to

Figure 1.5. Max Beerbohm, *Studies of the Heads of the Pre-Raphaelites*, 1917–18. Mark Samuels Lasner Collection, on loan to the University of Delaware Library. © Estate of Max Beerbohm. Reproduced courtesy of Mark Samuels Lasner.

the feelings of dissatisfaction and sorrow that inspired it, and its failure reflects much about the predetermined failure of the nostalgic project.

However, though the project was not completed, the process of thinking it through seems to have allowed Beerbohm to indulge in the artistic equivalent of the temporal inversion that the manuscript describes. Engaging in pastiche gave Beerbohm the opportunity to occupy an aesthetic manner of another moment, to sketch himself into another period. In the many drawings that he generated while working through this concept, there is evidence of real pleasure in trying his hand at Rossetti's style, at camping Rossetti's practices, and imagining himself into another artist's time and body. The Mark Samuels Lasner Collection at the University of Delaware includes a page of these sketches that reveal Beerbohm enacting an even more exaggerated version of Rossetti's style than the mimicry practiced in *Rossetti and His Circle*. This Jane and this Lizzie appear like penciled specters rising from the oils and watercolors on which they are based (Figure 1.5). In the manuscript in the Taylor collection, Beerbohm has sketched a copy of Rossetti's *Sir Launcelot's Vision of the Sanc Grael*, the elusive image that figured in the Oxford Union fresco, allowing himself the pleasure of re-creating a work that had faded away. If the project could not be completed, the attempt to do so provided moments of escape during the 1910s, fostering and nourishing the development of Beerbohm's post-Victorian camp aesthetic.

"Enoch Soames," another tale of time travel and temporal inversion, also emerges from this period. A failed Decadent poet travels a hundred years into the future to encounter his legacy in the reference works in the British Reading Room only to find he has been completely forgotten. Again, Beerbohm offers up a fantasy of a much more mutable form of temporality, a world in which one can shuttle easily between periods. This is exactly the sort of thing that might appeal to an audience firmly situated within a violently troubled era. "Enoch Soames" is one of Beerbohm's best known and beloved works and, like the *Rossetti and His Circle* caricatures, one that might allow a traumatized public contact with an at once nostalgic and satirical vision of Victorian aestheticism. In this case, it is the Decadence of the 1890s that Beerbohm simultaneously celebrates, mourns, and ridicules – the "odd apparitions" of the period, the young writers who "strove earnestly to be distinct in aspect."[67] Interwar readers are ushered into the domino room of the Café Royal, led to the offices of the Bodley Head publishing firm and through Chelsea to drink absinthe beside a "dim," "sad" Decadent figure.[68] Decadence here is not a disturbing locus of sickness and perversion but a quaint and somewhat silly form of eccentricity. Here we can see yesterday's avant-garde truly operating as a source of comfort and nostalgia for a distressed population. What was once a thorn in British readers' sides emerges here as a sweet, silly specter from a lighter time brought into the present by a dandy who smirks at the bohemianism he has reanimated.

This was an intensely generative moment for Beerbohm, a period that produced the majority of his most beloved works, but he insisted that his caricatures were not appropriate for display in wartime. He canceled an April 1915 exhibition of his work at the Leicester Galleries, arguing that "my caricatures, exhibited while England is in the throes of a life-and-death struggle, would not merely fall flat: they would be an offence against decency.... Imagine a nation being called on, in the midst of a whole world's tragedy of suffering and horror, to enjoy my little jokes.... The idea is inconceivable."[69] While he himself seemed to find great solace in humor, he felt that this antidote should not be shared with the public. "The war," he wrote, "is no laughing matter; and the war is *the only matter* in the present and in the near future."[70] He, however, refused to depart from his oblique and delicate dandyism and speak explicitly about this matter. A minister of the government asked him to complete some propaganda cartoons, but he declined, and Lieutenant Colonel Charles à Court Repington invited him to do political drawings for the Sunday papers, and again he refused.[71] In a 1914 letter to Edmund Gosse, he wrote, "It seems absurd to write to anyone about anything but the war. It seems to argue a lack of sense of proportion. But if I wrote anything about the war, not less guilty should I seem of that lack. What could I write that would not seem utterly trivial in proportion to this theme?"[72] He wrote in a similar vein to Arnold Bennett in 1915: "No, I don't think I shall do any war cartoons. My drawing is too *funny*. A tremendous grimness seems to me the only way; and *I* can't be grim or tremendous."[73] While he did agree to contribute a series of cartoons of "Artists on the Front" to *Reveille*, a literary quarterly for the "Disabled Soldier and Sailor" edited by John Galsworthy, for the most part, he withheld his work from the public until hostilities had ceased.

In the years following World War I, however, Beerbohm released a flood of material on the public. There was a series of exhibitions at the Leicester Galleries in 1921, 1923, 1925, and 1928. *Seven Men* (1919), *And Even Now* (1920), *Around Theatres* (1924), and *A Variety of Things* (1928) – the last two part of a ten-volume collected edition of Beerbohm's writings – were published along with four collections of caricatures: *A Survey* (1921), *Rossetti and His Circle* (1922), *Things New and Old* (1923), and *Observations* (1925). The public demonstrated an enormous appetite for these post-Victorian Decadent productions. As Evelyn Waugh argued, Beerbohm was "regarded as a man of the 1890s but his full flowering was in the 1920s."[74] The publication of the Rossetti caricatures and "Enoch Soames" gave a traumatized public, one that had been witness to much ugliness, access to a moment and a milieu preoccupied with beauty above all things. While Beerbohm might satirize the excesses of aestheticism and Decadence, his camping of the Pre-Raphaelites or the Yellow Nineties might have been even more palatable to that public than a straightforwardly sentimental nostalgia for the consummately aesthetic past. That delicate past must have seemed somewhat incomprehensible to a readership that just came through the war. His satirical treatments of aestheticism and Decadence allowed the interwar public to consider the allure of the cult of beauty while acknowledging its historical situatedness in a moment much different than their own.

The Rossetti caricatures were particularly well liked, and reviews of the collection frequently made note of the opportunities for contact with beauty that the works allowed. The *Times* reviewer, for example, argues that "each [drawing] is worth a whole volume of sermons on ideals in art and life."[75] Critics also tended to note the loving manner in which Beerbohm lampooned Rossetti's circle. Henry McBride states in the *Dial* that Beerbohm "expresses love with whacks."[76] Lloyd Goodrich's review in the *Arts* notes that Beerbohm is "not one of those caricaturists who stand at a distance and deal resounding blows. He treats his victims with a degree of consideration, almost of tenderness, that reminds one irresistibly of the attitude of a collector of butterflies towards his specimens."[77] The reviewer for the *Connoisseur* asserts that Beerbohm's representations of the Pre-Raphaelites seemed more intimate than his caricatures of contemporary personages, individuals Beerbohm knew personally, and that this sense of intimacy arises from Beerbohm's gentle and precise mode of satire: "The fun is both genial and witty, and, best of all, one feels that one more fully realises the characters of the circle and its environment because of it."[78] These works serve as windows into another, more beautiful time, but the artist seems strangely to stand on both sides of that window, intimately aware of the world being caricatured while clearly comprehending that the represented moment is fully and finally over. He is at once detached from and intimate with the objects of his satire, and he similarly enables his audience to come into close contact with a more beautiful past while poignantly entering into a realization that they occupy a very different present.

Beerbohm's capacity for Decadent detachment played a large part in his appeal to audiences of the 1920s. In a 1925 review of an exhibition at the Leicester Galleries, Yvonne Cloud argues that Beerbohm's disinterestedness holds a particular value during a period of tumult and passion like the interwar period: "When the recluse, the hermit comes amongst the people his word is attended by all wise men and in these days, particularly, where everyone has a blunt axe on his person, the opinions of the detached looker-on are greatly instructive. He sees the world through twinkling eyes. What funny axes! he says and with both hands, for he is not himself encumbered, he sets about neither to steal nor to grind the axes of others, but to show how exquisitely humorous they are."[79] In *Max Beerbohm in Perspective* (1921), Bohun Lynch celebrates Beerbohm's lack of earnestness: "We mean by 'earnestness' . . . that seriousness which is set forth not only without humour but which makes manifest the impossibility of there being a sense of humor behind the sense of importance. Earnestness is an inalienable and indispensable quality of propaganda, of the sermon."[80] Beerbohm's satirical vision, his skepticism, and his apartness allow him to speak in measured terms, to avoid the earnest fervor and passion of the sermon or propaganda, and it is this kind of disinterestedness that is needed most at the moment. Beerbohm remains stubbornly aloof from the intense passions that govern the interwar years. Not fully tied to any perspective, he is able to properly consider and to critique them all. In Lynch's words, he "keeps the balance true."[81] All political positions are equally subjected to Beerbohm's satirical scrutiny. As Lynch argues in response to Charles Marriott's critique of Beerbohm's caricatures of Labour, "Max has satirized the social outlook from all three points – Aristocracy, Labour, and Business,'" so "none of them need complain."[82] He "recognises that all stories have two sides to them, and no truth is absolute."[83] His aloofness allows him to see clearly during a period of rampant blindness. In *Experiences of a Literary Man* (1926), Stephen Gwynn connects Beerbohm's detachment to a pacifist ethos, stating that he "should like to paper the office of the League of Nations – or better the Chancellories of Europe – with Max caricatures. No other pacifist has given such trenchancy to his attack on bullying. [He] sets a picture before, it may be France, or it may be Ireland, and says, 'Look at your vicious self.'"[84] As much as Beerbohm endeavored to represent himself as separate from the twentieth century, 1920s critics, who did acknowledge his detachment, nevertheless insisted that he was intensely necessary to the very present to which he insisted he had no connection.

Following the war, Beerbohm allowed himself to depart from the extreme obliqueness of his wartime work and speak directly to the political realities of the moment. These works reveal on Beerbohm's part a rising disgust with the post-Edwardian world, its violence and incivility, and they often make explicit the pacifist sensibility implied in the earlier works. In a cartoon published in *A Survey*, for example, Beerbohm presciently represents the development of a weapon so powerful that it could be "dropped from an aeroplane . . . destroy all human and other animal life throughout an area of 500 square miles."[85] The Eminent Soldier to which the weapon has been presented finds it "marvellous" and notes how much "it makes one wish that one was a youngster and *sure* of being in the Next Great War."[86] The soldier's brutal enthusiasm for the weapon's destructive capacity is matched only in intensity by his jingoistic paranoia as he expresses concerns about whether the "other Powers [have] got anything of the sort."[87] In interwar political cartoons such as this, Beerbohm expresses an aesthete's distaste for a world growing increasingly vulgar.

It is important to note, however, that some of what Beerbohm perceived as vulgarity might be perceived as progress. He was troubled by the rise of Labour and a bit upset by the change in women's roles at the turn of the century. His post-Victorian dandyism and nostalgia did not always produce the most optimal political results. While there might be something admirable in his cosmopolitanism and his pacifism, this cannot fully displace the more conservative elements of his thinking, his reverence for tradition when it came to issues such as class and gender. Because of this intermingling of the conservative and the progressive in his thinking, Beerbohm's politics are notoriously difficult to categorize, and he only contributed to this confusion by describing himself as a "Tory Anarchist."[88] Lawrence Danson connects the difficulties in categorizing Beerbohm politically to the ongoing disagreement concerning the politics of parody. As he argues, "parody has often been seen as a conservative force," represented by critics like George Kitchin as "a bullying prefect defending the old school against anything foreign or new."[89] Conversely, Bakhtin's work encourages a consideration of the more progressive effects of parody. He argues that parody resists repression by "[introducing] the permanent corrective of laughter" and forming "a critique of the one-sided seriousness of the lofty direct word, the corrective of reality that is always richer, more fundamental and most importantly *too contradictory and heteroglot* to be fit into a high and straightforward genre."[90] Beerbohm's work seems to enact both elements of parody, launching a defense of tradition while at the same time lampooning the past, demonstrating a deplorable anxiety concerning the progressive developments of the twentieth century as well as an admirable resistance to the jingoistic nationalism of the period.

The peculiarity of Beerbohm's temporal and political positioning in the interwar period, the extent to which he seemed so contemporary and so anachronistic, so conservative and yet somewhat radical, registers even more clearly in his reception by the high modernists. While Beerbohm worked avidly to link himself to the Victorian past, to enact an anachronistic posture and insist that his time was very much over, the young men and women of the 1910s and 1920s treated him as admirable and significant rather than passé. Roger Fry invited him to visit the Omega Club in 1917.[91] Beerbohm's visitors' book indicates that T. S. Eliot, Ezra Pound, Wyndham Lewis, and Ernest Hemingway sought him out at Rapallo in the 1920s.[92] When he wrote in 1918 to express his admiration for Lytton Strachey's *Eminent Victorians* (1918), the response he received matched and exceeded the reverent tone of his original missive. Strachey refers to Beerbohm as "*cher maître*."[93] He writes that he, since he was a boy, thought of Beerbohm as "the *one* truly distinguished and classical master of the English tongue" and that, as he wrote his book, he often wondered "what Max, if he ever saw it, would think of it."[94] Strachey indicates how present and central Beerbohm remained in the modernist imagination, giving the lie to Beerbohm's protestations concerning his marginality to the period.

Beerbohm's most interesting exchange with modernism, however, occurred when he began his correspondence with Virginia Woolf. Woolf states that she highly admires Beerbohm's style in "A Flying Lesson" (1920) and "The Modern Essay" (1925), asserting that the "spirit of personality permeates every word he writes."[95] Writing to Woolf to praise *The Common Reader* (1925) in 1927, Beerbohm thanks her for being "nice about [his] essays" and expresses delight in her *Mr. Bennett and Mrs. Brown* (1924).[96] He also notes, however, that he wishes she could be a bit more conscious of readers like him in her novels: "In your novels you are so hard on us common readers. You seem to forget us and to think only of your theme and your method. Your novels beat me – black and blue."[97] He insists he admires her creative work immensely, "but only in a bemused and miserable manner."[98] And he contests her claim that "a new spirit exacts a new method," arguing that "a hundred years from hence fictional narrative will be thriving . . . on the old method" practiced by Homer, Thackeray, and Tolstoy.[99] In a postscript he teases her about her enthusiasm for the novel and the modern, asking, "Aren't you just a trifle over-loyal to this particular era?"[100] Woolf's reply exhibits much of the same reverence and enthusiasm on display in Strachey's correspondence with the "*maître*." She begins by stating that his letter reached her as she was on her way to Hardy's funeral, where she "had a ticket as [her] father's daughter."[101] However, she notes, "now that Mr Beerbohm has praised me I have a right to half a seat on my own account."[102] She states that she looks upon Beerbohm "as one, perhaps the only one, who is withdrawn far, far above us, in a serene and cloudless air, imperishable, aloof. And then suddenly you let down a ray from your sky and it rests! – behold! – upon me! If you knew how I had pored over your essays – how they fill me with marvel – how I can't conceive what it would be like to write as you do!"[103] She moves on to reply to his "kindly criticisms."[104] She asserts that she cannot write other than she does and she does so simply to amuse herself, and she then insists that she must say a word in favor of "freaks in general," works such as *Tristram Shandy*, Thomas Love Peacok's *Gryll Grange*, and Beerbohm's own *Zuleika Dobson*.[105] His work, she implies, does not fit squarely within the tradition of the "old method." Works like *Zuleika* might have more in common with the torturous freaks she composes than with Thackeray or Tolstoy. She grows at once more playful and aggressive in asserting that, as Beerbohm lives with the immortals, he cannot understand the horror of being forced to rub shoulders with the Bennetts and Galsworthies of the world: "If the tradition breeds them, with all their innumerable virtues, then to

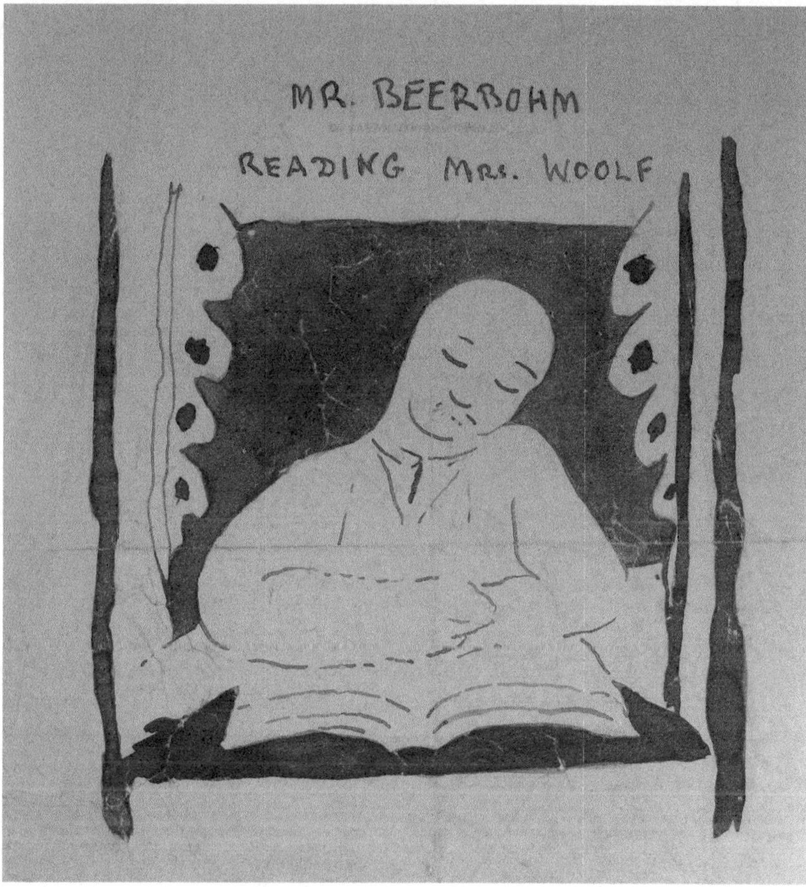

Figure 1.6. Max Beerbohm, *Mr. Beerbohm Reading Mrs. Woolf*, on verso of ALS to Miss Peyton, February 19, 1928. Mark Samuels Lasner Collection, on loan to the University of Delaware Library. © Estate of Max Beerbohm. Reproduced courtesy of Mark Samuels Lasner.

my thinking, the tradition had better be snuffed out and extinct."[106] She contests directly Beerhom's aesthetic conservatism while insisting that he does not even belong on the side with which he's identified.

Beerbohm followed this exchange with a note a month later to a "Miss Peyton," thanking her for sending him *Mr. Bennett and Mrs. Brown*, a "delightful work" that should serve as "a perfect model of how to behave as a lecturer."[107] The verso depicts *Mr. Beerbohm Reading Mrs. Woolf* (Figure 1.6). The drawing lightly undercuts the praise on the recto by

Figure 1.7. Vanessa Bell, cover of *Mr. Bennett and Mrs. Brown*, 1924. © Estate of Vanessa Bell, courtesy of Henrietta Garnett. Reproduced courtesy of the Harry Ransom Center, University of Texas at Austin.

referencing the difficulty Mr. Beerbohm tends to encounter when dealing with Mrs. Woolf's prose. The Mr. Beerbohm in the picture seems to have fallen asleep. The image, however, is a pastiche of Vanessa Bell's cover for *Mr. Bennett and Mrs. Brown*, which represents a similarly sleepy woman with her arms draped over a book in just the same posture (Figure 1.7). The post-Victorian satirist, who tends to implement pastiche as a method for traveling into the past, has here allowed himself the pleasure of playing with the forms of the present. Although the content of the picture seems to indicate that he is unable to comprehend the modernist aesthetic, the form shows him playfully trying his hand at a modernist style. The exchange with Woolf and the Bell pastiche together highlight the tension in Beerbohm's strange positioning during the interwar period, the manner in which his avowed aloofness and anachronism were complicated by his intense engagement with the political and aesthetic present. This tension became even more evident in the years leading up to World War II, as Beerbohm moved to a new medium that allowed him to bring his post-Victorian Decadent persona to a much larger and even more receptive public.

III. The Last of the Dandies Radiates: 1935–1956

On October 28, 1935, Moray McLaren of the BBC invited Max Beerbohm to participate in a new series of talks being broadcast on Sunday nights under the general title of "Revisited." "The idea," the invitation states, "has been to ask some distinguished author or journalist to return to the town or city with which his early youth was associated and to broadcast from there a partly reminiscent and partly observant talk on the changes or lack of changes which have taken place between then and now."[108] Beerbohm's reply indicates that the idea of "radiating" on the subject of London interested him very much. However, he notes, "I am essentially a private, non-radiant person, by nature and habit," and so "only a rather heavy bribe would tempt me forth. I should want – I was going to say £100, but won't grossly say that: I will delicately say £90. Do you think this outrageous? If so, tell me so; and have no fear that my feelings will be hurt."[109] McLaren's response expresses delight at Beerbohm's interest, but he also acknowledges that the fee Beerbohm asks is "certainly out of the ordinary," so much so that he will have to put the question to the BBC executives.[110] The internal memo in which McLaren makes his case for acceding to this extraordinary request indicates much about Beerbohm's reputation during this period. Although he continually cast himself as archaic, passé, a time traveler from the 1890s who could hold no possible interest in the modern moment, the fact remains that his fame probably reached its apex in the years following World War I. By the 1930s, he was a beloved fixture in the English public's imagination, a fact McLaren emphasizes in his memo, noting that "Max Beerbohm is about the only living writer of English who is universally liked."[111] McLaren stresses that there will be "an enormous public for this talk."[112] Beerbohm is also, McLaren notes, "a rare bird," one who spends most of his time in Italy but has been forced back to England by the state of affairs in his adopted country.[113] Owing to both his elusiveness and his appeal, the English public is hungry for contact with Beerbohm, and this, McLaren notes, could be the first and the last opportunity that the BBC might have of broadcasting him. McLaren concludes the memo by noting that "the recollection of London of the past and the comparison of old London with the London of to-day is one of the subjects on which he is most brilliant and most nostalgic."[114]

In his broadcasts for the BBC, Beerbohm often plays up a vision of himself as a tottering old man, up past his bedtime, "one of the relics of an older, an easier, and more pleasant yet formal world than this one."[115] However, he also subtly upsets his listeners' expectations, injecting into his dreamy stories of the Victorian past a certain tautness and an air of fundamental dissatisfaction that runs counter to their desire to doze off while listening to a silly, sweet, and benign antique. In fact, during his very first broadcast, the aforementioned talk on London, he warns his auditors, "I am going to be depressing. Perhaps you had better switch me off."[116] His talk is peppered with pleasant anecdotes about a goat that lived in Piccadilly and the two milkmaids who once milked two cows in St. James's Park, but these rosy images give way to something much more acidic. London in the 1880s and 1890s, Beerbohm, notes, had "a demure poetry about 'her,'" but "nowadays she cannot be called 'she': she is essentially it."[117] "London has been cosmopolitanised, democratised, commercialised, mechanised, standardised, vulgarised, so extensively that one's pride in showing it to a foreigner is changed to a wholesome humility. One feels rather as Virgil may have felt in showing Hell to Dante."[118] When one encounters the new houses that have been built and considers the "significant houses, the old habitable homes, that were demolished to make way for them, and when one sees how what remains of decent human architecture is reduced by them to the scale of hardly noticeable hovels, then one's heart sickens, and one's tongue curses the age into which one has survived."[119] Beerbohm manages his own disgust by engaging in the type of bizarre temporal inversion for which he is most well known: "As I go my rounds, I imagine that the present is the past. I imagine myself a man of the twenty-first century, a person with an historic sense, whose prayer that he should behold the London of a hundred years ago has been granted."[120] He is able to "console" and "brace" himself with this imagined time travel, which transforms the objects of his contempt into souvenirs of a bygone age for an appreciative twenty-first-century man. Nevertheless, he insists, "there is always a deadweight of sadness in me. Selfish sadness: I ought to keep my pity for the young people who never saw what I have seen, who will live to see what I shall not see – future great vistas of more and more commercialism, more machinery, more standardisation, more nullity."[121] Following this eruption of bitterness and sorrow, Beerbohm immediately tells his listeners to "forget this talk. Or at any rate discount it. Remember that after all I'm an old fogey – and perhaps rather an old fool."[122] Assembling about himself once more the costume of a meaningless fossil, he feigns irrelevance and exhaustion, a posture entirely belied by the content of almost every sentence that preceded these statements.

This tension between nostalgia and critique played a key role in the discussions that preceded his 1942 broadcast on "Advertisements." Beerbohm's response to a 1942 invitation to speak on the *Yellow Book* circle reflects his willingness to operate as a source of historical contrast but not as a form of meaningless escapism: "I daresay I might be quite fairly good on the theme that you suggest: the Yellow Book time. But here again I am averse. Last January I seemed to be generally liked in the character of the dear old gentleman. But I think it would be a mistake to repeat those effects. There are other elements in me. There is for instance some 'snap' left in me still and I should like to give that a turn."[123] He suggests instead that he might deliver a talk on advertisements. In his anxious reply, C. V. Salmon states that Beerbohm's proposed subject "frightens [him] a good deal": "Advertising is about as prickly a subject for us as you could have chosen. On the one hand, our being a monopoly makes it easy for us to 'talk in a superior way about the vulgarity of advertising,' and, on the other, the fact that we derive revenue from advertisements in the Radio Times makes it difficult for us to deal impartially with it at all."[124] Beerbohm's response notes, "But you would *not* be talking about it in a superior or any other way. It is merely I myself that would be saying some things about my own private and personal dislike of the too vast quantity of advertising that goes on in peace time. . . . My touch is a light one – and an irresponsible one; and the B.B.C. could not, I think, conceivably be compromised by my expression of my own aesthetic fastidiousness in this matter."[125] He concludes his letter with one additional taunt: "I invented a slogan the other day, 'Nothing in this world is worth buying'; and this I should be inclined to quote. Do you think the advertisers would be injured?"[126] Beerbohm was finally able to deliver the talk, and in an internal memo that followed the broadcast, G. R. Barnes, the director of talks at the BBC, notes that if he were Kenneth Adam, the BBC's head of publicity, he would "tell the advertisers that Max has made an international reputation by pulling all sorts of legs (some of them even more distinguished than those of advertisers) since the days of the Yellow Book."[127] Here it is his ties to the past that endow him with the right to mock. Far from a quiet fossil, he is an esteemed and established satirist (who nevertheless has some snap left in him) whose reputation ensures his freedom to speak critically.

To say that Beerbohm functioned as nothing more than a facilitator of nostalgic retreat during the war and the years leading up to it would be somewhat reductive. In his talks, with their "irresponsible touch," their ironic tone, Beerbohm nimbly brandishes his trademark silver dagger prose style. He is light yet precise in his rapierlike attack on the conditions of modernity. His 1936 broadcast on "Speed," for example, seems to be concerned simply with the danger posed to pedestrians by motor cars. However, the rhetoric Beerbohm employs concerning the omnipresent threat of physical harm in the modern world subtly gestures toward the larger spirit of dread that marked the early twentieth century. In response to the press's call for the public to be more "traffic-conscious," Beerbohm replies, "There is really no need to tell us we must be so. How could we be otherwise? How not be concussion-apprehensive, annihilation-evasive, and similar compound words? When the children of this generation, brought up in fear, shall have become adult, what sort of ailments will their progeny have, one wonders?"[128] The public, he argues, seems to be in need of "rousing" to confront the "habitual carnage" that has become commonplace in the modern world. He playfully scolds his listeners, "You are ashamed that in years not very remote from ours young women were worked to death in the factories, and children in the coal mines. You blush at the barbarities of criminal justice in the eighteenth and early nineteenth centuries. What do you think posterity will think of *this* age?"[129] The modern fascination with speed, he argues, has resulted in pervasive and omnipresent danger. This message is relayed, however, with a spirit of levity within a talk that advertises itself as preoccupied with nothing more serious than pedestrians' rights.

Linda Hutcheon argues that it is the ironizing of nostalgia in postmodernism that "[creates] a small part of the distance necessary for reflective thought about the present as well as the past."[130] Beerbohm's post-Victorian camp nostalgia similarly enabled criticism as opposed to escape. The nostalgic dandy with a dagger reflected on both the past and the present in his radio broadcasts with a spirit of affectionate malice. Even when he finally did as he was asked and spoke about the men of the Yellow Nineties, he did so in a Decadent camp style that lovingly called the figures of the fin de siècle forth while at the same time having much fun at their expense. In the years following the war, he delivered a series of talks on Yeats, George Moore, and Henry James, and the audience responded warmly both to the opportunities these talks provided for returning to a more aesthetic past and the satiric spirit with which the speaker did so. The Audience Research Report for the talk on Yeats (which received an "appreciation index" of 73), for example, quotes a pleased "clerk" who was particularly enchanted by Beerbohm's "velvet-pawed malice towards his contemporaries."[131] A "student" stated that Beerbohm "must be the perfect broadcaster – modest, malicious, velvetly ironic, cynically good natured, witty and individual. . . . He is never either haughty or over-enthusiastic."[132] A "translator" similarly noted in the talk "a charming vein of reminiscence and also a captivating absence of reverence for the great."[133] It is his critical detachment, his camp sensibility, that the listeners mention repeatedly. He reminisces, but he does not reminisce reverentially. Beerbohm, in fact, thematizes his capacity for detachment in the Yeats broadcast by discussing his own immunity to Yeats's charms: "I often had the pleasure of meeting Yeats, and I liked him. But merely to like so remarkable, so mystic and intense a creature, to be not utterly under his spell whenever one was in his presence – seemed to argue a lack in oneself and to imply an insult to that presence. Thus the pleasure of seeing Yeats was not for me an unmixed one. I felt always rather uncomfortable, as though I had submitted myself to a mesmerist who somehow didn't mesmerise me."[134] It is difficult to envision a mesmerist who might overwhelm the skepticism and apartness of Beerbohm. Yeats had a reputation for aloofness, too, Beerbohm acknowledges, for being "apart from the rest" and "not primarily of this world."[135] Yet, he asks, didn't his "management of the Celtic Renascence" seem to contradict that vision, proving Yeats to be "a practical man"?[136] Beerbohm hesitates about drawing that conclusion, noting that, despite the "pamphlets, letters to newspapers, lectures in America, speeches," Yeats seemed to be "[bombinating] in the void, never for an instance in any vital relation to the audience."[137] This sounds very much like the inverse of Beerbohm, who carefully and archly radiated rather than bombinated to an audience with whom he was in extremely vital relation. The content of the Yeats broadcast and the response it elicited taken together serve as a rich example of Max Beerbohm's post-Victorian Decadent form of camp nostalgia and the appeal it held for twentieth-century audiences, for whom he provided, not an escape from the present or an idealized vision of the past, but a skeptical and critically engaged form of reminiscence.

The radio broadcasts solidified Beerbohm's position in the mid-century cultural imagination. As Clair Price wrote in 1939, "for British listeners the radio has transformed him from a legend of the distant Nineties to the most enchanting of living voices."[138] The *Times Literary Supplement* similarly asserted that the morning after his very first broadcast, "Max" was "a household word in suburban trains and homes."[139] "In the midst of the war," when "that same voice," "very calm, very precise, quietly assertive of the reality of civilized values," spoke again, "the cult could almost be heard growing."[140] Listeners wrote to Max to tell him of the pleasure the broadcasts brought to them. The sculptor Kathleen Bruce, an old friend of Beerbohm's, wrote in 1942, "How enchanting you were last night. I was afraid that sort of perfect style, perfect wit, perfect humor, had vanished from the earth – It was a very keen delight – a perfect thing to happen while the air warning was on."[141] Siegfried Sassoon wrote following the London broadcast to say that "it was a triumphal success" during which he "felt the wisdom of the ages . . . and the glory of exquisite art and the affirmation of exquisite courtesy. . . . Everything was there which I love and value deeply."[142]

When the lectures were published as a collection in 1946, the response was similarly warm. The reviewers often made the case that the collection indicated how critically engaged Beerbohm remained with a present from which he seemed so often to be turning. In a review titled "The Perfect Trifler," for example, Louis Kronenberger asserts that the lectures reveal that "Max has not been living, placidly oblivious of the present in a fin de siècle dream. He is too constantly jarred by the present not to be uncomfortably aware of it. All the things he loves . . . are not much valued in our day. All the things he hates . . . are ubiquitous. . . . Again and again he can only shudder at what he sees, and sigh for what is vanished."[143] His nostalgia, Kronenberger argues, possesses a highly critical valence. The review in the *New York Times* similarly argues that "what this little book proves despite its nostalgic backward look, despite its regret for things lost and dead, is that Beerbohm is no gallant anachronism. His quality is ageless."[144] The broadcasts were perceived by the mid-century public as highly relevant to and engaged with the modern moment.

While Waugh may have been correct that Beerbohm flowered most fully in the 1920s, the audience and affection for his work grew enormous in the 1930s, 1940s, and 1950s. He was featured frequently in the popular press as "The Last of the Exquisites," the last remaining dandy of the fin de siècle.[145] In 1937, the Fungoids, a society dedicated to the "Preservation of the Memory of Enoch Soames," was founded at Yale. William Borst wrote to notify Beerbohm and to inform him of their plans to publish a volume of Soamesian poems titled *Absinthesis*.[146] In 1946, Harold Hobson published *The Devil in Woodford Wells*, a work of fantasy in which Enoch Soames again travels into the future, in this case to the 1940s, and encounters the effects of World War II on London.[147] A Maxoc Society was founded at Oxford in 1940. When he turned seventy in 1942, the Maximillian Society, whose members included Clive Bell, Desmond MacCarthy, Augustus John, Graham Greene, and Leonard Woolf, honored him with a party at the Players Theatre. When he turned eighty, he received a telegram from Winston Churchill and a book filled with written tributes from almost fifty admirers. Augustus John's entry foregrounds Beerbohm's complex and inverted temporal positioning: "Max is said to have been born old, which is no doubt why he grows younger, not older, and at this rate will end in the cradle."[148] And Evelyn Waugh highlights the appeal that Beerbohm's Victorian civility and his links to a superior past held for him as a young man: "At the time I lived mostly among people who thought mad manners rather chic. They were the hall-mark of the '20s. I suddenly heard a voice from a better age and it has rung in my ears ever since."[149]

If Beerbohm had seemed necessary and relevant following the First World War, the sense of his relevance was only compounded by the Second, and it was again his aloofness and anachronistic civility that remained central to his appeal. Clair Price's 1939 feature in the *New York Times Magazine* notes that "for nearly thirty years he has cultivated the habit of detachment. He has been an observer of the social and political turmoil around him, never a fighter in it."[150] His ability to remain separated from the fray endowed him with the capacity to see and understand that fray more clearly. In a 1952 essay, Bertrand Russell makes a similar claim, stating that Beerbohm's "view of the world is impartial": "His version is extraordinarily just and extraordinarily detached."[151] He notes that to the "tortured nerves" of modern men, Beerbohm's oblique, delicate, and detached work may seem frivolous or inappropriate: "The shrieks of Jews in Auschwitz and the torture of slave-labourers in the Arctic have numbed men's capacity for delicate appreciations."[152] Russell acknowledges that "such work," work that is delicate and perceptive and just, "can no longer be produced": "Our turbulent world gives little opportunity for the development of fine shades . . . and in this sense I fear it is only too true that he belongs to a past epoch. This is not to condemn him but to condemn the present."[153] It is, Russell argues, Beerbohm's post-Victorian positioning that renders him so attractive and fascinating to a traumatized modern public. E. H. J.'s "A Posy for Rapallo" (1952) also makes a case for the relevance of Beerbohm's work to the postwar world: "It is my firm opinion that any man who is truly civilized and who shows forth the graces of civilization in his work may be doing as much as any didactic teacher to lift mankind out of barbarism and society out of chaos. The world is in trouble and fear not so much from lack of ideas and idealisms as from lack of the truly civilised temper. If literature is not, before all things, the pioneer and guardian of civilised manners – then the cause is well on the way to be lost."[154] Beerbohm is described as the heir of those writers who never shout or scream, never show temper or act fanatically, such as Jane Austen or Henry James. He is a "civilized writer" who "feels more deeply than anyone else the ugliness of human violence and folly" but "will not use its barbarous weapons" to fight against it.[155]

In 1943, Beerbohm delivered the Rede lecture at Cambridge. His topic was Lytton Strachey, but like his obituary for Beardsley, the lecture seemed more properly to describe the nature and appeal of his own work. Strachey's *Eminent Victorians*, Beerbohm argues, came at a serendipitous moment "in that the Great War (as we impresciently called it) had been going on for two and a half years."[156] The moment demanded work like Strachey's: "In war, inevitably, rightly, voices are loud; and war, even when the omens are propitious to our own causes, is a tragic, a painfully astringent theme. And then the sound of a quick voice suddenly discoursing on well-remembered figures that had flourished in halcyon years not long gone by was bound to give us something very like the sense of relief that is ours in escaping from the din and crush of a metropolis to some dear little old familiar countryside."[157] Until his death in 1956, Beerbohm continued to provide a similar sense of relief to the British public, an alternative to the din and crush of twentieth-century modernity, allowing an embattled population access to halcyon years not long gone by. In his post-Victorian Decadent camp nostalgia, his smirking detachment, and his purposeful cosmopolitanism, he insisted on a reality separate from the brutality of the early twentieth century, a type of civility and cool contempt for conflict that, though seemingly obsolete, retained its allure and its capacity to foreground the failings of the modern moment.

CHAPTER 2

Pacifism and Post-Victorian Decadence

Vernon Lee at the Margins of the Twentieth Century

When World War I began, Vernon Lee was on her annual summer trip to England, and she was unable to return to her home, Il Palmerino, in Italy, until the war ended. This was a painful experience for her, and she longed throughout her stay to return to Tuscany. In a 1919 letter to Logan Pearsall Smith, Lee expressed relief to be back on her hillside, among her furniture, "all so unchanged."[1] She also expressed surprise at finding *herself* so unchanged: "*Unchanged as ghosts are*. For in this Elysian empty peacefulness, there is a sense of... well! Shall we say *finality*? A looking on – and as little as possible of that – on a world one no longer belongs to & has no duties towards; for it must be pleasant to feel, as I suppose ghosts do, that they have no limbs or vitals or voice, but my eyes... the most they can do is to rustle & disappear, which is what I am hastily (& agreeably) doing."[2] She represented herself to Smith as a spectral and disappearing presence, a remnant of the late-Victorian past, silent and receding, with no responsibility for or obligation to the present. This self-characterization, however, seems somewhat disingenuous. Lee's speaking role in public intellectual drama was far from over at this point. She published six more books before her death in 1935.[3] Her enormous and angry response to the war, *Satan the Waster* (1920), would not be published until the following year, and she continued to study and engage with the most recent developments in the humanities and social sciences until her final days. If she no longer belonged to the present, as she insisted in her letter to Smith, she certainly continued to feel a sense of duty, a responsibility as an intellectual, to engage with and intervene in public debate.

Six years after sending this letter, Vernon Lee published a short work titled *Proteus, or The Future of Intelligence* (1925) in Kegan Paul's Today and Tomorrow series. The Today and Tomorrow series, as its name suggests, positioned itself at the forefront of public intellectual debate in the 1920s. Publishing more than a hundred titles, such as Bertrand Russell's *Icarus, or the Future of Science* (1924), Anthony Ludovici's *Lysistrata, or Woman's Future and Future Woman* (1925), and J. B. S. Haldane's *Daedalus, or Science and the Future* (1924), the series, as a reviewer for the *American Journal of Sociology* put it, offered "readable, challenging statements in popular terms of what their authors believe to be some of the implications of the findings of modern science for the human life of the future."[4] Many of the works were purposefully controversial, such as Haldane's *Callinicus, a Defence of Chemical Warfare* (1925), which encouraged the English public to overcome their squeamishness about the use of poisonous gases. These tiny texts were received by the press as incendiary, "thought-compelling" barbs.[5] The *New York Times* referred to them as "the mildest appearing 16mos that ever scuttled our human complacency with the picture of such vast horizons or such acute despairs," and the *Commercial Tribune* noted that "each is a compendium of science and excitement. You can read any one of them in an hour and be certain of shocks, surprises, and intoxicating ideas. They violate the literary Volstead act, and may well be suppressed or denatured."[6]

These works represented decisively modern or novel turns in twentieth-century thinking. What place, then, did Vernon Lee, an aging representative of what George Bernard Shaw referred to as "the old guard of Victorian cosmopolitan intellectualism," have in such a series?[7] How could a hastily disappearing ghost scuttle human complacency? The jacket for *Proteus* seems to struggle with this, billing Lee as an author "who for forty years has been known as an authority on art, literature, poetry, and other subjects," while heralding the novelty of her "new theory of intelligence" and the "revolutions" this quality "may yet accomplish." Lee is at once of the past and the future, a remnant of the fin de siècle who is devoted, almost stubbornly, to innovative and decidedly twentieth-century thinking. In this chapter, I would like to use Lee's peculiar position within this series to begin thinking about the role she played in twentieth-century political and aesthetic discourse. How does her temporally marginal position enable a particularly incisive mode of political thinking? In foregrounding her own marginality and outsiderism, how does Lee simultaneously highlight her own unique capacity for political insight? Although she had a slightly more conflicted relationship to Decadence, Lee was, like Beerbohm, linked in the public's imagination to the 1890s and the later phases of aestheticism, and, like Beerbohm, she compounded the sense of her own anachronism by channeling an earlier form of aestheticism, in this case the aestheticism of her former mentor Walter Pater.[8] It should be noted that Lee's relationship to Pater was complex and shifted throughout her career. During the late-Victorian period, she expressed reservations about Pater's work. In

Renaissance Fancies and Studies (1895), for example, she notes that Pater's *Studies in the History of the Renaissance* (1873) left one with a feeling of "caducity and barrenness" because of its overwhelming emphasis on variety of experience at the expense of the concepts of morality and character. Nevertheless, she also finds in this text "the characteristic germs of what will develop, extrude all foreign admixture, knit together congruous qualities, and give us presently the highly personal synthesis of *Marius* and the *Studies on Plato*," works that, in Lee's eyes, reflect Pater's later interest in "beauty of the spiritual kind."[9] During World War I and in its aftermath, she returned to Pater's thinking about beauty and pleasure with a renewed enthusiasm, and Paterian aestheticism played a key role in her critical response to the war. As a remnant of the fin de siècle, she hovered between the 1870s and the 1920s, operating as a bridge between the heyday of the Aesthetic Movement and the interwar period. By turning to Pater, she highlighted her disappointment with the present while at the same time insisting that Pater's ideas about beauty, pleasure, and detachment, which played such a central part in the Decadence of the 1890s, might speak to and heal the modern moment.[10]

In *Proteus,* Lee manufactures a post-Victorian Decadent remedy for the traumas of the post-World War I period. *Proteus,* although far less explicitly political than *Satan the Waster* or the anxious essays Lee wrote for the periodical press during wartime, bears the mark of recent violence and the sense that further danger might be near. Lee notes that the current moment is marked by scaremongering, that "encyclopaedic science and journalistic emphasis are being applied to make our flesh creep with prophecies of Perils. . . . Peril from black, brown, yellow races; from Semites, Mongols, Latins (in Nordic countries), Teutons (in Latin countries), Celts all over Anglosaxondom, Jews throughout the globe."[11] Genius, which tends toward "exaggeration, contrariness, and . . . megalomonia," cannot properly decipher or evenly respond to such conditions. It is Intelligence that will be needed to "steady our nerves and allow us to recognize the real dangers of which, heaven knows, there are plenty."[12] In describing the manner in which Intelligence functions, Lee relies on a vocabulary of selection, using terms that serve to link Intelligence to taste as theorized in the works of Pater and Wilde. She refers to Intelligence's "active rhythm of grasping and acquiescing; a process of assimilation and elimination in which the already experienced and accepted selects that which shall be accepted or rejected."[13] The terminology Lee uses to describe this hybrid of aesthetics and ethics that is Intelligence is reminiscent of the vocabulary Pater used to describe the ideal critical spirit. In *Marius the Epicurean* (1885), for example,

Pater describes Christianity's relationship to ancient life as "a spirit which, in its dealing with the elements of ancient life, was guided by a wonderful tact of selection, exclusion, juxtaposition."[14] The "selective action" of Intelligence, the action that is required to direct the nations away from further disaster, seems to bear a striking resemblance to the "wonderful tact" of the critic, to the mode of perception, selection, arrangement, and juxtaposition celebrated by Pater and by Wilde, who, in "The Decay of Lying" (1891), argues that selection "is the very spirit of art."[15] Intelligence will allow for the selection of true concerns and the rejection of useless paranoias. In addition, the "mental eye" of Intelligence facilitates the "taking of Otherness into account," the ability to see that Otherness "has ways of its own and does not exist merely to suit our likings."[16] Much as Pater mingles discourses of morality and taste in his representation of the tactful selectiveness of early Christianity, Lee's formulation of Intelligence in *Proteus* posits perceptiveness, critical capacity, and aesthetic sense as the foundation for ethical action. She uses a markedly late-Victorian vocabulary drawn from aestheticism and Decadence to articulate an antidote to twentieth-century violence, paranoia, and militarism.

In the years leading up to World War I and in its aftermath, Lee insisted on a separation between herself and the present. Although she consistently engaged with the escalating aggression and nationalism of the early twentieth century, in works such as *Proteus,* she foregrounded her own marginality to the spirit of the times, returning again and again to the language of late-Victorian aestheticism and Decadence to speak to the problems of the modern moment. I am interested in particular in the manner in which Lee audited and found unsatisfactory a whole host of theories of the subject in the aftermath of the war, theories that worked to explain the incredible violence and devastation that had just occurred. Lee's marginalia in the works of psychology and sociology that she read in the 1910s and 1920s indicate that she found most of these theories fundamentally lacking. Situating herself on the margins of these conversations, she highlighted their inadequacy, while at the same time generating in her own works of the twentieth century a decidedly late-Victorian alternative theory of the subject. Her insistence on the centrality of the aesthetic impulse, as opposed to sexual, aggressive, or gregarious instincts, allowed her to maintain a sense of hopefulness about a future marked by decency and beauty rather than nationalism and warfare during the interwar period. Drawing on a Paterian vocabulary of taste, pleasure, and selection, she combated the pessimism of the post-World War I social sciences with an aesthetically inflected vision of the individual. Lee's utopian optimism, which looks forward to a future of intelligence, emerged directly from her affiliation with the past. Her position as a post-Victorian Decadent outsider allowed her to disentangle herself from the energies of the early twentieth century to articulate an alternative aestheticist theory of the subject.[17]

I. Selection and Rejection: Vernon Lee and the Interwar Social Sciences

In an April 1920 letter to Leo Stein, who was at the time living close to Il Palmerino in Settignano, Lee asks Stein to lend to her some "specimens" of Freudian analysis so she might overcome her repugnance for psychoanalysis and be "converted" to Freudianism.[18] She acknowledges that she possesses an "intense special . . . aversion to Freudianism," but she insists that this aversion does not arise from mere misoneism.[19] This aversion results instead from her skepticism about the "the excessive weight given to the sexual . . . factors" in Freud's thinking.[20] Nevertheless, she insists she wishes to "*overcome this resistance*, or to reduce it to a rational even if hostile criticism."[21] Her curiosity about Freud seems to have been linked to her efforts to think through the war, as her letter was sent along with "the psychological notes" that accompanied her "forthcoming War-Play," which she offered to Stein as proof of the fact that certain elements of Freudianism had already become integrated into her own thought.[22] The letter is very confusing. Lee describes herself as at once hostile to Freud and willing to be converted, as in need of education in his theories while at the same time already conversant in psychoanalysis. Lee's conflicted response to Freud indicates much about her state of mind following the war. Exasperated and disheartened, she cast around desperately, hoping to find in the social scientific disciplines some account of the subject that might render the recent past comprehensible. However, the "selective action" of her own Intelligence frequently forced her to reject the conclusions of those psychoanalysts and sociologists who posited the sexual or aggressive impulses as central to human nature. She turned to their works in hope of an answer but turned away in favor of an aestheticist account of a subject for whom the drive toward beauty is the central impulse.

During and after the war, Vernon Lee, as was her habit, read widely and across the disciplines. The Vernon Lee Collection at the British Institute of Florence contains numerous works of sociology, biology, political economics, and psychoanalytic theory that Lee read in the late 1910s and early 1920s. Lee wrote all over these books, inside the covers, in the margins, lengthy notes that ran from page to page, and she added to the books themselves, pasting in relevant periodical essays, and situated them discursively, peppering her marginal notes with references to relevant further reading. She constructed for her future readers a unique archive of intensely revealing artifacts. The texts in the collection resemble decorated books, art objects that provide a window into the thought processes of a remarkable late-Victorian intellectual. Although the work done in the margins and on the title pages of these books, the contradictions and the questions, the linking of individual authors and arguments to other books and lines of thought, often resulted in critical essays, the two are not equivalent. To read Lee's rebuttal to Wilfred Trotter in *Satan the Waster* is something quite different from actually witnessing her processing an argument she finds despicable. Sitting in the reading room at the British Institute, reading alongside Lee, I became increasingly convinced that Lee intended her annotated books to be encountered by scholars, that she looked forward to a future when critics might wish to know how she arrived at the conclusions she did and might wish to watch her argue with and digest the works of her contemporaries.

As Hilary Fraser has noted in her work on Lee's marginalia, "correction was one of the main purposes, in Lee's own view, of her prodigious annotation of books."[23] Fraser draws the term "correction" from the words inscribed at the end of Lee's copy of George Bernard Shaw's *Intelligent Woman's Guide to Socialism and Capitalism* (1928): "But what a fine book! how full of wisdom and humanity. Only, like every book, it requires a Reader to correct it."[24] Annotation allowed Lee to correct and to select, to discriminate, which, according to Lee, facilitates ethical action. She writes in the conclusion to *Gospels of Anarchy* (1908), "My marginal notes reveal the need of saving that part of my teacher's teaching which I could subscribe to from the mass of illogical notions in which it is embedded."[25] Her marginalia are material evidence of the attention she devoted to the process of selection and rejection.

Writing in the margins also allowed Lee to materially foreground what Hilary Fraser has referred to as her "interstitial identity," her status as a sexual and national outsider. In his work on marginalia, H. J. Jackson emphasizes the "attitude of defiance" in which marginal notes are produced. Marginalia, according to Jackson, "express the separate (usually contrary) views of the marginalist, and thereby assert a separate personality."[26] Although Lee always seemed to carry with her a sense of separateness, her outsiderism was compounded in the twentieth century, by the war, by the advent of new cultural avant-gardes, and new developments in the social sciences for which she did not feel much sympathy. Rather than seeking to alleviate this sense of separation from the present, she reinscribed it, voluntarily occupying the margins, placing herself at the edges of new thought, on the outside of theories that required correction.

A multitude of dark visions of humanity circulated during the 1910s and 1920s. As Paul Crook notes, "wartime theories in a range of disciplines presented man as a 'fighting anima' whose primal instincts were tragically at odds with advanced culture. . . . Instinct theory – which stemmed from animal psychology, physiology and the genetics revolution – encouraged the belief that pugnacity had been programmed into the ancient part of the human brain as a result of evolutionary pressures dating from prehistory."[27] Although some theorists expressed hope that reason and morality would triumph over these pugnacious instincts, the incredible devastation of World War I provided convincing evidence to support these bleaker hypotheses concerning human behavior. As Lee, a staunch pacifist, watched the nations at war and then watched those same nations explain the war to themselves, more and more seemed in need of correcting, in particular those intellectual discourses that sought to explain and defend warfare.

Wilfred Trotter's *Instincts of the Herd in Peace and War* (1916) attracted an immense amount of attention, engagement, and ire from Lee. It is, in fact, one of the most annotated texts in the collection in Florence. As Gillian Beer notes in her discussion of Lee's notes on Trotter, "Lee writes wry, witty, sometimes outraged comments, not only alongside the text in the margin, but sometimes in loops round and round the printed page – which allows her to get more of a say in reply to Trotter and entoils him satisfactorily."[28] The marginalia in *Instincts of the Herd* reveal multiple strands of disagreement on Lee's part. Whereas Beer focuses on Lee's resistance to Trotter's organicism and his reliance on crowd theory, I would like to focus on Lee's critique of Trotter's representation of the Germans as a species apart motivated by aggressive instincts.

Wilfred Trotter is widely known for popularizing the concept of the herd instinct in the early twentieth century. Trotter argued that, along with the three major elemental instincts discussed by social psychologists and evolutionary biologists, sex, self-preservation, and nutrition, the gregarious instinct must be understood as one of the primary motivations guiding human behavior. Animals that possess the social instinct sacrifice in autonomy what they gain in protection. Although they are far more sensitive to suggestion from other creatures within the social group than solitary animals, they are shielded from the immediate effects of natural selection by the larger unit. Gregariousness, according to Trotter, should be understood, not as a recent development of human evolution, a product of civilization, but as a fundamental and primary characteristic of the species, an influence as integral as sexual desire or hunger.

To illuminate the nature of the human social instinct, Trotter discusses comparable forms of the gregarious instinct as exemplified in three types of animal groups represented by the hive of bees, the herd of sheep, and the pack of wolves. The beehive represents to Trotter the utmost development of the social instinct, in which individuals sacrifice identity almost entirely to the group, willing to work themselves to death to support the function of the hive. The herd of sheep, united for defense, alert to danger, prepared to communicate about and escape from threats, represents the protective type. This type is somewhat less socialized and altruistic than the bee but more socialized than the wolf pack, the aggressive type, which is united only for attack. It is here that Trotter's thinking takes a turn for the unsettling, moving in a direction that the decidedly cosmopolitan Lee would find distasteful. He extends this typology to the nations of Europe, using it as a framework through which to read the war. England as a nation occupies a point on the continuum somewhere between the fully socialized bees and the amiably protective sheep, but Germany's lineage is lupine. Germany is a throwback to the least socialized and altruistic of the gregarious types. It relies for its unity on perceived threats from without and dwells permanently in alternating periods of aggression and preparation for aggression. These instincts are so essential to Germany's constitution that the war between England and Germany must be understood as a "war not so much of contending nations as of contending species."[29] Therefore, Trotter contends, it is useless to seek peace with this essentially warlike species, as peace stands in opposition to German instinctual behavior. "The destruction of the German empire is," according to Trotter, "an indispensable preliminary to the making of a civilization tolerable by rational beings."[30]

This conclusion would, of course, be upsetting to Lee, who had spent time during her childhood living in Germany and thus felt a certain sympathy for the nation. In addition, Lee was firmly cosmopolitan and would find any such attempt to essentialize national identity troubling. Her extensive marginal notes indicate that she found manifold flaws in Trotter's logic. Following Trotter's discussion of the difference between protective and aggressive gregariousness, Lee comments, "The point to observe is that there is no structural reason why any race of men should be aggressive to other men. The reasons are always economic or intellectual."[31] Lee is incredibly wary of positing aggressiveness as a primary instinct. This is not a definition of the subject with which she can concur. In the final chapters of the text, in which Trotter makes his assertions about

Germany's lupine nature, her aggravation and impatience escalate. Trotter asserts that Germany has cultivated the wolflike instincts in its people, throwing them back into "the anachronism of a lupine society," and the success of this movement cannot be "accounted for by even the power of the immense machine of officials, historians, theologians, professors, teachers, and newspapers by which they were, in season and out of season, enforced. The immense success that was attained owed much to the fact that suggestion was following a natural, instinctive path. The wolf in man, against which civilization has been fighting for so long, is still within call and ready to respond to incantations much feebler than those the German state could employ."[32] Lee counters by arguing, "Surely a people perpetually butchered by others like Germany in the past would have the ideal of force at any price. The sheep, if it had an ideal, would . . . like to be a wolf. Ideals are nine tenths the expression of a painful reality; they are theoretical reversals of the present order."[33] The explanation for Germany's pugnacity lies not in some murky evolutionary past but in the scenes of recent history. Lee, in fact, encouraged the European public to take Germany's past traumas into consideration, publishing in the *New Statesman* in 1915 an essay titled "Bismarck Towers," in which she discusses the "uneasy, humiliating embryonic national life" from which Bismarck delivered the nation.[34] According to Lee, "for two centuries the poor, weak Germany of earlier days had been invaded and raided, girls dishonoured and lads taken for foreign service," a past by which Germany continues to be "haunted."[35] Trotter, conversely, wholly ignores historical explanations for German pugnacity, preferring to dwell in essentialist notions of national identity based in bizarre animal analogies. Lee grows increasingly skeptical as Trotter's argument progresses. In a footnote concerning the evidence of German lunacy in German nationalist writing, Trotter notes that attending to these works can be useful, as "the howlings of a pack of wolves . . . betray to us with who we have to deal, betray their indispensable needs, their uncontrollable passions, the narrow path of instinct in which they are held, enable us to foresee, and, foreseeing, to lay our plans."[36] An exasperated Lee writes beneath the footnote, "The only result being leave not one wolf cub alive, I suppose."[37]

Lee was not only troubled by the use of psychological theory as a rationale for warfare. She also responded skeptically to the psychoanalysis of diplomacy in avowedly pacifist texts, such as Caroline Playne's *The Neuroses of the Nations* (1925). An internationalist and cosmopolitan thinker, Caroline Playne was a member of Britain's National Peace Council, the Emergency Committee for the Relief of Distressed Aliens, and the Nailsworth Peace

Association. During the war, she arranged a postal service for correspondence between warring countries and worked to locate missing persons. In the years after, she endeavored to increase public understanding of the "group-insanities" of France and Germany so as to "[build] up preventative psychiatry" that might "inoculate German, French, and British readers against being quite so vulnerable to mass media propaganda again."[38] Playne was also, like Lee, a member of the Union of Democratic Control, and in her deep-seated aversion to warfare, she certainly had much in common with Lee.[39] However, Lee's marginalia in *The Neuroses of the Nations* indicate that Lee was skeptical of the less careful modes of analogical thinking that might result from pathologizing international relations. Her notes in Playne's text are particularly playful and contrary, arch and shrewd, offering historical counterevidence to Playne's ahistorical assertions and calling into question the very idea of importing concepts from the discipline of psychology to illuminate political history. Vineta Colby notes that Irene Cooper Willis communicated with G. Lowes Dickinson in the late 1920s about a series of books Lee hoped to promote on "the psychological preparations for war in various countries."[40] Lee clearly believed that there was something to be gained from subjecting the prewar mind-set of the nations to close scrutiny. However, her disparaging remarks in the margins of Playne's *Neuroses* indicate that she was suspicious of the potentially misleading conclusions in which the misapplication of psychological concepts to national behavior might result.

In *The Neuroses of the Nations*, Playne seems to draw on a strange brew of Le Bon, Trotter, Freud, Simmel, and Nordau to argue that World War I was the necessary result of the escalating "neurasthenia" of the modern moment. She argues that the accelerated temporality and excessive "sense-stimulations" of the modern world had depleted the nervous systems of men at the turn of the century.[41] "This was especially apparent," according to Playne, "wherever men were collected in clusters, in concourses, in parties, in self-conscious national groups; for these groups, these collectivities were so excited that their emotions were out-of-hand, uncontrolled and uncontrollable. They became possessed of anxieties and ruled by anxiety-fear."[42] The stress and strain that the modern world placed on the nerves produced individuals and nations vulnerable to paranoia, hysteria, and the "emergence of primitive, instinctive passions."[43] The war, according to this vision, was not an incomprehensible atrocity but the natural outgrowth of modern conditions.

Playne's argument concerning the impact of modernity on the human mind draws on the theories of neurasthenia that had been in circulation since the latter half of the nineteenth century. However, her assertion that "group aberrations . . . were furnishing an impulsion which might cause society to roll back into barbarism" more specifically mimics Max Nordau's warnings concerning modern decay. In his *Degeneration* (1892), Nordau discusses the proliferation of fatigue, exhaustion, hysteria, and neurasthenia at the turn of the century, the effects, according to Nordau, of "contemporary civilization, of the vertigo and whirl of our frenzied life, the vastly increased number of sense impressions and organic reactions, and therefore perceptions, judgments, and motor impulses, which at present are forced into a given unity of time."[44] Nordau claims that these conditions have resulted in a proliferation of "degeneracy" at the fin de siècle. Nordau, of course, went on to diagnose the aesthetes with degeneracy, positing their "emotionalism," eccentricity, and immorality as symptoms of the quickened temporality and accelerated experience of the modern age.

Vernon Lee was deeply troubled by Nordau's claims. Her critique of *Degeneration*, "The Deterioration of Soul," which was published in the *Fortnightly Review* in 1896, focuses on the ethical limitations of Nordau's diagnosis of degeneracy. She argues that it is "dangerous to draw a hard and fast line between ourselves and any of our fellow creatures. . . . To make such a crude distinction does as much harm to us, who account ourselves sane, as to these whom we brand and pen up together as degenerate."[45] As Richard Dellamora has argued, Lee's response to Nordau emerges from a very specific cultural moment, the immediate aftermath of the Wilde trials, and her "Deterioration of Soul" might be read as a deeply encoded defense of Wilde.[46] However, Lee's critique could easily be extended to the manner in which Playne implements theories of neurasthenia in *The Neuroses of the Nations*. Playne begins her study by acknowledging that the "present volume lies open to the criticism that other nations than one's own have been searched and found to be seriously wanting in nervous stability and sanity," but she counters this critique by asserting that she is well aware that the "neurasthenical mind" existed in Great Britain before the war. In fact, according to Playne, "its history needs study as much as the history of the maladies of the two nations [France and Germany] among whom were first generated the obsessing fears, jealousies and hatred which distinguished the [prewar days]."[47] Yet the fact remains that her study dwells in and disseminates anti-German sentiment, drawing a "hard and fast line" between England and other nations, and it is this, perhaps, that put Lee off of a text that advertised itself as part of the pacifist project.

Lee's critical marginalia in *The Neuroses of the Nations* harp on Playne's ahistoricism and her excessive reliance on what Lee refers to as an "absurd jargon of 'neuroses.'"[48] What is perhaps most frustrating about *The Neuroses of the Nations* is the frequency with which Playne will move from real historical and political analysis to less insightful conclusions about national mental maladies. For example, following immediately upon an extended discussion of Caprivi's attempt to enlarge the German military, which was defeated in part due to economic concerns, Playne compares Germany's concern about being perceived as "unable to find the means for sufficient military protection" to the "pathological self-consciousness" of teenage girls: "Like neurasthenic girls in their 'teens, Germans were troubled as to what other nations might think of their vain displays."[49] Historically grounded explanations for the diplomatic failures of the early twentieth century are typically overlooked by Playne in favor of a more sensational vision of national neurasthenia, a tendency that must have troubled a reader like Lee, with such a deep commitment to historical thinking.

Lee's marginalia in the works of interwar social science in the British Institute's collection indicate that she was averse to any vision of the war that posited that atrocity as the natural outgrowth of the modern human condition, as the unavoidable consequence of modernity. Presumably she was troubled by the manner in which this explanation for the war elided the real historical conditions that had facilitated the escalation of violence and cleared individuals and nations of responsibility for their acts of aggression. To say that modern men have been irreparably crippled by modernity, that they are unable to resist the passions and paranoias that led to war, is to foster a dark vision of the subject and posit violence as natural and inevitable. In her marginalia in *Neuroses*, for example, Lee continually "corrects" Playne's sensational and ahistorical characterizations of modernity and the modern subject. Her escalating impatience with Playne's ahistoricism becomes evident in her marginal response to Playne's rhetorical question, "Does not every historical period exhibit group mental-maladies?"[50] Lee retorts, "Just so."[51] Playne responds differently to her own question, insisting that the "regression" and "uprush of primitive instincts" evident in the years leading up to the war reflect a historically unique proliferation of national neuroses.[52] "Owing to the stress and strain of a mechanicalized, industrialized age," Playne argues, "the nervosity which upset the world produced more all-pervading folly and fury in masses of men than ever before."[53] To justify this specious claim, she turns to Baron von Hügel's assertion that "the ancient Greeks and Romans, the entire medieval world of modern times . . . possessed no term for what we, unhappy recent generations, now popularly mean by 'nerves' and 'nervousness.'"[54] Lee rejoins, "They called it spleen, demonic possession, insanity. Nerves was already a scientific & humanistic notion."[55] Her irritation finally reaches its peak at the end of a chapter on "The Nature and Symptoms of the German Neurosis," and at the beginning of the next chapter, "Its Origins and Growth Traced in History," Lee has scrawled, "If we must talk in this absurd jargon of 'neuroses' that of Germany was an inferiority complex established already in the 30 years war & reinforced by Napoleon & after."[56] In this moment of frustration, Lee sarcastically implements the vocabulary of psychological theory to represent real historical conditions, to insist that it is not German neurosis that led to war, that the war has a history, that it was the result of political and military events of the past rather than the essential nature of a nation or the fractured nature of modern minds.

In 1919, Lee encountered a work to which she was much more sympathetic, so much so that she, in fact, dedicated the prologue to *Satan the Waster* to its author, G. F. Nicolai. Nicolai was a German heart doctor and the chair of the Department of Physiology at Berlin University. He openly protested when Germany violated Belgian neutrality and was consequently imprisoned in Graudenz Fortress, where he composed his pacifist treatise, *The Biology of War* (1915). The work is an interdisciplinary interrogation of the causes of war, engaging with contemporary instinctivist theory while at the same time relying, as Paul Crook has argued, on "linguistic and psychological analysis" to "establish the horrifying and brutalizing effects of total war."[57] An English translation of *The Biology of War* first appeared in 1918 with a sensational preface by the translators, detailing the imprisonment of the author, the smuggling of the controversial manuscript into Switzerland, and Nicolai's escape from Germany aboard an "old-fashioned" airplane accompanied by a German subaltern.[58] The preface concludes with a sentence seemingly cribbed from a spy thriller: "At present it is better to refrain from giving details of this escape."[59] The translators position Nicolai as a brave and heroic opponent to militarism, and this vision of the author was warmly received by both British and American reviewers, who celebrated the text as "remarkable, considering its environment."[60] Lee seems to have responded positively to the portrait of a selfless and courageous pacifist comrade painted by the translators of *The Biology of War* and to the antiwar argument articulated by Nicolai. Her marginal notes in Nicolai's text more properly resemble what H. J. Jackson refers to as "docile" or "*professional* marking, . . . the more or less systematic underlining of passages, noting down of topics or key words, and similar means by which readers since the birth of print have tried to improve their grasp or recall of the works they read."[61] She rarely takes issue with Nicolai's assertions, and the majority of her annotations simply note the topic under discussion, such as "war and property" or "drawing the sword for an idea." It is easy to see why Nicolai's argument would have been much more pleasing to Lee than Trotter's. Although troubled by the escalation of nationalist violence in the early twentieth century, Nicolai expresses the hope that the intensification of warfare in the twentieth century heralds "the Death Agony of the War Giant," for "whenever anything is to die a natural death, it must grow great; that is, reach its maximum size. . . . Everything which is big must and will die, because, in conformity with the inevitable law of growth, it will grow beyond the limits of what is possible."[62] Nicolai's optimistic assessment of the "War Giant" acknowledges the excessive brutality of the present while looking forward to a peaceful future.

Nicolai's hope for future peace would certainly have appealed to Lee, but the vision of the subject articulated in the opening pages of *The Biology of War* does not correspond with her own. Nicolai alludes to the "delight in" or "hankering after" war as an "instinct" that is "in a nation's very blood."[63] He points to the nations' vulnerability to "war fever" as evidence that this instinct is "innate to the human race, ever ready to break out."[64] However, this vision of essential pugnacity gets revised in later sections of the treatise, as Nicolai argues that human agency may operate as an antidote to the war instinct. Animals might not be able to adapt to new surroundings that are incompatible with their instinctual behaviors, but, according to Nicolai, man "*can* change. He is not like a bacterium, always obliged to do what is 'in accordance with his nature.' Man is able to act differently, . . . to adapt himself to new circumstances."[65] In fact, Nicolai comments, "human beings who still continue to abandon themselves enthusiastically to their lust for war always involuntarily make me think I see a dog scratching for a time with its hindlegs on the asphalt pavement of some modern town after relieving nature."[66] Lee marked Nicolai's optimistic discussion of the power of human agency (seemingly in approval, as she has not written around it in circles) as well as another passage in which Nicolai advances a vision of the source of warfare that seems to contradict his earlier assertions concerning essential pugnacity. She underlined the statement "Wherever there is nothing to be had, however, no fighting takes place" and marked a paragraph in which Nicolai argues that "there is nothing natural, nothing great, and nothing noble about war. . . . It is merely one of the numberless consequences of the introduction of property!"[67] According to this later formulation, then, war is not a primitive instinct but a product of the notion of private property. Any move away from the idea of the naturalness of war would have been far more pleasing to Lee, who opposed any conception of the human subject as fundamentally belligerent.

The element of Nicolai's argument that Lee seems to have found the most attractive was his critique of the misapplication of Darwinian principles in the defense and celebration of warfare. Nicolai notes, in a passage underlined by Lee, that, although "most of the theoretical defenders of war to-day are wholly ignorant of natural science," they have "heard enough of Darwinism to know that Darwin was said to have stated that all living creatures achieve victory by means of struggle, and that everywhere the unfit are exterminated and the fit survive, and thus the race is perfected." Nicolai rails against the "blind [transferal]" of the "doctrine of selection being effected by the struggle for existence" to war between human beings, asking how "these so-called Darwinians know that it is the wheat which is left and the chaff which is removed."[68] Lee's "professional marking" of this section summarizes the passage in a phrase that succinctly dismisses the concept under discussion: "supposed winnowing."[69] She has marked in approval as well a paragraph describing the "selected type" that would emerge from this manner of winnowing, a "rabbit-like creature," accustomed to dwelling in the trenches, with "but *slender intelligence*," a "half-idiotic, troglodyte race," "agile and nimble" with "*no refined requirements*."[70] However, it is not simply that "these so-called Darwinians" have blindly transferred the principle of the struggle for existence to warfare. They have in addition misunderstood the principle itself, falsely equating it with an assertion on Darwin's part concerning the centrality of violence to the natural world. Lee marked a paragraph in which Nicolai responds to these assertions, arguing that "it is a mistake to insist that struggle for existence must necessarily be horrible or even brutal."[71] This error in vulgar Darwinist thinking arises from a narrow understanding of the principle of "struggle": "The struggle for existence is concentrated upon procuring free outlet for Man's mental capacities, and thus rendering the maximum amount of energy available for mankind."[72] War, as Lee notes in the margins, is "a struggle not *for*, but *against*, existence."[73] Nicolai similarly asserts that war has nothing to do with the struggle for existence, "save for the fact that it is perpetually destroying a fraction, even if only a small fraction, of mankind without in reality helping in the struggle."[74]

In correcting vulgar Darwinism, Nicolai moves toward a more optimistic assessment of the subject. He notes that vulgar Darwinists neglect Darwin's emphasis on the social instinct. "However noisy and self-assertive the impulses of hate may be," according to Nicolai, "the social instincts, their opposites, our oldest inheritances, have long been lying dormant in our brain."[75] Nicolai insists that "universal brotherhood" is "older and more primitive than all combat," that we have "dead tracks" in us that might lead us back to our essentially social nature, that "love is older than hate," and we may return to our inherently gregarious nature by rejecting the impulse to make war.[76]

Nicolai was clearly influential for Lee, assisting her to see beyond Trotter's jingoistic sociology and Playne's vision of a world of fractured neurasthenics to a future-oriented vision of a pacifist subject. However, her own pacifist theory of the individual, articulated in works such as *Proteus* and the longer, and perhaps stranger, *Music and Its Lovers* (1932), relies on aesthetic theory rather than the concept of gregariousness to rethink human belligerence. Like Nicolai, she contradicts vulgar Darwinism by redefining essential human nature in terms of a desire for harmony as opposed to bloodshed, but her optimistic reassessment of humanity centers on the aesthetic as opposed to the social instinct. Drawing on her previous work in psychological aesthetics, she argues that the individual craves beauty rather than violence. Human beings instinctively seek out the aesthetic to buttress the health of the psyche. Much as Kit Anstruther-Thomson, with whom Lee had conducted experiments in "psychological aesthetics," noted the manner in which the contemplation of symmetry and balance in a work of art caused her to straighten her shoulders and breathe more regularly, Lee argues that our need for beauty refines and perfects us.[77]

II. Ethical Aesthetics: Cosmopolitan Detachment and the Aesthetic Drive

Although Lee began her career expounding an aggressively aestheticist credo concerning art's separation from moral concerns, her understanding of the relationship between ethics and aesthetics became progressively more complex over the course of her career. In her later work, such as *Gospels of Anarchy*, she argues that taste underwrites and creates the possibility for moral behavior. The aesthetic and moral faculties are connected through their capacity for judgment, and moral judgment, according to her formulation, operates according to aesthetic principles. In her early aesthetic writings, such as *Belcaro* (1881), Lee echoed Walter Pater's assertion that "art comes to you proposing frankly to give nothing but the highest quality to your moments as they pass."[78] She argued that "beauty, in itself, is neither morally good nor morally bad; it is aesthetically good, even as virtue is neither aesthetically good nor aesthetically bad, but morally good."[79] She initially rejected Ruskin's particular brand of aesthetic morality, arguing that "he has made the enjoyment of mere beauty a base pleasure requiring a moral object to purify it, and in so doing, he has destroyed its own purifying power."[80] According to Lee's early aesthetic theory, aesthetic experience is good because, and only because, it is a source of pleasure. However, Lee qualified and complicated the arguments in *Belcaro* over the next three decades. *Miss Brown* (1884), Lee's novelistic satire of the Aesthetic Movement, indicates that as Lee became more critical of aestheticism's hedonistic tendencies, her attachment to the "art for art's sake" credo became more complex. Her understanding of Ruskin seems to have followed a similar route. As her career progressed, Lee found it increasingly possible to integrate Ruskinian ethics with Paterian aesthetics, and by the early twentieth century, she began equating the desire for beauty with the desire for goodness.

Taste, according to the later Lee, facilitates, and is in fact the foundation of, moral behavior. The aesthetic and moral faculties are connected through their capacity for judgment, and moral judgment, according to her formulation, operates according to aesthetic principles. In a chapter on Emerson in *Gospels of Anarchy*, for example, Lee opposes the logical faculty, which "reduces all things to cause and effect, making them all equally important or unimportant," to the "aesthetic and moral faculties which are essentially selecting, preferring, and which arrange all things in a long scale whose bottom means abhorrence or contempt, and whose top the fervidest love and admiration. These and only these are qualifying activities; the mere logical intellect can only recognise and connect, it cannot judge."[81] "Qualifying activities," those activities that involve judgment, allow the subject to discriminate, to prefer, and to choose, to select the beautiful and the good while rejecting that which is abhorrent or unjust.

In her early-twentieth-century writing, Lee theorizes the subject in aesthetic terms, arguing that human beings *instinctually* select and prefer the beautiful and the good. She locates the inextricably interlinked aesthetic and moral impulses at the center of human activity. "We are," according to Lee, "so constituted that evil cannot please nor chaos satisfy us."[82] Our "human instincts . . . decide for good against evil."[83] "The soul of man protests against the contact of foulness and baseness, injustice and pain, however much legitimated by logic. The soul will not be satisfied with a divinity that governs mere cause and effect – it requires a moral, an aesthetic rule."[84] Lee theorizies an essentially aesthetic, and therefore essentially ethical, subject. It is, in her eyes, when we are at our most aestheticist, most interested in and driven by the pursuit of beauty and pleasure, that we seek out the finest things and become our finest selves. And this is, in her eyes, our natural state. We are inclined to seek out the beautiful and the good.

Human beings are, according to Lee, guided by aesthetic desires that direct them toward that which is admirable and just.

This is a vision of the subject that might be difficult to preserve in wartime. However, the connections drawn between morality and taste in these works served as the source for Lee's later response to post-World War I thinking about the nature of the subject. Both during and after the war, Lee maintained that her earlier thinking about the relationship between ethical capacity and aesthetic sensibility remained relevant and true. In her post-World War I writing, she actively engaged with the escalating violence and jingoism of the early twentieth century while insisting on the centrality of ethical aesthetics to human behavior.

Much of Lee's earlier writing dwells on the ethical value of the aesthetic capacity, but Lee's *Satan the Waster* foregrounds the political utility of Paterian modes of perception. *Satan the Waster* is perhaps Lee's most radical and experimental text, composed primarily of ancillary material (an introduction, epilogue, and lengthy notes) meant to illuminate her pacifist play, *The Ballet of the Nations* (1915), a nightmarish vision of a violent allegorical dance choreographed by Satan. The play had been published on its own five years earlier, but in its 1920 incarnation, the commentary and notes outweigh the play itself. In these newly appended notes, Lee meditates on the recent war and the "vital lies" and "delusions" that facilitated the escalation of violence. She decries the diminished vision in which nationalism results, opposing jingoistic blindness to the hyperkinetic sensitivity of the aloof aesthete.

Wartime patriotism comes under fire in *Satan the Waster*, and the spirit of national pride is criticized primarily in terms of its effects on perception. In a chapter devoted to the nature of patriotism, Lee notes that "the love entering into Patriotism . . . is a love which is governed by the *first personal pronoun*; and manifests itself in the *possessive case*. It is love due to possession; not love . . . by *preference*, attraction, suitability, choice, desire."[85] It is "love for one's country *because it is one's own*. . . . Such love due to possession does justice neither to the real qualities of its object . . . nor to the qualities of all the other things in creation." The argument that possessiveness handicaps perception had also been rehearsed by Lee earlier in, for example, *Laurus Nobilis* (1909), in which she argues that it is "like the tension of a muscle, this constant keeping the consciousness aware by repeating 'Mine – mine – *mine*.' And this wearisome act of self-assertion leaves little power for appreciation."[86] As I have asserted elsewhere, Lee's representation of collectors in her short fiction equates possession with critical blindness.[87] Lee's collectors accumulate objects to shore up their own sense of identity with little or no true interest in the collected object's alterity. Ownership, according to Lee's formulation, relies on the appropriation rather than the appreciation of difference, limiting the possibility for true contact with otherness. Lee's critique of patriotism can in this sense be understood as a continuation of her earlier critique of the shortcomings of possessiveness and the ethics of capitalism. According to Lee, possessiveness desensitizes us to difference, and patriotism, which relies on possessive impulses, inhibits our capacity to contemplate and engage with the world around us.

Lee clarified the political implications of her critique of the limitations of possessive perception in a 1912 article on "The Sense of Nationality" published in the *Nation*. Lee, presumably in an attempt to defuse escalating jingoism before the war, responds to a call made by Maurice Barrés as well as "sundry less exquisitely gifted literary craftsmen in England" for a "Sense of Nationality," a call that had, according to Lee, only stimulated the growth of "the natural crop of Chauvinism."[88] Chauvinism is defined by Lee here as "the preference of ourselves, *because we are ourselves*," while a true sense of nationality should be understood as "sensitiveness to national qualities and differences."[89] Lee argues that the forms of chauvinism being cultivated by Barrés and his English inferiors are not simply distinct from the sense of nationality. The sentiments inspired by chauvinism, in fact, serve to inhibit the sense of nationality: "Chauvinism is to the sense of nationality as a nettle to a wheat-ear; not only different but incompatible, a weed (and difficult to handle!) in itself, and taking the ground, the air, the possibility of life from the useful plant so difficult to cultivate."[90] The possessive, chauvinist, egoistic forms of feeling that underwrite nationalism and patriotism inhibit the capacity to see and understand other nations and nationalities.

Lee's notion of the ideal type of perception, freed from the limitations of chauvinism and possessiveness, resembles the Paterian model of aesthetic consciousness, which Jonathan Freedman argues "refuses to be captured by any one sense experience; endlessly mobile, indeed acutely hyperkinetic, it comes into being under the injunction to refuse any sense of 'possession or leverage in an indeterminate situation.'"[91] In the conclusion to *Studies in the History of the Renaissance*, Pater cautions his readers against "acquiescing in a facile orthodoxy of Comte, or of Hegel, or of our own."[92] To remain alive to the world and to the sensory information we receive, we must, according to Pater, reject any "theory or idea or system which requires of us the sacrifice of any part of . . . experience."[93] Patriotism, which removes us from the realm of "contemplation and appreciation" to place us in the realm of "passion, action, desire, and effort," is exactly the sort of theory or idea against which Pater cautions his readers. While under its sway, according to Lee, we inhabit the sphere "not of *seeing* but of *taking, grabbing, clinging to, keeping, defending*; and, in the course of such taking or keeping, frequently *destroying*."[94]

Lee posits a Decadent model of detachment that she refers to as "aloofness" as the antidote to the blindness of possessiveness and the destructiveness of patriotism. Aloofness, as conceptualized by Lee, enables the subject to maintain the hyperkinetic mobility and clarity of vision that Pater celebrated. Lee traces her own aloofness to her peculiar, cosmopolitan upbringing, which "made [her] know, admire, love, but also mistrust, several nationalities; and while intensifying [her] appreciation of the splendid or delightful qualities special to each of them, made [her] incapable of identifying [herself] with the whole of any."[95] During the war, Lee contributed to the *Atlantic Monthly* a short piece titled "The Heart of a Neutral" (1915), which posits a more mythical explanation for her capacity to remain aloof from rising violence. According to the story, the fairies came to her christening. These fairies, invited by her parents, were the different nations, and "each brought [her] the gift of understanding [each nation's] greatness and beauty, and enriching [her] life with such knowledge. . . . And all of them said, 'This child shall have the joy of loving us.'"[96] Yet Lee's parents forgot to invite another, more seemingly malevolent fairy. This fairy could not take away the other fairies' gifts, "for even a fairy and an angry one has no power to remove fairy gifts," so instead she simply added her own, a gift that had the potential to spoil the rest: "For with the knowledge of the good of each nation, this child shall know in sadness the weakness and folly also of them all. And every nation shall say to her, 'You are an alien and though you love me, shall have no power over my heart.'"[97] However, another fairy came forward later in her life, and she gave to Lee another gift: "When all the nations shall welter in the pollution of warfare, this child's eyes shall remain clear from its fratricide fumes; she shall drink deep of sorrow, but recognize and put away from her lips the sweetened and consecrated cup of hatred."[98] Lee acknowledged the fact that her aloofness during the war must have appeared monstrous and even hostile to her more patriotic friends, but it was this very aloofness that allowed her to see the war and its causes clearly, to penetrate the delusions and vital lies that made this catastrophe possible. In her introduction to *Satan the Waster*, she notes that she came to her views of the war by not being able to be "as the current phrase goes, *in the war*. . . . It was [her] initial aloofness which made [her] see the war as a common catastrophe, in which this country's real danger was its danger as a portion of the whole war-imperiled world, instead of seeing only [her] country's danger at the enemy's hands."[99] Though her detached position might have seemed cold and cruel, "holding thus aloof [she was] able to see the war under a certain angle and in certain of its aspects which would have been hidden from [her] had [she], as the phrase goes, *been in it.*"[100]

Lee's concept of aloofness owes much to the Victorian tradition of theorizing detachment as described by Amanda Anderson in *Powers of Distance*. Anderson is attentive to the fact that many Victorians felt wary of the rootlessness and alienation that might accompany detachment. While they valued the perspective detachment might provide, they also exhibited a deep ambivalence about the ethics of detachment. However, Victorian writers returned again and again to the question of detachment, indicating that their wariness about impartiality did not prohibit them from perceiving the ethical value of self-overcoming.[101] Lee's interest in the suppression of personal preference, nationalism, and possessiveness, then, should be understood as emerging from an ongoing debate about the value of distance in the nineteenth century, a conversation in which Mill and Arnold as well as Eliot and Dickens played an enormous role. However, the concept of cosmopolitanism was very much a part of modernist conversation as well. Rebecca Walkowitz has recently noted that, whereas Victorian images of cosmopolitanism tend to promote detachment, modernist images "assume more integration among cultures and less uniformity within them."[102] Lee's commitment to "knowing and admiring" many nations while at the same time resisting identification with any nation in particular seems to position her as hovering between the two tendencies described by Walkowitz. While she remains wary of full-fledged national affiliation, she shares with her modernist peers a desire to engage and associate with difference.[103]

Walter Pater, however, should be understood as Lee's most crucial and immediate influence as she theorized and enacted aloofness during the war. We must, according to Pater's conclusion, avoid forming habits, reject facile orthodoxies, and eschew any belief system in which faith might limit our capacity for perception. Lee echoes Pater's hymn of hyperkinetic detachment in *Satan the Waster,* using a vocabulary drawn directly from her mentor to describe the ideal method of perceiving and responding to an ever-shifting and changing reality. She argues that "Principles and Ideals," which are meant to serve as "an unshakable anchor against the tides and storms of passion and delusion," might be one of the most dangerous of "man's most personal attachments."[104] While these Principles and Ideals might at times "steady man against the buffets of passion and the floods of delusion," this is only the case when these Ideals stand in opposition to escalating passion and delusion: "For when, as in war time, the Principle, the Ideal, the Standard, Usage or Commandment, happens to be on the same side as the passions and delusions, then this mechanism of moral and intellectual moorage becomes a mere hulk, clinging to which, as it floats on the dominant currents, we become only the more submerged and blinded by the perilous seas of unreality."[105] When the Ideal or the Principle is understood to be "supreme and perfect like a godhead," any attempt to think critically about it, to perceive it clearly, amounts to a "sacrilegious outrage."[106] Lee advances the Paterian claim that adherence to Ideals frequently cripples one's vision and intellect. To see with the finest senses, she argues, requires the strict avoidance of Principles that might veil reality from view.

Lee similarly seems to draw on Pater's description of the perpetual motion of physical life and of the individual in her discussion of the nature of Reality and the mode of perception that Reality necessitates. Reality, according to Lee, is fundamentally multiple: "it always has *other* sides; the sides you do not happen to see or think of; the sides that don't interest you at the moment; the sides which happen not to be in any manner, yourself."[107] To perceive this multiple and complex reality, one must, as Pater said, be able to pass swiftly from point to point and not be hindered by our ties to orthodoxy and habit.[108] Or as Lee puts it, reality "requires successive and various orientations and focuses, requires the telescope and also the microscope."[109] Echoing Pater's discussion of the "strange, perpetual weaving and unweaving of ourselves," Lee insists that one must be able to shift perspective quickly and freely, to understand that one is a part of a particular reality, but "a part never two seconds in contact (bodily or mental as the case may be) with the same other parts. You are not even a stable pattern of the same parts of yourself, but, like a kaleidoscope, you drop into all manners of combinations at the impact of the variously-changing combinations of everything else."[110] To move freely between telescopic and microscopic perception of reality as one's very self shifts and changes in a kaleidoscopic manner, one must not be hindered by passions and delusions, Ideals and Principles, that might hamper this hyperkinetic activity. Thus war passions and war delusions, which "make us see only one side of realities, and see that in wrong proportions and erroneous connexions," must, in Lee's eyes, be understood as an "outrage on the Reality of Things." By uniting one country against another, these passions "cut . . . Reality in two, hiding one half thereof," fixing us within one portion of reality, disabling our capacity to shift and transform our own identities and to perceive and engage with otherness.[111]

Pater's influence is also evident in Lee's later work on music, in which she generates an alternative theory of the subject that posits the subject as driven by the desire for beauty. In the teens, Lee began a project with the working title *Hearers and Listeners.* This work would take her more than twenty years to complete, not appearing in print in its entirety (under the title *Music and Its Lovers*) until 1932.[112] In this extended research project, Lee investigates the possibility that music might improve and benefit human subjectivity and argues that human beings actively and instinctively seek the moral improvement that music might provide. This conception of the subject, like Lee's conception of ethical aloofness or moral detachment, relies on Paterian thinking and a fundamental belief in the ethical value of the aesthetic to counteract the dark conclusions about humanity circulating during the interwar period.

The idea that music might improve and benefit the subject recurs frequently in Lee's work. For example, in 1915, Lee published an essay on "Bach's Christmas Music in England and Germany" in the English suffragist magazine *Jus Suffragii.*[113] The essay recounts Lee's visit to the Temple church on Christmas Eve in 1914. Listening to Bach, Lee muses upon the idea that "there beyond the sea and the war chasm, in hundreds of churches of Bach's own country, . . . there, at this very moment, were crowds like this one at the Temple, listening to the self-same Christmas Music . . . praying for the same mercies: Give us, O God, strength to live through these evil times, . . . teach us to forgive the cruel folk who hate us; give us such peace as will never be broken."[114] In Lee's hopeful vision, the two nations become united by their shared listening experience: "They are united, these English and German crowds, in the same hopes and fears and prayers, even as, unsuspecting, they are united in the same sequences of melody, the same whoofs of harmonies wherewith, across two hundred years, that long dead but undying organist of Leipzig enmeshes, draws together, nooses and nets our souls to lift them, clarified, close embraced, nay consubstantial, into the presence of the new born, the eternally reborn, Hope of the World."[115] The souls of the churchgoers are clarified by Bach's harmonies, and they are lifted from their nationalist prisons to travel across the war chasm and acknowledge the common humanity of English and German subjects. The argument developed here seems to be an outgrowth of the larger *Music and Its Lovers* project.

Music and Its Lovers was an immense research project that involved the distribution and analysis of more than 150 lengthy questionnaires concerning the nature of the human response to music. This text, like all Lee's post-World War I writing, bears the marks of brutality, but it also articulates a theory of the subject that should be understood as a direct contradiction to the dark vision of essential human belligerence developed by, for example, Wilfred Trotter. Rather than positing aggression or gregariousness as primary instincts, Lee instead focuses on the aesthetic drive. She argues that the material elicited by her questionnaires might "suggest how the desire for music as something to be listened to has gradually evolved out of a primitive need for music as something to stir inert, or release pent-up, emotions and to induce such day-dreams as restore and quicken the soul."[116] The need for music is not a civilized counterpoint to or constraint on our essential human nature. It is, in fact, as fundamental to human nature as any of the darker and more destructive drives on which sociologists and psychologists have chosen to focus.

Subjecting our desire for music to scrutiny could, according to Lee, illuminate the nature and significance of our drive toward beauty in general. She commences her study by citing Pater's statement that "all art tends to the nature of music," noting that "this saying had long haunted" her.[117] Pater's assertion seems to suggest that knowledge of music "would afford the best clue to the aesthetics of other arts less simple in their tasks and less seemingly intimate in their processes."[118] What we stand to gain from the examination of our thirst for music, then, is a fuller understanding of the role that the aesthetic as a category plays in human life.

Lee argues that listening to music promotes ethical development. This ethical development results from the impersonal form of happiness that music elicits. As evidence for music's ability to diffuse self-interest, she cites the responses to her questionnaires, which describe the fundamental uniqueness of the "musical emotion," an emotion disentangled entirely from instrumental or egotistical concerns. Mme. Louise notes, "It DEPERSONALISES me," and Barbara says, "It takes me out of myself."[119] Bettina writes, "Music which really lays hold of me, stirs and soothes, does not evoke. What it does is sometimes deeper and vaguer . . . a longing for self-surrender, for an oblation of myself which would not be self-sacrifice, but the highest fulfillment of life."[120] This depersonalization or oblation of the self increases one's sensitivity to alterity, to that which lies beyond the boundaries of the subject. According to Lee, "while so much of our individual social life seems silly or cruel, all contemplative activity which concentrates attention upon what is not ourself nor subservient or detrimental to ourself . . . but upon the qualities and relations of some otherness is such as our moral judgment selects and fosters, or . . . sympathetically condones. These exclusions and inclusions result in the plane of contemplation being felt to be a sanctuary, a region of purification as well as peacefulness."[121] In contemplating music, we become more moral, more pure, more peaceful. We become good. Countess Sophie notes that while listening to music, she "always has the distinct impression of a moral influence reaching down 'from a higher, happier sphere.' The 'best' of her being is 'vivified.'" Bessie echoes this sentiment in her assertion that music is "moral in the sense that it makes one less of a beast."[122]

Lee returns to the question of fundamental drives in the conclusion of the study. She argues that the need for purification through art may be "a state which . . . existed before all art and which all art . . . has deliberately or unwittingly . . . set about appealing to [and] reinforcing."[123] According to Lee, the need for excitement may be more "fundamental and older" than any of our other drives, "underlying everything else."[124] The crude desire for excitement can be satisfied in drink, gambling, and love making, but we tend also to crave "something nobler, for excitement no longer crude but transfigured into spiritual exaltation."[125] She builds on this assertion in an attempt to account for the recent war. Unlike Trotter, however, Lee does not posit warfare as unavoidable or aggression as essential. She instead asserts that aggression results from the misdirection of our instinctual craving for excitement. During the war years, the need for exaltation was satisfied by nationalist literature and propaganda, but Lee insists that this desire might have just as easily been fulfilled by the contemplation of music. The final sentence of *Music and Its Lovers* recounts Lee's recollected wartime thoughts, the "childish wish" she made from the sidelines of nationalist discourse: "Oh, if only these gifted people would stop for a while speaking and preaching and writing; and slake their unexpected thirst for aesthetic excitement and enthusiasm by listening silently to some great Symphony."[126] According to Lee's formulation, then, the human subject is not instinctually aggressive nor instinctually peaceful. Human beings are rather naturally drawn in pursuit of excitement. This need, however, can be gratified as much by beauty as by bloodshed.

Lee's revision of twentieth-century theories of the subject, as articulated in works like *Proteus* and *Music and Its Lovers*, relies on Paterian vocabulary and aestheticist and Decadent concepts to argue for the centrality of beauty, taste, and contemplation to the makeup of the human being. She reimagines the individual as a seeker of higher planes of aesthetic experience and pleasure rather than of battle. She aggressively rejects the body of knowledge that sprang up in response to the war and harkens back to Pater's celebration of music, "intellectual excitement," and the "courting of new impressions." Hers is a nineteenth-century antidote to a twentieth-century problem, a bit of post-Victorian Decadent annotation in the margins of interwar social science.

Whereas Lee might have operated from the margins of aestheticism and Decadence during the late nineteenth century, voicing critiques of aestheticism's sexual politics and, as Stefano Evangelista and Francesca Billiani have argued, "[oscillating] between loose affiliation [with] and vocal rejection" of the Decadent Movement, in the twentieth century, she seems to have grown more fond of and nostalgic for the avant-gardes with which she was associated in the late-Victorian period.[127] The Lee of the 1880s and 1890s was troubled by the hedonistic tendencies of aestheticism and Decadence, but Lee in the 1920s found in these movements a tremendously useful arsenal of tools for approaching the problems besetting the modern moment. Richard Dellamora has encouraged us to take note of the fact that "Lee [wrote] from within the very movements that she [critiqued]," asserting that a novel like *Miss Brown*, which might seem to simply bash aestheticism, is in its sensational excess "not only Aesthetic but Decadent."[128] He argues that "it is her role as an internal participant-observer that lends force to the observations she makes from a feminist subject-position."[129] Her ability to hold ideas in tension, to articulate a nuanced criticism of an aesthetic while at the same time implementing that aesthetic, is what made her such a thoughtful practitioner of political critique. Her capacity for complex political and aesthetic positioning was showcased once again in the twentieth century, in the complicated manner in which Lee situated herself temporally, as at once within and without the World War I era, astounded by its violence but never so shocked that she turned away altogether. She gathered together those tools of previous British avant-gardes with which she had always been in such conflicted relation and utilized them to fashion a response to a new set of particularly troubling political conditions. She drew on these instruments of the nineteenth-century past with a full awareness of their shortcomings as well as a newfound optimism about the wisdom that they might offer to the twentieth century.

Lee's post-Victorian Decadent pacifism did not, however, charm and attract twentieth-century audiences in the same manner that Beerbohm's post-Victorian Decadent camp nostalgia managed to. Her pacifism was far more earnest, explicit, and direct than Beerbohm's camp mode of critique and thus alienated the broader public. Whereas Beerbohm's statements about his own anachronism and irrelevance should be understood as performative, Lee's understanding of herself as a marginal or outsider figure was in many ways accurate. Certain leftist or bohemian figures such as

George Bernard Shaw did respond enthusiastically to her strident critique of wartime patriotism. Shaw, for example, argued that the notes to *Satan the Waster* proved that Lee "has never been wrong once since the war began" and that "by sheer intellectual force, training, knowledge, and character," she had "kept her head when Europe was a mere lunatic asylum."[130] While Lee appreciated Shaw's warm response, her thank-you note to him emphasizes the fact that her work on the war had been otherwise neglected. She notes that, prior to Shaw's review, "[her] *Satan*" had been "suffering under an interdict, or excommunication," and she bemoans the fact that she found herself during the war "at hopeless variance with even her own small public."[131] When *Satan the Waster* was reissued in 1930, a review in the *Spectator* confirmed Lee's assertions concerning the interdict placed on her pacifist work, noting that, on its initial publication, *Satan* was "completely ignored by all the critics (except, of course, Mr. Bernard Shaw)," and that was because "the state of public feeling at that time would not have rendered it possible for such a savage and whole-hearted condemnation of war to succeed."[132] This is a bit of an exaggeration. Reviews did appear in many periodicals, including the *Times Literary Supplement*, the *New Statesman*, and the *New Republic*. However, the majority of these reviews express astonishment or disappointment with Lee's aloofness and her unmitigated contempt for the war. The short discussion of her work that appeared in the *Manchester Guardian* criticizes the fact that Lee chose "to deal with the whole great tragedy in a spirit of supercilious repudiation and ridicule."[133] The review that appeared in the *Times Literary Supplement* argues that "about the war, . . . we are not in the mood for satire," and insists that "if your main desire is to prove that some action or proposition or state of mind is wrong, you do not ridicule it, you try to prove it wrong; and the effort to do that will not lead you into satire."[134] Unlike Beerbohm's playful and oblique humor, Lee's incisive satire offended twentieth-century audiences.

This is not to say that Lee's pacifist work was without impact. Though she was not able to convince H. G. Wells of the justness of the pacifist cause, her public debates with him allowed for the further dissemination of her critical vision of the war.[135] Some figures, such as Austin Harrison, the editor of the *English Review*, who expressed disdain for her views during the war, eventually came to see the appeal of her arguments. Harrison, for example, carried no review of *The Ballet of the Nations* when it first appeared, but in 1919 he accepted the prologue and epilogue to the play, which later appeared in *Satan the Waster*, for publication in the *English Review*.[136] C. K. Ogden, the editor of the Today and Tomorrow series, clearly was not put off by her explicit condemnation of the war, for he chose to invite her to contribute *Proteus* to the series after *Satan the Waster* appeared in print. Ogden, however, was, like Shaw, quite leftist in his views, having founded the Cambridge Heretic Society in 1909, and supported pacifism, worker's rights, and universal and women's suffrage.[137] The reviews of *Proteus* demonstrate the fact that her appeal was for the most part limited to dissident figures such as Shaw and Ogden. The review in the *Living Age* argues that Lee "interprets intelligence as a highbrow dilettantism" and that her "outlook seems to savor more of a weak discontent with the bustle of progress or of an apology for self-conscious aestheticism than of a valuable contribution to the thought of 'to-day and to-morrow.'"[138] The reviewer for the *Virginia Quarterly* confesses to "feeling more at home" with the people of the past, whom Lee describes as "stupid," than "among the Intelligent" and states that *Proteus* "is destined to a place in my library alongside its more famous predecessor," "The Hunting of the Snark."[139] Her work appeared to many twentieth-century readers too elitist, too aestheticist, too highbrow, too cosmopolitan to make much sense during their own war-ravaged moment. She spoke from the margins and was heard most enthusiastically by others who occupied those margins. It was, however, by dwelling in the margins, separate, aloof, apart from the violence and passions of the period, that, in Lee's eyes, one might most effectively see and in turn speak to the problems besetting the modern moment.

CHAPTER 3

"Towards Aristocracy"
Baron Corvo and the Corvine Society

In an essay published in the *London Mercury* in May 1934, Mary Butts mourns the death of a fairy tale. The recently deceased fairy tale was the story of a "beautiful priest" who "knew the secrets of the Borgias and the ancient gods of Italy, who loved and suffered and died young and wrote books of genius no one ever read."[1] The myth had been dispelled by the publication of an "experiment in biography" by the post-Victorian dandy A. J. A. Symons. The founder of the First Edition Club and the editor of *An Anthology of Nineties Verse* (1928), Symons had made a living on his knowledge of the fin de siècle, his capacity for pleasure, and his enjoyment of curios. He finally made a name for himself with *The Quest for Corvo* (1934), in which he demonstrated how one might enjoy the rarest and strangest of Decadent curios, Baron Corvo (Frederick Rolfe, 1860–1913).[2] According to Butts, *The Quest for Corvo* destroyed her vision of the beautiful, suffering priest, replacing this vision with a far grimmer account of less romantic trials.

Baron Corvo was not, in fact, a priest. He was a convert to Catholicism who had hoped to be a priest, but those desires were frustrated, leaving him embittered against the church. He was also not a baron. He came from a family of piano manufacturers, but he exhibited, according to an old acquaintance, a "tendency to 'swank.'"[3] He claimed that his title had been bestowed on him by an Italian noblewoman, and, regardless of his impoverished circumstances, he remained invested in the concept of aristocracy for his entire life. But he *did* die young and write books of genius that few people read. He spent a good part of his life hungry and struggling and generating countless schemes to amend those problems. He painted, and he photographed. His photographs were mainly nudes, but he also experimented with color photography and claimed to have invented a method of submarine photography. He wrote quite a bit, dense and elaborate historical novels written in a Macaronic combination of Latin and English, heady short fiction populated by beautiful Italian adolescents, and poetry about boys bathing. He published in the *Yellow Book* and spent some time at the fringes of that circle before moving to Venice, where he spent his final years often homeless, still hungry, and at war with the British expatriate population.

The Quest for Corvo details Symons's remarkable efforts to piece together the strange story of Corvo's life and uncover missing works by the "strangest artificial orchid of the Nineties."[4] The story he assembles from bits of letters from acquaintances and conversations with surviving friends is not a particularly pleasant one, as Corvo seems to have been perpetually involved in quarrels, and Symons struggles with the information he acquires about Corvo's sexuality. *The Quest* reads like a harrowing literary detective story, revealing a rather tragic figure who seems to have spent a good part of his life angry and at odds with everyone.

Butts insists that Symons had debunked the Corvine fairy tale, replacing it with a much more "horrible story." I, however, would argue that Symons exchanged the fairy tale for yet another myth. The "beautiful priest" becomes in Symons's hands a paranoid eccentric, an inexplicably cantankerous man, an inveterate Tory, the possessor of a "fascinating, distorted temperament," which leads him to alienate all and forever insist on his own superiority to the world around him.[5] The beautiful priest and the elitist paranoiac remain equally distant from material conditions and political events. Both stories neutralize or veil from view the economically driven rage that registered in nearly every moment of Corvo's career. With the publication of *The Quest*, Corvo became less ethereal but no less incomprehensible. He is represented by Symons as a pathological curiosity in possession of curious conservative qualities. Like a more sinister Oliver Twist, Symons's Corvo is untouched by material circumstances. He lived in poverty, but he retained an aristocratic temperament, and, according to Symons, nothing but his "strange, tormented spirit" inspired him to lash out irrationally at the world around him.[6]

Butts's essay is by her account inspired by reading *The Quest*. However, before reading *The Quest*, she had ordered and consumed Corvo's works on her own, driven by "an impassioned need to know more," an insatiable curiosity about the motivations of this strange man.[7] Drawing on her own knowledge of his work, she represents Corvo harshly yet astutely, attending to his anger and its economic sources. Though she begins her essay by lavishing praise on Symons's "truth," her short portrait draws out much that is absent from the pages of his biography. Her Corvo is first and foremost oppositional. Generally "white hot against our society," his rancor is directed in countless directions, but his grievances against society circulate around a single topic: class hierarchy.[8] In nearly every book, Butts argues, on every page, one finds the palimpsest "Here am I, Rolfe, Baron Corvo – and a man of my genius has as much right to call himself Baron as any porkbutcher who's had his from a king with a title filched by politicians from a worthier house. Here am I, to tell the world what I think of it – Stinking cads! Stinking cads! Stinking cads!"[9] "The scream," according to Butts, "is embedded in the style, with all its colour and affectations, archaisms and involutions."[10] Every word, then, Corvo's entire aesthetic, is permeated by this sense of injustice, this contempt for things as they currently are, this exasperation with structures of inequality, and an unshakable conviction in his own value and his right to privilege. Corvo's preoccupation with status finally repulses Butts, as she becomes increasingly disgusted by the "evidence of spiritual vulgarity" in his works, "the approach of the *parvenu*, the unction, the concealed swagger. The kind of insistence on breeding that is itself ill-bred."[11] And the grand discovery that looms over Symons's entire quest, the "Venice letters," in which Corvo entreats the recipient, Charles Masson Fox, to come to Italy to enjoy the sexual favors of young gondoliers, becomes in Butts's account much more than what Symons described as "perverse sexual indulgence," the remorseless "destruction of the innocence of youth," all in some way linked up with that senseless paranoia on which Symons continually insists.[12] According to Butts, the scream is embedded in the Venice letters as well, for "[pandering] for male prostitution" was his "revenge," his angry rebuttal to being "thwarted, starved, exposed to all the brutishness of our society."[13] While others shared this experience, Corvo's unique egoism led him to strike back in this peculiar way.

Butts's Corvo emerges as a markedly different sort of creature, one who is angry for a precise set of reasons and not simply pathologically paranoid, but it is, of course, Symons's Corvo that is most well known. *The Quest for Corvo* has probably been encountered by more readers than all of Corvo's works combined. His Corvo is the one that we have inherited. His is the Corvo reflected in mid-century works like Pamela Johnson's "The Fascination of the Paranoid Personality: Baron Corvo" (1963).[14] His is the Corvo that emerges in recent criticism, a cantankerous elitist who serves in Regenia Gagnier's work as a representative example of all that is unsavory about the Decadents: their fear of "loss of boundaries" and "engulfment by the mass," their "recuperative attempts to fortify the rigid boundaries of the self and British society against the barbarians at the gates," and their delight in rigid hierarchies.[15] What is absent within this critical tradition is an awareness of the scream embedded in the style, as

Butts described it, as well as the sorrow. The delight in rigid hierarchies on display in Corvo's work emerges from something far more tragic than straightforward conservatism or elitism. He feigns fear of being engulfed by the masses while wrestling with the knowledge of his own kinship with the barbarians. His title, his sham nobility, his "tendency to 'swank,'" emerge in this light as anxious attempts to assert his right to respect from the world around him. His works are an account of degradation, humiliation, and privation as experienced by a subject who defiantly insisted on his own value. While his thinking does not move in the direction we might like or expect, toward socialist cooperation, comradeship, and democracy, his tendency to "swank" resulted from the same privations and poverty that produced those movements. Gagnier critiques Decadence's use of art as "an escape from, not a transformation of, daily life," but for one like Corvo, who saw no means available for the transformation of daily life, who starved and struggled and wound up in the workhouse, utopia, revolution, salvation for the poor must have felt quite distant and impossible.[16] His novels dwell on fantasies of wrongs righted, of value recognized and rewarded. A man who was rejected from the priesthood becomes pope. A beautiful boy murdered by a usurper becomes king. The injustice of the world is inverted. In some ways, these fantasies speak just as eloquently to injustice as the democratic poetics of socialist aestheticism.

This is not the Corvo that we have been handed, however, and in this chapter I would like to attempt to account for this fact by focusing on Corvo's reception in the 1920s and 1930s, his strange canonization by a group of post-Victorian dandies led by Symons and the equally interesting Maundy Gregory.[17] Corvo functioned as the centerpiece for a peculiar circle of connoisseurs, men with their own set of class anxieties living in an age marked by economic crises, "Bolshevism," and an emergent Labour Party. For these men, Decadence, or a revised and simplified version of Decadence, served as a soothing antidote to the political realities of the interwar period. Both Gregory and Symons were themselves *parvenus* "with an insistence on breeding that was itself ill-bred." Symons cultivated his appreciation for the rare and the fine in an effort to pass as what he was not. Gregory did much the same and, in turn, facilitated similar behavior on the part of others, selling honors to newly wealthy war profiteers. Although it might have been Corvo's class anxiety that initially attracted them to his work, they carefully elided the scream from the portrait that they chose to circulate among their fellow dandies and collectors. Corvo became in their hands a rare curio and a marker of elite taste. Symons and Gregory together founded the Corvine Society. The banquets of this society created a space where epicurean men could engage in decadent behaviors in a manner that reflected their exceptional taste and their esoteric knowledge. At the Ambassador Club, while consuming the finest foods and cocktails, book collectors and connoisseurs delivered speeches emphasizing that Corvo's works were fine, editions of them were rare, and exposure to or ownership of these texts was a privilege as well as a marker of distinction. These events were integral in the production of an elite, homosocial circle of post-Victorian dandies, a community of reactionary men who stood in opposition to progressive political change. By rallying around a particular vision of Corvo, the rarest of curios and the most elitist of conservatives, these post-Victorian dandies signaled their dissatisfaction with early-twentieth-century political realities. This chapter, then, considers the role that this vision of Corvo's Decadent texts played in the solidification of a certain kind of class identity during the interwar period.

I. The Principle of Aristos: Corvo and the Erotics of Inequality

In this chapter, I hope to trouble the traditional representation of Corvo as nothing more than an archconservative. However, it is the case that his works demonstrate a real preoccupation with hierarchy and imbalanced power relationships. For example, while ephebophilia was often considered in terms of its democratic possibilities by fin-de-siècle authors and artists, Baron Corvo's representations of adolescent boys celebrate fixed and stable hierarchies, chivalrous friendship, loyalty, and obedience. Rather than stressing the mentoring or "raising up" of a beloved boy, Corvo's works dwell on the erotics of asymmetrical relationships, submission, and service. The boys in his fiction wait hand and foot on the older men who are their masters. The young models in his photographs present themselves submissively to the presumably older spectator, often in presenting poses with their hands clasped behind their backs or tied behind them. His works carefully preserve rank and order. However, while I acknowledge the extent to which Corvo's works exemplify the reactionary conservatism of Decadence as described by Regenia Gagnier, this chapter also contextualizes these works in an effort to illuminate his complex political stance.

Corvo's politics were much more conflicted than recent critics have been willing to admit. He did compose a poem titled "Towards Aristocracy" that was meant to serve as a "counterblast" to Edward Carpenter's Whitmanesque celebration of freedom and equality, *Towards Democracy* (1883–1902), and he often lambasted socialism.[18] But he also wrote for a socialist newspaper, the *Aberdeen Standard*, and lived with its founder, the socialist leader Henry Hyde Champion. He donated money to the Fabian Society and corresponded with its founders, including Hubert Bland and E. Nesbit. Socialism, despite all the contempt he often displayed for it, seems to have exercised quite a pull on Baron Corvo. In addition, his infamous Venice letters often articulate deep sympathy for the suffering of the gondoliers. Although he tried desperately to maintain a distinction between himself and the servants and gondoliers he encountered in Venice, he spent much of his time in the city struggling, often starving, frequently homeless. His vision of friendship was conceived of in direct opposition to Carpenter's ideal of comradeship, but the impoverished gondoliers emerge in his Venetian correspondence as his comrades nevertheless, as his sympathies transgress the very class boundaries he worked so hard to preserve.

Corvo's fantasy visions of injustice inverted, in which wrongs are righted and the last become first, must be understood as emerging from the experience of poverty and degradation. His most reactionary works are also deeply preoccupied with the question of injustice. His representations of ephebophilia and chivalrous friendship functioned in complex, often contradictory ways, advertising themselves as part of a conservative, Decadent reaction against democratic politics while at the same time voicing a poignant critique of economic injustice. His critique of socialism similarly should not be taken at face value, emerging, as it did, from a long and protracted consideration of the merits of the concept of equality as opposed to a clean and complete rejection of democratic comradeship. I begin here by focusing on the elaboration of an elitist and aristocratic politics in Corvo's works, before turning to an examination of the screams and sorrows that inspired his excessive tendency to "swank."

While the primary post-Victorians of this chapter are the members of the Corvine Society, Corvo positioned himself as out of place in and disapproving of the modern age. His *Hadrian the Seventh*, for example, speaks a markedly Victorian, Decadent language, but it speaks that language to a set of twentieth-century problems. First published in 1904, the novel looks with longing to an ordered and stable past almost as much as it gazes with horror at the impending violence and disorder of the coming decades. Though Corvo's fantastical revision of history hysterically represses the rise of Labour and conflict between the nations, his hysteria speaks to and presciently predicts both World War I and the success that the Labour Party experienced in the 1920s and 1930s. In every way, Corvo shuts his eyes to the realities of the coming era, and on every page of *Hadrian the Seventh*, those realities insistently surface.

As the novel opens, Corvo's alter ego, George Rose, watches fearfully from his tiny attic apartment as chaos begins to reign over the twentieth century. He sits in his shabby brocade armchair reading newspaper articles titled "THE GATHERING OF THE STORM," "SIGNS OF SMOULDERING REVOLT," and "ANARCHY ADVANCING."[19] Revolutionary fever has taken hold of the working classes. Workman's riots are taking place in St. Petersburg. Nihilists are agitating in Berlin. In response, Rose fills a notebook with reactionary phrases and opinions in his purposefully archaic handwriting. He quotes Gabriele d'Annunzio approvingly: "Old legitimate monarchies are everywhere declining and Demos stands ready to swallow them down his miry throat."[20] But within this fantasy reconstruction of the turn of the century, Demos can only stand ready to swallow tradition *until* George Rose becomes Hadrian the Seventh. In an unlikely turn of events, the Sacred College elects Rose, who had, like Corvo, previously failed in his candidacy for the priesthood, to the position of pope. The deeply conservative pontiff defeats Demos and goes on to change the Church and the world. To do so, he must contend with a treacherous socialist leader, an awful scorned woman, the rising tide of anarchy, and the problems of Russia and France, but he handles himself beautifully, and order is restored by Hadrian's hand.

Hadrian the Seventh holds socialism responsible for many of the modern era's problems. The novel's central villain is the aforementioned treacherous socialist leader, Jerry Sant, who hopes to blackmail Hadrian into forcing English Catholics to vote for members of the "Liblab Fellowship," a union between the Social Democratic Foundation and the Independent Labour Party. Hadrian, however, stridently opposes socialist principles and refuses to capitulate to Sant's demands. When the members of the Liblab Fellowship misunderstand Hadrian's call for reform in his *Epistle to All Christians* to be an endorsement of the "doctrine of Equality," Hadrian issues a Pontifical Breve to debunk that doctrine.[21] Equality, Hadrian declares, is "scientifically, historically, and obviously false and impracticable," and the doctrine of Equality is nothing but "a diabolical delusion for the ruin of souls."[22] Men are not equal but infinitely different from one another, and to deny this fact is to deny the very nature of the Divine Creator's scheme. The claim to equality, Hadrian argues, is "so indecently unjust that it only could emanate from inferiors who hoped to gain by degrading their superiors."[23] Socialists are only "actuated by their lust of improving their own condition at the expense of their brother," and their incessant outcry is "by no means . . . the bitter groan of oppressed poverty, but rather the grumbling vituperation of envious discontented mediocrity anxious to affect an appearance, which was sham and not its own, and to wallow in luxurious conditions which it had not earned."[24] After debunking the doctrine of Equality, Hadrian endorses the principle of Aristos, "The Best."[25] "Rights, inherited, meritorious, conferred by legitimate authority," he declares, are "sacred" and not to be contested by the "essentially selfish and venal" demands of the Liblab Fellowship.[26]

While deflecting socialist blackmailers, Hadrian must also contend with the escalating militarism and aggression of the early twentieth century. Alliances are being formed as empires expand. "Each nation," we are told "[fears] the other; and all [fear] France and Russia."[27] But the impending world war and the problem of socialism are dealt with summarily before Hadrian is assassinated by Jerry Sant in the novel's final pages. Hadrian passes, yet he leaves the world much for the better. Europe has been divided into a Northern and Southern Empire; England's "Ninefold King" rules over Ireland, Wales, Scotland, Asia, Africa, Canada, Australia, New Zealand, and All Islands; and socialism has perished from Germany, Italy, and England. The Church has severed itself from worldly concerns, and the "diabolic ebullience" of the persistently unruly France and Russia has been "restrained and stamped out."[28] The world has been remade according to the principle of Aristos. Three strong rulers control the world. The unruly nations that contributed most to the escalating tension between the nations are under martial law, and "the sordid selfishness" that is socialism has been eradicated.[29] When the novel ends, Corvo has successfully staved off the advancement of anarchy by retreating into a highly ordered, strictly monarchical fantasy realm.

Hadrian the Seventh could certainly serve as a representative example of all that is unsavory about the Decadents. The novel does seem to be the height of, almost a caricature of, the most awful forms of conservatism that Decadence has to offer. The attitudes on display here are part of a larger current within Corvo's oeuvre. He first made a name for himself in the pages of the *Yellow Book* with his Toto stories, heady, homoerotic tales in which a lovely Italian boy explains Catholic mythology and Italian folklore to an older English man.[30] These stories dwell on the erotic possibilities of imbalanced power relationships. Toto revels in his position as servant and the narrator in his as master, often scolding, punishing, and whipping Toto for minor infractions. The Toto stories are quintessential fin-de-siècle Decadence, but Corvo outlived the 1890s, and his aesthetic became increasingly reactionary in the 1900s and 1910s as he greeted the twentieth century's upswing in anarchy.

Corvo was quite aware of the rich thinking about friendship, fellowship, and cooperation taking place in the circles associated with aestheticism at the turn of the century. However, he chose to repudiate the socialist utopianism of William Morris and Edward Carpenter and to perversely revise their optimistic vision of bonds between men in his own writing about friendship. In his semiautobiographical *The Desire and Pursuit of the Whole* (published posthumously in 1934), Corvo describes his response to Carpenter's Whitmanesque celebration of freedom and equality, *Towards Democracy*. He apparently found the language "splendid," but "its doctrine set him in revolt."[31] His disgust inspired the composition of a "counterblast" titled "Towards Aristocracy."[32] Though this work has never been found, his *Hubert's Arthur* (published posthumously in 1935), which was composed during the same period, might be understood as a fictional equivalent. This what-might-have-been history, which concerns itself with the contested succession following the death of Richard the Lionheart, revels in hierarchy, domination, and obedience. Told from the point of view of Hubert de Burgh, who slavishly admires and obeys the young Duke Arthur of Brittany, the novel celebrates a model of chivalrous friendship that contests and revises Carpenter's vision of fellowship.

Like *Hadrian the Seventh*, *Hubert's Arthur* aggressively represses the rise of democracy, rewriting a new and firmly aristocratic future for England, successfully eradicating monstrous Demos in favor of a newly healthy and inviolable Aristos. The novel revises England's past to ensure a firmly aristocratic future. According to the mythology of English democracy, John's injustices and Henry's inadequacies served as a fertile soil for the growth of modern political institutions. The precedent set by the signing of the Magna Carta during John's reign facilitated further agitation for reform during the reign of Henry III. Corvo allows the signing of the Magna Carta to occur in his own what-might-have-been history, but he nips democracy in the bud by replacing Henry III, "ambitious yet unsure of himself," with a confident and noble King Arthur who defeats Simon de Montfort.[33] In reality, Arthur disappeared in 1203 and was rumored to have been murdered by John. Corvo's Arthur, conversely, survives and takes the throne, and thus the troublesome reign of Henry III is avoided altogether, and the rumblings of democracy that began during John's are silenced and forgotten. Arthur renegotiates England's relationship to the Church and preserves the concept of Aristos. Through Arthur, Corvo makes for England a new future, monarchical and Catholic.

The novel's representation of friendship reinforces the political valence of Corvo's revision of historical fact. In reality, Hubert de Burgh served as justiciar to both John and Henry, but in Corvo's alternative history, Arthur's beauty, his carriage, and his unmistakably kingly manner tear Hubert from the usurper John's service, and Hubert dedicates himself to placing Arthur in his rightful place on the throne. On first sight, Hubert is inflamed with servile passion and abject admiration for the boy, falling immediately to his knees and promising to be his "true man henceforward."[34] Because of Hubert's previous ties to John, Arthur is slow to trust Hubert, and Hubert seems to relish the opportunities for humility and suffering Arthur's suspicions provide: "My heart bled for the stern stony loneliness of that white child. Not that I let him see how I pitied and loved and adored him. Not that I gave him any inkling of how hot I was to serve and worship him."[35] Hubert is hot to serve. This passage, more than any perhaps, best illustrates the manner in which friendship is conceived in this novel. The pleasures of submitting and serving are privileged above all else. Arthur's youth compounds the thrill of the relationship, as Hubert voluntarily submits to one much smaller, much younger than he, and he does so in deference to hierarchy. He surrenders to his duty as a servant to the disinherited king, taking pleasure in the young king's severity, expressing reverence for his natural right to rule. This is the erotics of Aristos, of sacred rights inherited, an inversion and rejection of the democratic eros of Corvo's contemporaries such as Edward Carpenter.

Corvo's fascination with the erotics of inequality is similarly evident in his photographs of adolescent boys. Corvo possessed a great enthusiasm for the "Arcadian" photography popular at the turn of the century, practiced most famously by Wilhelm von Gloeden. As Donald Rosenthal has noted, these pictures, in which young male models posed in classical costumes in the outdoors, facilitated for homophile men an escape "from a world of social disapproval to an idealized earlier time when, it was thought, same-sex desires and relationships were honored."[36] However, while many Arcadian photographs represent groups of men and thus seem to celebrate camaraderie or fellowship, Corvo's photographs typically subject one young man to erotic scrutiny. The subject here does not seem to be bonds between men but rather the act of looking. And although he does at times photograph boys in pairs, his models so rarely express interest in one another that they tend to remain desired objects as opposed to desiring subjects. Forty percent of von Gloeden's photographs depict multiple interactions.[37] His models flirt and communicate and examine one another. Corvo's models, conversely, present themselves submissively to the viewer, often in "presenting" poses, with their hands behind their backs or tied to a tree in postures reminiscent of St. Sebastian.[38]

While Corvo's interest in adolescents does seem tied to his interest in power imbalance, ephebophilia is not, of course, always bound up entirely within an erotics of inequality. As Richard Dellamora notes in his discussion of male friendship in the Victorian period, within the Athenian institution of pederasty, a mentor directed the education of a protégé in the "virtues required for participation in the government of the city."[39] The objective of these relationships was "emergence of the younger member as a citizen and equal of his older friend."[40] Corvo, however, does not seem to want the young men he eroticizes to mature into equals. In the Venice letters, he speaks with disgust of the maturation of adolescents: "He'll be like this till Spring, say 3 months more. Then some great fat slow cow of a girl will just open herself wide, and lie quite still, and drain him dry. First the rich bloom of him will go. Then he'll get hard and hairy. And by July, he'll have a moustache, a hairy breast for his present great boyish bosom, brushes in his milky armpits, brooms on his splendid young thighs, and be just the ordinary stevedore to be found by scores on the quays."[41] And he does not represent his contact with these working-class boys as a source of liberation. In another letter to Fox, he disparages the "slavish tendency" one encounters in some of the Venetian young men, but he also notes that "the best method is to begin with slaves and educate them out of slavery into intelligent and faithful servants."[42] The final goal, he implies here, is not equality but more capable service.

II. "Queer Ideas about Money": Degradation, Privation, and the Search for the Divine Friend

Though Corvo's works certainly represent hierarchy and inequality in eroticized terms, this is only part of the story. At the very time that Corvo wrote some of his most deeply conservative, reactionary works, he was, much like the gondoliers discussed in the Venice letters, struggling, often hungry, frequently without a home. He lived for a time aboard his boat while composing *Hubert's Arthur*, fending off swimming rats and ferocious crabs. He told Fox he was "simply dying of cold and hunger" and that he looked "so hideously shabby that [he] daren't shew [himself] in the street by day."[43] Of course, even at his most abject, Corvo retained his sense of Aristos. He noted that he could not solve this problem by simply going about at night, for "after dark, the place swarms with people who are not respectable: and [he was] not going to be mixed up with them."[44] And he did, as Gagnier notes, use money from patrons to attempt to maintain rank. He thanked Fox profusely for sending him the money necessary to tip the servants of a family with whom he was staying, noting that, had he been unable to do so, the servants "would have treated [him] as one of themselves; and their insolent familiarity would have become intolerable."[45] In the end, however, the boundary between Corvo and those less "respectable" proved too difficult to maintain, and he did become "mixed up with them." In 1909, he wrote in search of a position as second gondolier, asserting that he "would be a good servant, in uniform or blouse," and that he knew "how to do brown boots better than any valet."[46] In a letter to Horatio Brown, he insisted that he was "so sick of people of [his] own class that [he would] jump at the chance of entering the class of menials."[47]

As Corvo's pretensions to "swank" grew more tenuous, he became increasingly white hot against society, and the scream Butts notes intensified. The 1909 Christmas greeting he sent to two former collaborators, Harry Pirie-Gordon and Robert Hugh Benson, alters Matthew 25:35–41 to express anger and resentment rather than gratitude: "For I was an hungred, & ye gave me no meat: I was thirsty, & ye gave me no drink: I was a stranger, & ye took me not in: naked, & ye clothed me not: sick, & in prison, & ye visited me not. Depart from me, ye cursed, into everlasting fire, prepared for the devil & his angels."[48] Inverting the lines of the biblical passage so that they conclude with a threat, Corvo charges his former friends with neglect and promises them damnation in return. In a note on his Corvo collection, David Roth quotes from a private letter from "one who knew him well in the early 1890s": "He had queer ideas about money: he was convinced it was the duty of the world to keep him supplied with the elementary necessities of life."[49] During the final years of his life, as the world repeatedly failed him in this regard, Corvo grew increasingly indignant, seeing consistent evidence of a failure on the part of his friends to look after his well-being.

The escalating scream of this period speaks to Corvo's growing sense of injustice as he experienced ongoing suffering and degradation. However, the more he suffered, the more proud he became and the more he insisted on his right not to suffer. As Miriam Benkovitz notes in her discussion of the missing work "Towards Aristocracy," Corvo's rejection of the principle of democracy resulted from extreme privation rather than privilege: "His poverty had consigned him too often to a nameless place among the masses of people who allow the democratic process to function. From his experience, democracy offered neither service nor protection."[50] If democracy had failed to protect him, perhaps an alternative system, a hierarchical system, would allow him to thrive. Any discussion of Corvo's reactionary conservatism should take into account the conditions that produced his strange attitudes. It was, however, Corvo's shrill elitism rather than its causes that seems to have attracted the Corvine cult of the 1920s and 1930s, and, to posit Corvo as the centerpiece of such a circle, much of the tragedy, sympathy, and interest in connectedness or collaboration present in his writing had to be minimized. Before moving on to a discussion of the Corvines themselves, I would like to draw out those elements of Corvo's thinking that the Corvines were most careful to erase.

In *The Quest*, Symons posits the Venice letters as evidence that Corvo had degenerated into a "habitual corrupter of youth, a seducer of innocence," a reading that neglects entirely Corvo's poignant expression of affiliation with the sufferings of the gondoliers.[51] At times this kinship is articulated in terms that nevertheless preserve a sense of ethnic superiority. In an early letter, for example, Corvo asserts his intimacy with the gondoliers while at the same time foregrounding their exoticism and distance: "These Venetians, like all Orientals (for they really are Orientals, you know) are frightfully shy of strangers; and it always takes time to get them to unstiffen and to let themselves go. And that is just what happened. I do really think that all my actions and exertions of the past year only came into sudden flower at the moment when you were on the verge of going away. P. and C. and the rest knew me thoroughly by then. They had seen me in wealth and poverty. They had got over their fear of me and knew me for one of themselves."[52] In a protean response to the gondoliers, he first characterizes them as alien and then as fundamentally alike. He begins in condescension and ends with an admission of his own humble circumstances, comparable in many ways to those of the young men he initially subjected to erotic scrutiny. He acknowledges that as much as he looked longingly at them, they, too, could see, and they saw him at times of which he might not have been proud. However, the fact that they were alike in their circumstances allowed for a greater degree of intimacy. As the Venice letters progress and Corvo allows Fox ever more insight into his actual position, the author and his subjects become equally more fully realized and fully human. His own suffering intensifies, as does his sensitivity to those around him. The impotent sorrow Corvo feels while watching Peter, one of the gondoliers, suffer with syphilis is one of the most striking moments in the letters. Again, Corvo expresses this sympathy in conflicted terms, reflecting disgust with what is ugly and agony at the sight of another's pain: "Isn't it simply frightful about poor Peter. His weight has come down 58 chilogrammes to 15!!! I'm ashamed to say that I hardly dare look at him. It's no good for me to try to look at him as long as I can't do anything to help him. But with the first decent sum I get I shall run him off to Solfatara and give him a course of sulphur baths and plenty of good food to restore him."[53] The aesthetic sense that repels him from the sight of illness is counterbalanced by the ethical sense, the angry sense of helplessness as the impoverished "Baron" acknowledges his inability to solve another's problems. Yet the defiant belief in a comfortable future, present throughout Corvo's letters, in this case allows for a comforting fantasy of assistance and generosity.

In fact, in almost every Corvine work that I have just finished characterizing as awful in its aloofness and elitism, one finds evidence of an ethical undercurrent, a gnawing sense of obligation toward others, a persistent fascination with bonds based in equality and cooperation. In her discussion of Decadence, Gagnier stresses the need for "control, stability, and distance from others" on the part of writers such as Huysman and Corvo.[54] She argues that Corvo's work "bears all the marks of the most conservative Englishness: love of hierarchy and of ritual for its own sake, obsession with private property (including the Beloved), general inflexibility, and a deluded self-sufficiency. While he protests that he wants (comm)unity . . . , his boundaries . . . are armoured, impermeable. . . . Not risk, nor generosity, nor change (the values of the earlier socialist aesthetes) rule Rolfe's world, but the firm principle of exact exchange: you get back what you give, measure for measure."[55] Corvo, however, characterized himself much differently. He was, as he writes in *The Desire and Pursuit of the Whole*, "incapable of refraining from the mixture of his life with other people's."[56] In a letter to James Walsh, he notes that he both loathes and craves "communion with [his] fellow creatures."[57] He continually sought connection and cooperation, though his quests often failed, and he returned repeatedly to the concept of community and the principle of altruism.

Hadrian, for example, is a work of stunningly conservative Englishness, but it nevertheless ponders how one might improve the lot of those less well off while, admittedly, preserving one's own freedom and autonomy. The solution, Hadrian finds, is the concept of "individualistic altruism." As the novel opens, George Rose ponders his "psychical detachment" from other men and speculates that the explanation for this detachment lies in his highly developed "critical faculty," his dexterity at "the arts of selection and discrimination."[58] This turning of the language of aestheticism to cold and insular purposes certainly resembles the Decadence described by Gagnier. But moments later, Rose undoes this impermeable barrier, bemoaning his isolation to God, begging for freedom, power, and money so he may "make a few people happy, just to put things right a bit, just to make things easy, just to straighten out tangled lives whose tangles make me rage because I myself am helpless. . . . My aim is single and unselfish."[59]

He wrestles repeatedly with his conflicting aims and intentions, acknowledging his tendency to apartness while at the same time speaking of his desire for connection: "I seem to be a thing apart. I can't understand my neighbour. . . . I want to understand my neighbour in order to love him. But I don't think I know what love is. But I want to – badly."[60] Hadrian's reforms allow him to begin to put things right, to express generosity toward his neighbor and make a move outside the boundaries of the self. He abolishes pew rents. He gives to the poorest of the poor. He is accused of being Tolstoyan and of possessing "an anarchistical kind of enthusiasm," but he counters by insisting on his own conservatism, arguing that his only motto is "Cultivate, and help to cultivate individuality, at your own expense if possible, but never at the expense of your brother."[61] Hadrian's individualistic altruism, his desire to "help to cultivate individuality," sounds suspiciously like Wildean socialism, the unselfish individualism that revels in difference and recognizes "infinite variety of type as a delightful thing."[62] Corvo cannot, of course, be lumped in with the radical socialist aestheticism of Carpenter, but he is not entirely at odds at all times with the thinking of his progressive aestheticist precursors. Corvo's (and Hadrian's) bitterness and suspicion inhibit the capacity for unabashed kindness, but the impulse to connect and to assist, stunted and cautious though it may be, is there.

Corvo represents socialism in an exceedingly harsh light in *Hadrian*, but he did flirt with the movement before arriving in Venice. This element of Corvo's biography was not allotted much attention by the members of the Corvine Society. In fact, in a set of essays published in the 1960s, the Labour historian Henry Pelling repeatedly called Symons to task for his inattention to Corvo's socialist associations.[63] Symons did take brief note of Corvo's interactions with Henry Hyde Champion, a socialist leader, during the time he spent living in Aberdeen, but Pelling argues that Symons "failed to realize the significance of Champion's influence on Corvo and the degree of mutual sympathy that existed between the two."[64] According to Pelling, "one side of Corvo's career has been completely neglected by the biographers and by the literary critics, whose minds appear capable of comprehending only a part of their legitimate subject matter."[65]

In her 1977 biography, Miriam Benkovitz began to illuminate this overlooked side of Corvo's life. She noted that Corvo turned to Champion after being evicted from lodgings in his pajamas, then (unsuccessfully) seeking certification of insanity in hopes of living at the Asylum, and finally living on the streets and on a sand dune on the Aberdeen shore. Champion was in Aberdeen campaigning as a Labour candidate in the 1893 General Election. According to Benkovitz, a desperate Corvo sought out Champion at his home, and his "defiant account of his situation and how he came to it" "caught the liking and sympathy of Champion."[66] He offered Corvo a position at his socialist weekly paper, the *Aberdeen Standard*; provided him with food and clothing; and allowed him to stay in his apartment.

Donald Weeks, the prominent collector and biographer of Corvo, insists that Corvo possessed "an inborn concern for his fellow-creatures" and that Champion was "the one man who moulded Rolfe into the literary personality he later became."[67] Whether Weeks is correct or not, works from this period in Corvo's life, such as the short story "An Unforgettable Experience" (1894), reflect a real engagement with Champion's vision of poverty and injustice. Benkovitz argues that the ambience of "An Unforgettable Experience," which tells the story of a woman in the slums incorrectly pronounced dead, "comes directly from Rolfe's association with Champion." The story is set in "a slum dwelling where the old and young alike live in crowded acceptance of human suffering. The woman in the coffin with the dead infant at her side, her other children writhing on a dirty bed 'like maggots in cheese,' her 'tipsy' husband, a barrow boy and his speech are elements of Rolfe's attempt to portray an environment about which he had not written before and would not write again."[68] The story, Benkovitz argues, must be understood as a marked departure from Corvo's tendency to elide and quickly forget his own experiences with poverty, treating each episode of homelessness and starvation as "a nightmare better forgotten in the light of deserved prosperity, an accident to be overcome by the exercise of imagination and will."[69] The dabbling in socialist reportage here is certainly unique, but, as Benkovitz indicates, the fact that Corvo preferred not to dwell on the experience of poverty emerges not from his conservatism but from his excessive knowledge of that experience. Corvo tended to repress, rather than dwell on, the details of suffering and privation, but during his time with Champion, he seems to have temporarily seen the value of conveying the nature of the slum experience to British readers. Champion apparently found the piece effective, for he called it to the attention of Jerome K. Jerome, the editor of *To-Day*, who accepted it for publication in his weekly in 1894.

The question remains, however, why Corvo, after such a seemingly positive and influential experience with Champion, chose to represent Labour in such a harsh manner in *Hadrian*. Pelling argues that Corvo often expressed sympathy with socialists "who, for one reason or another, were at odds with the organized labour movement," much as he, a devoted Catholic, spent his life at odds with the Church. Champion, for example, was highly unorthodox in his views and espoused something "more akin to

Tory Democracy than to Liberal Radicalism."[70] He criticized the Liberal tendencies of the founders of the Labour Representation Committee, and he was in turn accused of working for the Conservative Party. His letters were intercepted and used as evidence against him, and Champion was finally forced out of the movement, emigrating from England to Australia in February 1894. Champion's struggles with Labour inflect the representation of the party in the pages of *Hadrian.* For example, Champion, or "Dymoke," is referred to repeatedly by Sant as a "Tory spy."[71] Hadrian himself remembers Dymoke fondly as the "only capable fighting man ever possessed by socialism, . . . sponged upon for fifteen years by socialistic cadgers, sucked dry, ruined, and cast out, a victim of socialistic jealousy and treachery."[72] Apparently Corvo's sympathy with Champion persisted well after the time they spent together, and he seems to have remained fascinated with Champion's oppositional stance in relationship to his party.

The Champion interlude does not represent the sole moment of socialist affiliation in Corvo's career. Corvo engaged in an extended correspondence with E. Nesbit's husband, Hubert Bland, who, like Champion, was more of a Tory socialist. This tempered mode of socialism seems to have had some appeal for Corvo, and, though he insisted to Bland that all the socialists he had ever encountered (save Champion and Bland's family) "are people who make me sick," he also said that his decision not to become a socialist had mostly to do with fear concerning his "means of livelihood": "You see it is not that I am difficult, not a matter of my personal pleasure, not by any means that I'm violently addicted to the 'place to which it has pleased God to call me.' Oh no. It's just simply that I do what I do & live as I live because I know no better way. If I did, I should leap at it."[73] Corvo's relationship to socialism cannot be categorized as simple. He certainly did spend a great deal of time castigating the movement, its members, and their beliefs, but he also exhibited a persistent interest in socialist dissidents who went against the grain or tinkered with the movement's ideology, accessorizing democratic ideals with elements of conservatism.

Corvo's interest in collaboration similarly persisted throughout his career, and I would argue that the same conflicted impulses that underwrote his strange relationship to socialism rendered collaboration at once alluring and near-impossible for Corvo. He spent most of his adult life in search of *divo amico desideratissimo*, the "divine friend much desired," his "Other Half," who would, among other things, assist him in the composition of literary works.[74] In the semiautobiographical *Nicholas Crabbe* (published posthumously in 1958), he describes this ideal collaborative relationship: "In course of the work, the workers themselves came closer together, closer in amazement at and admiration of each other's extraordinary genius. . . . MS. after MS. was written and emended and revised and rewritten again and again until the two keen minds were wholly satisfied. Arguments and quarrels took place, without a vestige of ill-nature; and no difference was passed over until it had been threshed out thoroughly and solved. Each was willing to give. Each was open to conviction."[75] Corvo's ideal model of collaboration involves ever-escalating intimacy, trust, generosity, and patience as well as real engagement with the thoughts and opinions of another. However, each time Corvo located a prospective other half, the ideal in practice fell much short of this vision, and the collaboration disintegrated into bitter quarrels and contests over creative property. Corvo was perpetually interested in situations of involvement and comradeship, but these situations often required disorder and loss of control. A truly cooperative relationship, a friendship between equals that results in the production of beautiful things, emerges as the idée fixe, the thing most longed for in Corvo's novels and letters, but the vulnerability required to make such a friendship successful frequently proves too much for him. However, while he never established a collaborative relationship with any degree of permanence, some of his strangest and most interesting works, such as *Hubert's Arthur* and *The Weird of the Wanderer* (1912), which he wrote with Harry Pirie-Gordon, were the result of collaboration. He was, at least temporarily, able to lower the gates and invite influence from a friend, though embitterment and suspicion finally curtailed these endeavors. If the quest for the divine friend and ideal collaborator was finally a failure, it is worth remembering how much time and energy Corvo devoted to this quest. The impulse to share responsibilities, to share labor and profits, is marked in Corvo and serves as a significant counterpoint to his somewhat disingenuous performance of unfettered elitism and individualism.

III. The Corvine Cult: Post-Victorian Dandyism and Reactionary Elitism in the Early Twentieth Century

All of this, however, the caustic critique of economic injustice, the longing for affiliation, the sympathy with the suffering of others, does not receive much attention from the early Corvines. The picture that they paint is of a very different sort of man, one who is much more appropriate for and useful to their own project, a complicated attempt at passing that relies on elite forms of consumption. The strange manner in which the early Corvines handled the representation of Corvo's class politics has much to do with the class politics of their own era, a set of events to which Corvo himself had looked forward in *Hadrian* and with which his posthumous admirers had to wrestle. The ADVANCING ANARCHY and SMOULDERING REVOLT foreseen in *Hadrian* had by the 1920s and 1930s resulted in a truly different political landscape. The Labour Party, struggling to assert itself at the time of *Hadrian*'s composition, was by the time of the Corvine banquets in 1929 the largest party in the House of Commons. The onset of economic depression, mass unemployment, and a general strike during the same period only further complicated matters. A simplified Decadence, personified by Corvo, allowed the Corvines to negotiate the political realities of the modern moment by transporting themselves back to a mythical moment of fin-de-siècle epicureanism, of unfettered, guiltless hedonism and elitism.

A. J. A. Symons first began implementing Corvo in his efforts to infiltrate the ranks of the upper classes on October 23, 1926, when he delivered a speech about Corvo before the Sette of Odd Volumes.[76] The Sette of Odd Volumes was "a select and distinguished dining club" for bibliophiles founded in 1878.[77] This "elite gentlemen's club" consisted of twenty-one members, "this being the number of volumes of the Variorum of Shakespeare of 1821."[78] The club had strong links to the Decadent 1890s, as the Rhymers' Club had borrowed some customs from the Sette; former members included Richard Le Gallienne and John Lane; and, at the time Symons was elected to the club, Wilde's son Vyvyan Holland was also a member.[79] Symons had just recently been elected to the club, and, soon after his admission, each new "Odd Volume" was expected to "make a literary, scientific, or artistic communication to the Sette."[80] Membership in the club promised Symons strengthened connections to the literary culture of the fin de siècle and to elite society, and his choice of topic for his initial communication bears significance in relationship to both aspirations.

Symons hailed from a somewhat complex class position. He felt intense humiliation concerning the time he had spent as a teenager working as an apprentice to a firm of fur dealers, an experience he compared to Dickens's time at Warren's Blacking factory. His father, a Russian Jewish émigré, had made a small fortune during the war when he purchased the Moorgate Auction Rooms. However, this moment of prosperity came to an end in 1921 because of some unsuccessful speculations on his father's part. According to his brother Julian Symons, A. J. possessed a deep "grudge against the condition of life into which he had been born" and a "determination to escape from it."[81] He was, Julian argues, guided above all by a "determination to achieve a position of importance in the world."[82] He "rejected with indignation" the "political determinism of modern Socialist theory" and exhibited a "Carlylean admiration" for the "destiny-defying power of the strong man."[83] However, underneath his pride and determination lay "doubts and anxieties" about his capacity to ascend from his somewhat liminal class position.[84] Armed with the connoisseur's knowledge he had acquired in his father's auction rooms, which allowed him to play the part of one familiar with and comfortable around luxury, A. J. A. Symons spent the rest of his life working to attain social success. He founded the First Edition Club in 1922 and began making a name for himself as a connoisseur of rare books. According to his brother, this pursuit arose directly from his anxieties concerning his class identity: "The scar that [working as an apprentice to a firm of fur dealers] left on my brother's character remained sensitive almost throughout his life: and this . . . was the conscious force that drove him to . . . an interest in bibliophily which, since it is generally a pursuit of the well-to-do, might lead to interesting social contacts."[85] The impulse proved sound, as it was Dr. G. C. Williamson, a member of Symons's First Edition Club, who had proposed Symons as a member of the Sette of Odd Volumes. Symons gained contact with the society he desired by positioning himself as an elite consumer and purveyor of literary rarities, and membership in the Sette finally promised to dispel any lingering class anxiety: "The Sette of Odd Volumes permitted my brother to move out of the social half-world in which through sheer uncertainty he had scented frequently a hostility in others which existed only in his imagination, into the full light of upper class society. There was no doubt of the social standing of his fellow Odd Volumes, . . . and if there was at first something strange to him in this intoxicating social air, he soon became accustomed to its headiness."[86]

It is noteworthy that at this pivotal moment in his transition into upper-class society, Symons chose to align himself with one who was not only a notorious pretender to the aristocracy but a rancorous critic of oppressive social forces. However, the portrait of Corvo that Symons chose to deliver to the Sette bears little resemblance to the Baron "white hot" against economic injustice described by Mary Butts. Symons entertained the Sette with the story of a quaint, odd, and perhaps mentally ill man who wrote elaborate works for discerning readers. In his speech, Symons does not spend an undue amount of time on Corvo's poverty. He does acknowledge that, if one had the opportunity to speak with Corvo, he likely would have mentioned that he had "starved in every part of England."[87] This topic, however, would have been passed over quickly in favor of a topic that had little to do with material circumstances. During this same imagined conversation, "whatever else was said, the one thing certain was that he would refer to his enemies and their conspiracies against himself: for, though he was not mad like William Blake, nor deranged like Cowper, he was afflicted with a mild form of persecution mania, which made him an expert in the art of quarreling, and transmuted his powers into pugnacity."[88] The concept of "persecution mania" remains central to Symons's vision of Corvo in the 1920s and 1930s, functioning as an effective method for neutralizing the more political elements of Corvo's rage and transforming his anger into eccentricity as opposed to political critique. Similarly, rather than considering Corvo's desire to cooperate with other men as a complicated and interesting counterpoint to his elitist individualism, this element of his persona is also represented as a disorder. According to Symons, Corvo's frequent "proposals for joint work" were a result of his "craze for collaboration."[89] His anger and his tenderness are pathologized and depoliticized, transformed into meaningless curiosities rather than integral parts of a dizzyingly complex political vision. Symons also chooses to isolate the question of Corvo's false title from larger issues of inequality and injustice. Where Butts hears a defiant assertion of individual value, Symons "[prefers] to think that the title was a sardonic jest on the shape of his own nose."[90] As he moves through a brisk description of Corvo's travails, he grows cautious of "[tiring his audience] with tales" of his privations, noting quickly that "the worst thing that happened to him in Scotland was ignominious ejection from his lodging in pyjamas."[91] The starvation and homelessness become in Symons's hands silly anecdotes, sources of interest or humor rather than tragedy: "His picaresque career reads like a page from the *Arabian Nights*, or a column from *The News of the World*."[92] Lest his upper-class audience begin to suspect that Corvo wished to live off of the state, Symons cautions them against "[thinking] of him as a waster or a scoundrel."[93] This was not the case. Once "warmed and fed," he immediately set about earning his keep. He reinforces this assertion concerning Corvo's work ethic in the conclusion of the speech, noting that Corvo "had so many gifts, industry above all."[94] He similarly foregrounds Corvo's aversion to charity, concluding with the assertion that Corvo's "life was wrecked by his inability to receive favors."[95] Although he might have believed that he ought to have received more support from the world, "his wants were few," and, in a sense, this belief was somewhat justified, for he was "giving good work to the world."[96] Symons has taken great care to render the angry Baron palatable to the Sette, subtly separating him from questions of welfare, unemployment, and state assistance, routing the scream from the style altogether.

Much is made of the style, which is, of course, truly noteworthy. Symons devotes an entire section of his speech to reciting some of Corvo's unusual, obsolete, "corrected," and portmanteau terms, such as "eximious," "tractator," "mispresent" (for "misrepresent"), "diaphotick," and "contortuplicate."[97] He promises his audience that there is great pleasure to be had in Corvo's "neological" style and his "[artificial]" prose.[98] However, in allotting so much attention to the style, Symons elides some of the most significant content altogether. He carefully ignores the question of socialism, which plays such a central role in *Hadrian*'s narrative, in his abstract of the novel, dwelling instead on the "metaphors like lightning, similes that shine, and appositions that linger in the mind like verse."[99] His representation of Corvo begins to sound like those reductive characterizations of Decadence that posit the movement as preoccupied with style at the expense of substance. What makes Decadent texts like Corvo's remarkable is the extent to which they are intensely preoccupied with both, taking up the political in prose that represents a "revolt from ready-made impressions and conclusions."[100] However, Symons has been careful to strain from his discussion of Corvo's work any trace of the raging discontent present on almost every page.

Symons's paper was "exceedingly well received by the Sette," and his membership in the Club solidified his ties with fellow dandies and connoisseurs, such as André Simon, with whom Symons went on to found the Wine and Food Society.[101] In his debut into elite society, Symons relied on a set of tastes and strategies that remained consistent for the rest of his adult life. His consumer pursuits and his direction of others' consumption were expressly designed to forge a false identity. Consuming and modeling the consumption of fine and rare things played a central role in Symons's program of passing. His success in high society rested entirely on his capacity for connoisseurship. Symons's membership in the Sette of Odd Volumes and his activities at the First Edition Club facilitated his acceptance into a much-desired world, and he built on these successes by, for example, organizing an exhibition of "Books Illustrating the Art of Good Living" in 1931 and founding, in 1930, along with Desmond Flower, the *Book-Collector's Quarterly*. The declared object of his Wine and Food Society, which was launched in 1933, was the raising of the standard of cooking throughout the country. The Society also published a magazine, *Wine and Food*, and organized elaborate banquets with menus modeled, for example, on the dishes served by celebrity chefs of the past, such as Marie-Antoine Carême, who had served Napoleon I, George IV, and the Emperor of Russia. In each of these endeavors, Symons placed himself in a position of superiority, making it his duty to exemplify taste and sophistication to those with money to spend.

As much as Symons's speech before the Sette served to demonstrate his fine and obscure literary taste, the speech also served to advertise his links to the late-Victorian past. Positioning himself as an expert on and conduit to the fin de siècle, he was able to impress the bibliophilic world with his knowledge of a rarefied field. Throughout the 1920s and 1930s, Symons marketed himself in literary circles as a post-Victorian aesthete, a man born out of time who cared only for things of the past, and expressed bewilderment at the preferences of the present. This was certainly the role he played in his unlikely friendship with Wyndham Lewis. According to Julian Symons, "the two had apparently nothing in common. Lewis's literary interests were related to the *avant-garde*, in particular Joyce, Eliot, and Pound, while AJ's literary concerns were chiefly Victorian. Lewis was a master of modern painting, of which AJ had little knowledge and less liking."[102] He suggests that the two were joined by their avowed individualism and that "Lewis was evidently amused by AJ and interested in him, . . . although no doubt he was caustically funny at times about the young man's dandyism."[103] In 1928, Symons solidified his ties with the 1890s by publishing his *Anthology of Nineties Verse*. He also spent years working on a biography of Wilde, which brought him into close contact with Lord Alfred Douglas.[104] The two corresponded for years, and Symons resigned from a club after being reprimanded for bringing Douglas to dinner. This friendship seems to fall in line with Symons's pattern of attraction to the more conservative strains of Decadence, a pattern of which his revision of Corvo's politics is a part.

Symons's Wilde biography, like a much-discussed *Select Bibliography and History of the Books of the Nineties, with Notes on their Authors*, was never completed. As his brother noted, Symons lived a "literary life which had little to do with the creation of literature."[105] When it came down to it, Symons much preferred consuming to producing, and his career relied far more on liking things than making them. Symons represented himself to the public as an avatar of the 1890s dandy-aesthete, a seeker of pleasure and luxury above all else. In his devotion to connoisseurship, he seemed to consciously model himself on Dorian and Des Esseintes or Olive Schreiner's lampoon of fin-de-siècle man in "The Woman Question" (1899), a "curled darling, scented and languid, with his drawl, his delicate apparel, his devotion to the rarity and variety of viands, whose severest labour is the search for pleasure."[106] Symons reanimated a caricature and a set of fictions. The living, breathing British Decadents of the 1890s often paired their pleasure with ethical pursuits and political commitments, and fictional dandies like Dorian drank champagne within the punishing confines of a morality tale. Symons, conversely, lived out a simplified distortion of the Decadent lifestyle, hunting for enjoyment without the attendant caution ("Only be sure it is passion – that it does yield you this fruit of a quickened, multiplied consciousness") that accompanied the pursuits of previous aesthetes.[107]

It is not simply that Symons seems to have strained the political from 1890s dandyism, replacing the ethical complexities of fin-de-siècle Decadence with brazen and thoughtless hedonism. His investment in consumption often seemed like a calculated attempt to infuriate an economically troubled public. The Wine and Food Society was founded when "the depression of two years before was not yet forgotten."[108] As Julian Symons notes, many wondered at the time, "Should a society devoted to the niceties of eating and drinking be started at a time when so many were unable to fill their bellies?"[109] The *Manchester Guardian* seemed to think not: "To discuss food with affection – at the right time and season – is not without its charm . . . whether it should be discussed in public and at the top of one's voice – particularly in a world where a large number of people can not get enough of its simplest forms – often seems a little open to question."[110] Symons's editorial notes in the first volume of the *Book-Collector's Quarterly* (1930) similarly exhibit a studied insensitivity to the economic climate: "This *Quarterly* comes into being in a time of trade distractions, when men's minds are agitated by economic difficulties afflicting all nations alike though not equally. Such a time may seem to some an unfortunate one in which to ask for a hearing. The editors, on the contrary, believe it to be a very good one. The heady speculation which has marked the last few financial years is obviously at an end; and every office, workshop, and stock exchange throughout the world is adjusting itself to a more rational relation of credit and conduct. What better opportunity could offer for the collector to set his house in order?"[111] To recommend the collecting of rare books in the midst of a depression seems a bit tone-deaf. Symons displayed a far more egregious deafness to tone in his decision during World War II to issue an "Unration Book," a parody of the original Ration Book, which insisted that, regardless of wartime restrictions, there would still be "a plenitude of good things."[112] His brother kindly describes the publication as "an error in the assessment of public feeling," noting that "the disclosure that plover, doe venison, braised duck and roast blackcock were still unrationed acted merely as an irritant for those to whom rationing was a serious, and even a depressing, subject."[113]

This tendency to what is either ignorant insensitivity or perversity is similarly on display at what Julian Symons refers to as "the most fantastic of all pieces of Corviana," the meetings of the Corvine Society.[114] While these events were meant to celebrate a man who spent most of his life starving and homeless, the meetings centered on an excessive amount of high-end consumption. They were events of the grandest order. As the attendee A. T. Bartholomew exclaimed, "such food & *such* wines!!!"[115] The menu included "*caviar d'astrakhan*," "*epigrammes d'agneau pio nono en aspic*," "*caneton d'aylesbury farci Palermo*," and "*canapés Ambassador*."[116] The guests drank vodka, Montrachet, Courvoiser, and the toast wine, Corvo Gran Spumante. Sir Shane Leslie described the fare in more Corvine terms: "meats red and white, tyrinathine or nacre-coloured, . . . liparose soups, . . . lickerish dishes, . . . wines aureate or purrothrixine of hue."[117] Leslie, who wrote one of the earliest critical essays on Corvo, began each of the banquets with a eulogy for the Baron, and at the second banquet he acknowledged the incongruity of celebrating Corvo in such a manner: "This fantastic meal, with its rubious and diaphanous wines, and its exquisite meats of Gallicised rather than the Galvanized variety to which we are more accustomed in British Taverns, may seem out of place in celebrating the life-long poverty of a Baron, who once wrote a Brief of beggarly fulmination to the Earl Marshal of England to state that at the moment of script only four baked biscuits stood between him and starvation."[118] This reservation is summarily dismissed, however, for Corvo's "appreciation of the beauty and bouquet of wine was considerable."[119] The fact that material circumstances provided few opportunities for the practice of that particular taste seems to have been deemed irrelevant by the organizers.

The meetings of the Corvine Society placed Symons in control of a spectacle of excessive dandyish behavior. Drawing on the social and cultural capital he had accrued through the First Edition Club and the Sette of Odd Volumes, Symons orchestrated occasions in which he was not simply a member of high society but the arbiter of taste and purveyor of knowledge, the privileged expert among the privileged few. Literary elites, lords, scholars, and wine connoisseurs mingled at these strange events. Guests at the banquets included Grant Richards, Francis Meynell, Vyvyan Holland, the Galsworthy scholar Vincent Marrot, the Swift scholar Harold Williams, T. Sturge Moore, Wyndham Lewis, and two Corvine collaborators, Sholto Douglas and Harry Pirie-Gordon.[120] However, while it was Symons whose cultural capital investments doubled at the banquets, the events were funded entirely by the wealthy Corvine and "purveyor of honors" Maundy Gregory.

Maundy Gregory, like Symons, hailed from a less than auspicious background, but he had transformed himself into a gatekeeper to the aristocracy and a staunchly conservative defender of upper-class interests. He was the son of a clergyman, but, in the words of Tom Cullen, he "conned his way to the top where he was courted by royalty, as well as by ministers of Cabinet rank, and by young men aspiring to Parliament."[121] Though there is very little evidence to suggest that he possessed any royal blood, "with the slightest encouragement [he] would produce a 4 ft. long pedigree compiled for him by the College of Heralds and signed by the Garter King of Arms which suggested that on his mother's side Gregory was indeed of royal blood."[122] According to the friends and acquaintances Cullen interviewed, "Maundy was obsessed with power."[123] Like Symons, he built his lifestyle and his career around a falsely elevated class identity, successfully integrating himself into a culture to which he did not truly belong.

Gregory endeavored to surround himself with an air of mystery and luxury. He claimed to have "engaged in counter-espionage work 'in which he employed some 1000 agents'" during the war. He carried in his pocket a diamond that had once belonged to Catherine the Great, and he often removed the diamond and distractedly played with it during conversation. He traveled in a taxicab that he claimed to keep on permanent hire. This was necessary, he told friends, because of his role as a "principal co-organizer of the great secret anti-Bolshevist movement."[124] The taxi, in fact, belonged to him, and the driver was on salary. His offices were similarly meant to enthrall. A gothic antechamber with tinted glass and pointed windows was occupied by page boys wearing uniforms identical to those worn by government messengers. Gregory's office itself was decorated with photographs of celebrities in silver frames, and his desk was "cluttered with telephones, indicators which buzzed, coloured lights which flashed, and a Morse 'tapper' key for summoning his secretary."[125] Gregory carefully calculated every detail of his existence to convey a sense of intrigue and wealth.

The pomp and pageantry successfully captivated the imagination of A. J. A. Symons. In describing their first meeting in *The Quest*, Symons recalls the "expensive flower in his buttonhole, an air of constant good-living, an affable smile, a glittering watchchain, good clothes and (as I noticed when he sat down) very beautiful boots."[126] Gregory visited to inquire about Symons's interest in Corvo, and he offered to buy some of Symons's "less important treasures," making it clear that "money was no object" and that "he was immensely wealthy."[127] As Symons got to know Gregory better, his wealth only came to seem more marvelous: "He had at least a dozen cigarette cases, and never used the same one on two consecutive days.... He spent at a fabulous rate.... And all his payments were made in the crispest of brand-new banknotes, or else in the shiniest of brand-new money."[128] At their second meeting at the Ambassador Club, "costly courses appeared and disappeared. Champagne flowed, large cigars and brandy followed."[129] At the end of the meal, Gregory "whispered confidentially, 'Of course this place belongs to me.'"[130] Symons was captivated not just by the finery but by the mystery as well: "For all the discursiveness of his self-revelation, I could never find out his occupation or the source of his income."[131] Gregory enveloped his new friend in fine things, performing the thrilling part of an aristocratic insider and intelligence agent to a highly receptive audience of one. He told Symons that he "counted Lord Birkenhead among his closer friends; he held an important post in the Secret Service; he was an intimate of many royal houses, and was, indeed, actively engaged in promoting the restoration of several."[132] For a man like Symons, who wished more than anything for intimacy with the world described by Gregory, his appearance on the scene must have seemed miraculous.

While Symons chose to play out his class concerns within the realm of collecting and connoisseurship, Gregory's intense preoccupation with class identity drew him into more clearly political arenas. In the teens, he founded the *Mayfair and Town Topics*, along with Jack and Harry Keen-Hargreaves. The proposal for the periodical that he sent to the Keen-Hargreaves reveals a man already banking on his capacity to exploit the class anxieties of others: "I have been studying the magazine market, and my research indicates that there is room for a weekly where business and society can rub shoulders. Not to put too fine a point on it, there are no end of industrialists who will pay handsomely to have their portraits sandwiched between gossip paragraphs about duchesses."[133] The duchesses, of course, did not have to pay for their portraits to appear in *Mayfair*, but the "industrialists" shelled out between fifty and five hundred pounds sterling for the privilege of the designation "Man of the Day." After the war, Gregory continued in the same vein, making his fortune selling titles to newly wealthy war profiteers. His fascination with rank and hierarchy similarly seems to have inspired his decision to purchase *Burke's Landed Gentry*, for which he happened to hire Corvo's collaborator Harry Pirie-Gordon as editor.

Gregory also founded another periodical, the *Whitehall Gazette and St. James Review*, "an organ of extreme right-wing opinion" that aimed to conduct, in Gregory's words, "a consistent and insidious campaign on behalf of monarchy and against the growth of Bolshevism and Communism and their ramifications."[134] According to Cullen, Gregory aimed to mirror upper-class prejudices and opinions in the pages of the *Whitehall Gazette* by, for example, linking paranoia concerning working-class agitation with anti-Semitism. Bolshevism was represented as a "conspiracy of the unsuccessful Jews throughout the world," and readers were warned of a "confused rabble . . . pouring into Whitehall from the East End, led by Russian Jew tailors . . . armed to the teeth with any weapon that comes handy."[135] The General Strike was cast as a Soviet conspiracy hatched by "Hebrew-Russian brains."[136] The paper critiqued trade unionism and treated socialism as a highly dangerous source of potential insurrection. The *Whitehall Gazette* may be understood as a catalog of the left-wing causes and organizations that elicited anxiety in Gregory and his fellow members of the Corvine cult.

The *Whitehall Gazette*, similar to the *Mayfair*, also promised anxious parvenus the opportunity to mingle representations of themselves with portraits of dukes and archbishops in a section titled "Officials I Have Met." Like the duchesses in the pages of the *Mayfair*, the true "officials" did not pay to appear in the *Whitehall Gazette*. That privilege was reserved for the businessmen and industrialists who paid up to five hundred pounds sterling for a flattering profile accompanied by a photograph. Cullen argues that Gregory used the profiles to sound out whether the subject "would be willing to pay £25000 to become a baronet, or maybe just £10000 to become a plain knight bachelor."[137]

Gregory's highly lucrative exploitation of class anxiety came under threat repeatedly during the interwar period. Immediately following the war, the socialist politician Victor Grayson attempted to uncover Lloyd George's involvement with the selling of honors, declaring, "This sale of honours is a national scandal. It can be traced right down to 10 Downing Street, and to a monocled dandy with offices in Whitehall. I know this man, and one day I will name him."[138] The monocled dandy was Maundy Gregory, but Grayson disappeared under mysterious circumstances before having the opportunity to "name him." A Royal Commission on Honours determined in 1922 that "there is no doubt that there have been for some time, and recently in increasing numbers, persons who, for want of a better name, we may stigmatise as touts, who have been going about asserting that they were in a position to secure honours in return for specified payments."[139] The commission recommended that a committee of privy counselors scrutinize all nominees for honors and that all nominations be accompanied with a statement that "no payment or expectation of payment . . . was directly or indirectly associated with the recommendation."[140] In 1925, the Honours (Prevention of Abuses) Act was passed and the sale of honors became a criminal offense. Gregory began selling foreign titles to compensate for the loss in income, but he did continue selling honors in England as well. The new law, in fact, facilitated Gregory's swindles by making no distinction between sellers and buyers of honors: "The chief difference was that whereas 'guaranteed delivery' had been his slogan in the past, now he flogged the occasional 'non-existent' knighthood or baronetcy, safe in the knowledge that the victim of his swindle would not squeal" for fear of winding up in the dock himself.[141] In 1932, however, Gregory made the mistake of offering a peerage to Lieutenant Commander Edward Whaley Billyard-Leake. Billyard-Leake was already a member of an elite social set and, in addition, had no desire to be knighted. He reported his conversation with Gregory to a "third party," either his own solicitor or a detective from Scotland Yard, and an investigation began. When the case went to trial, Gregory pled guilty and, on February 21, was sentenced to two months' imprisonment. On his release, he left England and spent the rest of his life in exile.

In 1929, however, Gregory was yet to be disgraced, and it was his money that funded the elaborate Corvine events at his club, the Ambassador. The vision of Corvo that these events ushered into existence reflected both Symons's and Gregory's deep fascination with class identity and elitist connoisseurship. Much emphasis was placed on the fact that Corvo's works are only appreciated by the "Happy Few."[142] "The readers of Rolfe, and the cravers of Corvo" were described as "a literary elite."[143] The speeches delivered extended the portrait that Symons had begun in his speech before the Sette and operated as a foundation for the image Symons would perfect in his *Quest*. Leslie cooperated in this effort, working to dispel the rumor that "the Baron . . . was mean of hand."[144] The contrary, according to Leslie, was true: "When funds or cheque fell into his hands, his lavish beaugeste was swift to conquer one of the primary characteristics of that class from which it cannot be properly denied he was sprung."[145] Nothing could be done to conceal entirely Corvo's class background, but the fact that he became a spendthrift whenever able provided some comfort to the "Happy Few." In an interesting counterpoint to the apolitical vision of Corvo that dominated these proceedings, Leslie concluded his eulogy at the second banquet by *almost* discussing socialism: "All had failed him, and looking around for some society or cause whose fortunes were as hopeless as his own, and whose prospects were equally dim in the eyes of Church and State, he perceived the struggling Labour Party. How he joined their struggling propaganda, and endeavoured to make what was diaphanous diaphotick, and how he became the secretary of Mr. Champion, remains to be told on another evening."[146] But that other evening never came, and the story of this chapter remained untold in the banquets' true sequel, Symons's *The Quest*. The vocabulary used by Leslie to describe Labour, as "hopeless" and "struggling," seems particularly striking in light of the fact that the second Labour government was formed during the very same year that the banquets were held. If anything, Labour's star seemed to be on the rise. Leslie's attempt to foreground a past moment when the party's fate seemed far more uncertain reads like an anxious denial of the political realities of the present, a representative moment within the larger patterns of appreciation for Corvo in the early twentieth century. Like the speech at the Sette that preceded and the biography that followed the banquets, the meetings of the Corvine Society reflected the early Corvines' longing for a less democratic past and a less politically complex Corvo.

Symons began composing *The Quest* a few years after the banquets. He was at the time in financial straits, as the First Edition Club had gone into decline during the depression. He turned to writing as a potential source of income, and it was crucial for the Corvo biography to appeal to more than the "Happy Few." The resultant text appeals in so many ways. It is a highly readable narrative of literary detective work and suspense, a mystery that unfolds chapter by chapter as additional works and secrets come to light, focusing on the author's experience of coming to know the subject rather than the subject himself. Symons referred to the work as "An Experiment in Biography," and the text has been hailed as groundbreaking.[147] However, the attractiveness of the biography rests in large part, I would argue, on the event with which it begins, Symons's perusal of the "hair-raising" Venice letters, and the relationship with which it ends, the friendship between Symons and Gregory.[148] The chapters that bookend *The Quest* say much about the portrait of Corvo that emerges in the chapters between. Symons banks on the titillating qualities of the Venice letters to draw his readership into *The Quest*, and he concludes the story in an aura of luxury and wealth, an insider world of wealthy book collectors, transforming Corvo into the centerpiece of a world of elite tastes and a point of contact between dandyish men. The reader is left with the impression that Corvo was first and foremost a man who exploited youth and whom men of taste enjoyed. Much that complicates this fades from view in favor of the far more alluring and salacious material that encircles the rest of the story.

The biography opens with the story of another friendship, the friendship between Symons and Christopher Millard. Millard is perhaps best known for assisting Robert Ross in the editing of Wilde's collected works and for his own six-hundred-page Wilde bibliography. He was in a sense Gregory's inverse. Although both Gregory and Millard expressed investments in same-sex desire, Millard's politics could not be more different, nor could his economic circumstances. Symons describes him as an "ardent Socialist" living in "cramping poverty."[149] However, Symons broadens Millard's appeal by stressing his covert conservatism. He was, according to Symons, "of the sort that is satisfied only with good things," and "his Socialist views did not prevent him from incarnating most of the Conservative virtues."[150] Millard's "cramping poverty" does not exile him from the elite homosocial world of the Corvine cult. He is represented by Symons as a cultural aristocrat who "had an air and dignity which never left him."[151] *The Quest* begins and ends with intimacy between men that circulates around literary intrigues and the appreciation of fine things. Symons's intense bonds with connoisseurs facilitates the recovery of Corvo's story.

Beginning with Millard strengthens Symons's representation of himself as one with strong connections to the fin de siècle and further exacerbates the titillating effects of the contents of the Venice letters. It was Millard, according to *The Quest*, who introduced Symons to the works of Corvo in 1925. This story is an invention, as Symons was aware of his work well before this meeting. As Julian Symons notes, "Millard . . . may well have lent A. J. Frederick Rolfe's *Hadrian the Seventh* on that day when they talked together of unjustly neglected books in Millard's little garden; but this assuredly was not the first work of Rolfe's that my brother had read."[152] To credit Millard with his introduction to the work, however, links the quest more firmly to a fin-de-siècle lineage, as Millard assisted in the early establishment of Wilde's legacy, and to a set of scandals, for Millard had been jailed twice for "gross indecency."

Symons's narration of his introduction to the Venice letters emerges as by far the most sensational and engaging section of the biography. Millard first gave him *Hadrian*, and Symons quickly returned in search of more. Millard then passed him the letters in a morocco-bound quarto, saying, "Since you are becoming interested in Rolfe you had better read these too."[153] Symons glanced quickly at the material, and "the few sentences that caught [his] eye as [he] turned the pages were arresting," but the thrill of the full reveal was delayed until he was home alone at midnight.[154] As he read the "unwitting account, step by step, of the destruction of a soul," his "hair began to rise."[155] The letters "gave an account, in language that omitted nothing, of the criminal delights that waited for the ignoble sensualist to whom they were addressed. . . . Only lack of money, it appeared, prevented the writer from enjoying an existence compared with which Nero's was innocent, praiseworthy, and unexciting."[156] Symons represents himself as shocked, indignant, and saddened by the letters, but it might be more true to say that he was above all intrigued. The letters left him restless, sleepless. He lay awake, unable to banish Corvo from his mind, his "curiosity . . . unslaked": "In *Hadrian* and the letters I had (what I took to be) the opening and the close of the career. What story lay in between?"[157] "The desire to know swelled in [him] so urgently" that he nearly rose to call Millard in the middle of the night but restrained himself until morning.[158] So *The Quest* begins because of the "extraordinary letters."[159] Their specter haunts the rest of the story, and they solidify the bond that concludes it.

The pomp with which Maundy Gregory arrived on the scene has already been discussed. Symons displayed to Gregory his collection, and Gregory gazed at the objects with admiration and envy. While Corvo's letters to his publishers "moved him to reverence," the Venice letters inspired "awe."[160] At that moment, according to Symons, his "reserve vanished . . . like mist before the sun," and he "began to like Mr. Gregory."[161] Shared appreciation for the letters allowed them to see one another as linked, as mutual members of the "literary elite," the "Happy Few." Soon after their first meeting, Gregory purchased the Venice letters from Symons at six times the price Symons had paid Millard. Gregory and Symons became collaborators in the case of the missing Corvine manuscripts, and Gregory's endless funds seemed capable of producing miracles. He unearthed the last five copies of the missing novel *Don Renato: An Ideal Content* (printed in 1909 but not published until 1963) from a "rat-haunted cellar," and then a week later arrived with a copy of Corvo's translation of the songs of Meleager.[162] The biography, which, owing to the sufferings of its subject, might have been a bit of a downer, concludes on a note of excess and intrigue, with champagne, expensive cuff links, golden cigarette cases, and a man who claimed to be a spy hunting down lost books in scary basements. The workhouse and the question of charity are long forgotten. Corvo's scream has been silenced, his attack defanged, and the lingering economic questions raised by his suffering are displaced by something far more fun.

Over the course of a decade, the Corvine myth was created and disseminated. Symons, with the financial backing of Gregory, ushered into existence a sort of Decadence that served as a pleasing antidote to the spirit of the age. He offered men like himself the opportunity to turn their eyes from the rise of Labour, unemployment, financial crises, and the dissolution of past hierarchies toward an almost tangible prewar past and a Decadent stick figure who shouted elitist mottoes and lampooned socialism. Corvo became in their hands a cartoonish figure, riled up for seemingly no reason, with a pleasing affection for the concept of Aristos and a titillating tendency to exploit adolescent boys. For men preoccupied with the concepts of power and privilege, Corvo was, of course, a perfect match, as these concepts are the twin loci of his entire aesthetic. His treatment of these concepts, however, was incredibly circuitous, complicated, and contradictory. For his persona to be rendered palatable for an audience in need of simplicity, a good part of the picture had to be excised from the frame.

The reception of Corvo in the early twentieth century offers a necessary counterpoint to the more progressive examples of the political uses of post-Victorian Decadence described in earlier chapters. Although post-Victorian Decadence did often facilitate resistance to the more conservative nationalist and jingoistic ideologies of the period, the Corvine cult indicates that the elements of Decadence foregrounded by Gagnier in her discussion of Corvo (the elitism, the aversion to alterity, the fear of contact with "the masses") could be called on for less appealing purposes. What I have tried to demonstrate here is the extent to which this repurposing of Decadence required a misreading and the reduction of the complexity of its source material. The reception of Corvo in the 1920s and 1930s was itself a creative act, a post-Victorian production that wrote into existence a new vision of an elitist Decadent mascot for post-Victorian dandies wrestling with the political realities of the early twentieth century. It is my hope that a more thorough understanding of the reception of Corvo in the 1920s and 1930s might facilitate a reconsideration of the political valence of his works that attends more thoroughly to their rich and strange treatment of the concepts of inequality and injustice.

CHAPTER 4

Irish Decadence, Occultism, and Sacrificial Myth
The Martyrdom of Althea Gyles

In 1909, Aleister Crowley published a short story titled "At the Fork of the Roads" in the *Equinox*, the official periodical of his mystical order, the A .·. A .·. . The story focuses on the use of black magic in a struggle between Count Swanoff, a poet of "royal Celtic descent," and Will Bute, a "poetaster" and "dabbler in magic."[1] Bute has gained "subtle hypnotic influence" over a young woman named Hypatia Gay, and he sends Hypatia to Swanoff's rooms to obtain a drop of his rival's blood for use in a spell he wishes to cast on him.[2] That night, as a result of Bute's spell, Swanoff is visited by a woman whose "touch [wakes] the serpent of essential madness in him."[3] Resisting his lust, Swanoff struggles with the succubus, kills her, and absorbs her power. Following this victory, the same scene is reenacted each night for ten nights, but the power of the stolen blood is eventually exhausted. Bute sends Hypatia to obtain even more so he may continue to haunt and trouble Swanoff's nights. However, when Hypatia arrives at the Count's home, he forces her into his temple, where she is confronted with the sight of a skeleton and an "evil altar."[4] She falls into an embrace with the blood-stained skeleton, giving herself over to the abyss, "[writhing] and [howling] in that ghastly celebration of the nuptials of the Pit."[5] The story concludes with Hypatia visiting the offices of a publisher in Bond Street, whose face is "bloated with disease and drink; his loose lips [hang] in an eternal leer; his fat eyes shed venom."[6] He sees the "leprous light of utter degradation" in the eyes of the newly ruined Hypatia and "[licks] his lips."[7] Swanoff has emerged victorious by defiling his rival's favorite and sending her into the arms of a vulgar and hideous man.

Most who read the story would have easily identified Count Swanoff as a stand-in for Crowley himself, and they would have known that Will Bute was meant to be understood as Crowley's nemesis, William Butler Yeats, with whom he had struggled for the control of the Hermetic Order of the Golden Dawn. Those with more knowledge of occult and bohemian circles at the turn of the century might have been able to identify the young woman as Althea Gyles and the leering publisher as Leonard Smithers, with whom Gyles had an affair in 1899. Gyles has now been largely forgotten, but she was considered by many to be one of the most interesting illustrators and book designers working at the turn of the century. Oscar Wilde described her as "an artist of great ability."[8] Bernard Muddiman, in his *Men of the Nineties* (1921), referred to her work as the "acme of the period's realization of the weird," and Robert Sherard listed her in the index of his *The Real Oscar Wilde* (1916) as "Gyles, Althea, Miss, a genius."[9] Gyles designed the covers for Yeats's *The Secret Rose* (1897), *The Wind among the Reeds* (1899), and the 1899 edition of *Poems*. Smithers, the leering publisher with the fat eyes, released one of her most important works in 1904, an edition of Oscar Wilde's poem "The Harlot's House" accompanied by "five weirdly powerful and beautiful Drawings" by Gyles.[10] For a moment at the turn of the century, she seemed poised to become one of the more important woman artists of the period. However, she stopped creating pictures very abruptly after a breakdown in 1900. This period of depression and illness seems to have been precipitated by the affair with Smithers (for which Crowley seemed to believe he was responsible) and the response it elicited from Yeats and his circle, who ostracized her in the wake of the scandal. Though she continued to publish poetry in the periodical press until the 1910s, she eventually abandoned that pursuit as well. She lived until 1949, but her presence becomes increasingly difficult to trace in the years following World War I. In the years immediately following her death, however, she surfaces in the works of those twentieth-century women writers who stood witness to her alienation and poverty following what Faith Compton Mackenzie refers to as her "loss of caste."[11]

In this chapter, I read Gyles's work and her strange biography in relationship to the lives and writings of the two most prominent Irish Decadents, Yeats and Wilde, and I consider the extent to which her contact with these two writers facilitated her acceptance of and enthusiasm for a concept of martyrdom that produced such dangerous results in both her poetry and her career.[12] Yeats described her as "ready to face death for painting and poetry," and in the poetry she wrote during World War I and in her own representation of herself as a suffering artist, fallen woman, and eternal outsider, Gyles seemed to relish the idea of sacrificing oneself for a cause.[13] In this she drew on a rhetoric of sanctified suffering that she acquired through her contact with Yeats, the Hermetic Order of the Golden Dawn, and Irish nationalism's evolving ideas concerning martyrdom at the turn of the century. While Yeats's ideas about violence and sacrifice certainly underwent dramatic changes later in his career, Gyles was most intimate with him during the period in which he was most enthusiastic about the concept of heroic sacrifice.[14] Yeats, however, is not the sole source of Gyles's attachment to this concept. Her enthusiasm for sacrificial ideals also seems to have derived from her intense affection and admiration for Oscar Wilde, whose downfall she witnessed with great sadness and fascination. As she carried these sacrificial ideals into the twentieth century, their potential to inhibit her critical thinking and mar her happiness became increasingly clear. Twentieth-century women writers, such as Faith Compton Mackenzie and Eleanor Farjeon, encountered her as an apparition from the 1890s, a physical reminder of that period's promises concerning revolution and women's freedom and the fact that those promises were never truly fulfilled.

I read Gyles here as a post-Victorian Decadent wrestling with the cultural inheritance of Irish Decadence. As I have argued, post-Victorian Decadence often operated as an antidote to the violence, devastation, and belligerent jingoism of the World Wars. Decadent aloofness, apartness, and humor – the cosmopolitanism that the Decadent stance facilitated – were valued in the twentieth century because they generated skepticism and detachment at a time when those virtues were markedly scarce. However, Gyles was drawing from a slightly different Decadent tradition. Her contact with the particular brand of nationalism inflected by occultism and apocalyptic zeal espoused by Yeats in the 1890s along with her reverence for Wilde's martyrdom left her earnest and engaged and invested in ideas of heroism and self-sacrifice. As a critic writing for the *Saturday Book* notes, whereas the "hard, frigid line style of Beardsley and his imitators alienates the sympathy," Gyles's work is "warm."[15] This warmth was ignited and inflamed by the apocalyptic and sacrificial rhetoric that was so central to many of the turn-of-the-century movements with which Gyles was associated.

The fin de siècle was a moment when multiple utopian movements promised that a new era would come if enough individuals were simply willing to enter fully into the spirit of a cause and sacrifice themselves for the sake of a new age, and Gyles seems to have believed truly in the coming of a new era that had been promised to her by socialism, by Theosophy, and by the New Women and bohemian men of the 1890s. Matthew Beaumont has recently argued that "the fin de siècle was at the same time a period of spiritual and political optimism and one of pessimism caused by the constant deferral of hopes. A spirit of apocalypticism performed a compensatory function for those, like the socialists and the theosophists, who were expectantly waiting for proof of a political and spiritual transformation and who were disappointed by the unpunctuality of history."[16] According to Beaumont, occultism's promises concerning the dawn of a new era held a powerful appeal for disillusioned social reformists at the turn of the century whose hopes for a new age were perpetually deferred and denied: "Utopian promise always becomes especially important when the opportunity to implement real social change starts to seem more remote."[17] As Richard Kearney has argued, the sacred rite of blood sacrifice performed a similar function for certain strands of Irish nationalism, for the ideology of martyrdom subscribes to a mythic logic that transmutes defeat into victory. Kearney argues that the Irish nationalist ideology of martyrdom "is *sacrificial* to the degree that it invokes, explicitly or otherwise, a 'sacred' tradition of death and renewal which provides justification for present acts of suffering by realigning them with recurring paradigms of the past and thus affording these acts a certain timeless and redemptive quality."[18] The present failure of the sacrificial victim is minimized or dismissed in favor of fantasy visions of the new era that sacrifice might bring to pass.

Gyles's work and her career reveal the destructive potential of the intertwined ideologies of apocalypticism and martyrdom. When individuals are called to sacrifice themselves in order to initiate a new future and to link themselves through bloodshed with a mythic, heroic past, the destruction and the disappointment that result cannot dissuade them, for the mythic logic of martyrdom makes failure illegible to self-sacrificing subjects. The tragedy of Gyles's disappointment, however, emerges with distinct clarity in the works of the women who wrestled with her living remains in the twentieth century. Gyles was of interest to these women because of her status as a post-Victorian Decadent, her ties to Wilde and Beardsley and the Yeats of the 1890s. However, rather than operating as evidence of the continuing power of the Decadent aesthetic, she illuminated the failings of fin-de-siècle aestheticism, its troubling treatment of feminine transgression and its fetishization of tragedy and sacrifice. Her work and the response that she evoked in twentieth-century women writers can tell us much about what happened to the passionate revolutionary energies of the 1890s after the moment of promised revolution had come and gone.

I. Gyles in the 1890s: Occult Antimaterialism and Sacrificial Ideology

Although Gyles seemed unwilling to commit fully and finally to any particular strand of occultism, throughout her life she remained perpetually in conversation with varied brands of occult belief and practice. Yeats first encountered Gyles when she was living in Dublin in 1891, a "strange red-haired girl, all whose thoughts were set upon painting and poetry."[19] She had fled her family home in County Cork in the late 1880s to attend art school in Dublin, living off the proceeds from a sold watch and a meager income derived from placing stories in an Irish newspaper. She was taken in by F. J. Dick, a member of "the household," a Theosophical commune at 3 Ely Place, who "had discovered her starving somewhere in an unfurnished or half-furnished room [where] she had lived for many weeks upon bread and shell-cocoa, so that her food never cost more than a penny a day."[20] Life in the commune offered the aspiring artist contact with many strands of fin-de-siècle occultism and bohemianism. The walls of the household were decorated with "extraordinarily and weirdly fantastic" Blakean frescoes symbolizing the journey of the pilgrim soul designed and painted by another occupant, George Russell (Æ), in collaboration with Yeats, who spent much time at the household in the early 1890s.[21] Yeats described the space as a community of "young men struggling, with inexact terminology and insufficient learning, for some new religious conception, on which they could base their lives."[22] The practices associated with the community do, however, seem to have wandered at times in darker directions. Yeats recounts the following incident in *The Trembling of the Veil* (1922): "I get in talk with a young man who has taken the orthodox side in some debate. He is a stranger [i.e., not a member of the household], but explains that he has inherited magical art from his father, and asks me to his rooms to see it in operation. He and a friend of his kill a black cock, and burn herbs in a big bowl, but nothing happens except that the friend repeats again and again, 'O, my God,' and when I ask him why he has said that, does not know that he has spoken; and I feel that there is something very evil in the room."[23] In an 1898 essay on Gyles's work published in the *Dome*, Yeats foregrounds the impress of the time spent in this strange space on Gyles's aesthetic, arguing that the "beautiful, lithe figures of [Gyles's] art, quivering with a life half mortal tragedy, half immortal ecstasy, owe something of their inspiration" to the "company of Irish mystics" who occupied the commune.[24]

When Gyles moved to London to attend Pedders and then the Slade School of Art, she transferred her allegiance, as Yeats had done, from Theosophy to the Hermetic Order of the Golden Dawn. The transition for Yeats had to do with the appeal of what Ian Fletcher has referred to as a "more elaborate, but more pragmatic mode of mysticism."[25] He had become exasperated with Madame Blavatsky's Theosophists and their "purely theoretical approach to the world of the unseen," because he desired a more practical form of magic, a body of knowledge and a set of rituals that would allow an adept real mastery over the world.[26] He had been asked to resign from the Theosophical Society following his founding of an Esoteric Section devoted to practical experiments in magic. Around this time, he became acquainted with S. L. MacGregor Mathers, one of the chiefs of the Hermetic Order of the Golden Dawn, and he was initiated into the order on March 7, 1890. Gyles was not an official member or adept of the Order, but she spent much time in the company of those associated with the Golden Dawn, including Yeats and Aleister Crowley, and, according to Crowley, witnessed some of the practical applications of magic of which Yeats was so fond. Crowley claimed to have seen Yeats and Gyles attempting an astral vision of a red and white hawk and a deer in Yeats's rooms in London.[27] This period of occult contact had an enormous impact on her work into the twentieth century. Though Clifford Bax would later claim that "her occultism was skin deep," a review of her works published and unpublished reveals a sustained engagement with principles drawn from both Theosophy and the Hermetic Order of the Golden Dawn.[28]

The impress of her contact with the Golden Dawn registers visibly, for example, in the covers Gyles designed for Yeats in the 1890s. Alan Grossman has argued that Yeats's books of the later 1890s "are not merely books, but talismans or *grimoires*, that they have magical as well as literary significance, and that they express a desire for power and beauty which the literary vehicle alone cannot convey."[29] Yeats wished to create in cooperation with his book designers "total books" "clothed in effective representations of potent signs" that extended and reinforced the content of the text within.[30] Works like *The Secret Rose* commingled Irish mythology and hermetic occultism, and Gyles's designs extended this hybridization of Celtic folklore and magic through an almost excessive amount of symbolic and iconographic signification.

Although much has been said about the manner in which these covers illuminate Yeats's idea of the symbol, his investment in cross-gender collaboration, and his quest for the talismanic book, I am interested primarily in the manner in which they reveal Gyles's developing interest in warfare and an eroticized vision of death, enthusiasms that would serve as the foundation to her personal mythology of martyrdom.[31] The central image on the cover of *The Secret Rose* is the Tree of Life, or sephirothic tree, a Kabbalistic symbol in which each sephira represents an emanation from God and the ten sephiroth taken together represent the process of creation (Figure 4.1). The tree's trunk is composed of Celtic knotwork and emerges from the skeleton of a knight who continues, even in death, to clutch the handle of a spear. At the tree's center sits the rose-cross, a Rosicrucian symbol, and above this, two lovers share a kiss. Declan Kiely has linked

Figure 4.1. Althea Gyles, cover of *The Secret Rose* by W. B. Yeats, 1897. Reproduced courtesy of University of Washington, Special Collections, UW 36365.

Figure 4.2. Althea Gyles, *The Knight upon the Grave of His Lady, The Dome*, 1898. Reproduced courtesy of University of Washington, Special Collections, UW 36364.

the cover's design to the ending of Yeats's story "Of Costello the Proud, of Oona the Daughter of Dermott and of the Bitter Tongue," in which the branches of the ash trees planted above the graves of the lovers Costello and Oona reach for one another and intertwine. The kissing faces, according to Kiely, represent the risen spirits of the deceased lovers.[32] The cover unites Yeats's fables of Irish heroism and immortal love with some of the most significant emblems of the Golden Dawn. The spine is decorated with a spear identified by most critics as the spear of Lug. According to Irish mythology, this weapon so longed for blood that it could only be quieted and contained by soaking its head in poppy juice. Yeats refers to the spear in another story included in *The Secret Rose*, "Rosa Alchemica," as the "spear dipped in poppy juice, lest it rush forth hot for battle."[33] Gyles's cover integrates heady icons of belligerent passion and the impermanence of death into a complex web of Celtic occultism.

The drawings that accompanied Yeats's essay on Gyles, "A Symbolic Artist and the Coming of Symbolic Art," in the *Dome* the following year exhibit a similarly morbid preoccupation with bloodshed and tragic love. The content of these drawings also seems to rest on similar assumptions concerning mortality and rebirth. *Deirdre* and *The Knight upon the Grave of His Lady* both center on a grieving figure, and the act of grieving is eroticized as the weeping figure lies prostrate atop the deceased beloved (Figure 4.2). In *Deirdre*, the tragic heroine buries her face in the bare chest of the dead Naisi, and the accompanying legend, "There is but one thing now may comfort my heart, and that thing thy sword, O Naisi," exhibits a romantic fixation with the concept of self-sacrifice.[34] The story of Deirdre, which, like the tale of Costello and Oona, concludes with the limbs of the trees above the lovers' graves intertwining, treats death as impermanent. Gyles foregrounds death's impermanence in the drawing of the knight, a fact that Yeats highlights in his reading of the piece: "*The Knight upon the Grave of His Lady* tells much of its meaning to the first glance; but when one has studied for a time, one discovers that there is a heart in the bulb of every hyacinth, to personify the awakening of the soul and of love out of the grave. It is now winter, and beyond the knight, who lies in the abandonment of his sorrow, the trees spread their leafless boughs against a grey winter sky; but spring will come, and the boughs will be covered with leaves, and the hyacinths will cover the ground with their blossoms."[35] In a letter to Yeats, Gyles had specifically requested that Yeats draw the audience's attention to the hearts of the bulbs: "I needn't explain that they are the symbols of resurrection."[36] Again and again in Gyles's drawings and designs of the 1890s, death is at once fetishized and dismissed, rendered romantic and alluring while at the same time recast as a phase rather than final.

Gyles, like Yeats, must have derived much of her certainty concerning the impermanence of death from her contact with Theosophy's doctrines of reincarnation. This doctrine features prominently in much of Gyles's unpublished work. An untitled and undated play by Gyles in the collection at the University of Reading, for example, centers on the concept of reincarnation. The opening act reveals, through a series of exchanges between Irish women servants, that a Cardinal is visiting from Rome, planning to purchase Jacob Carew's "grand old place."[37] The servants also speak of a madwoman who has recently been disturbing the sleep of the town's inhabitants, wailing and screeching and laughing in the nearby glen. As the play proceeds, it becomes clear that the Cardinal is interested primarily not in the home but in a sixteenth-century fresco by the great painter Lorenzo that decorates its ceilings. On first visiting the house, the Cardinal wants nothing more than to contemplate the fresco. While observing the Cardinal as he appreciates the painting, Carew's son, Raimond, and his beloved, Ethne, notice the madwoman watching the Cardinal from the window with a "dreadful," murderous look on her face.[38] The Cardinal and his doctor, Aloysius Beauchamp, are warned of the madwoman's malicious glare, but they greet the news with composure and interest, reassuring the young people that together they plan to found a sanctuary for the insane, and they will be able to assist the troubled woman. The Cardinal diagnoses the woman as suffering from a case of "slipping back."[39] He informs Ethne's father, Lord M, that he and Aloysius have discovered that many cases of nervous trouble "are people who – through shock, long strain, etc. have relapsed into past lives."[40] The Cardinal himself seems to be "slipping back" in a more controlled manner. He acknowledges that he was once Lorenzo himself, and Ethne was Gemma, the child of Lorenzo's closest friend whom the painter adopted following her father's death. The young girl cross-dressed and stowed away aboard the ship traveling to Ireland when Lorenzo came to paint the fresco, and then Lorenzo's jealous wife, Lisa, cut the ropes supporting the scaffolding while the two completed the last touches on the painting. Lorenzo held Gemma tight in his arms to protect her as they fell, and he took the brunt of the fall and died. The madwoman is slipping back to her vexed past as Lisa, still consumed with jealousy and anger. She does finally attempt to stab the Cardinal, but the Cardinal and Aloysius struggle with her and take her dagger. They then load her into an ambulance while assuring her that they will treat her with color and vibratory cures. Reincarnation is treated within the play as a fact accepted by innovators in the medical sciences, and the partnership between Doctor Aloysius Beauchamp and the Cardinal, who speaks often of his reverence for the Druids and his belief in Karmic debts and astrology, represents occultism's capacity to function effectively in cooperation with representatives of the modern world.

An unpublished and undated fragment of a novel titled *Pilgrimage* in the collection at Reading similarly focuses on the concept of reincarnation.[41] In this case, it is love at first sight, as opposed to madness, that is interpreted as proof of the individual's connection to past lives. Wilmot Upton and her son, Basil, encounter a young woman in the forest with whom Basil feels an immediate and overwhelming connection. "What is love at first sight but love remembered?" the narrator inquires.[42] Wilmot, too, takes the girl's hand at once. It is only later that any of them are struck by "how strange it was that they had all clasped hands as old friends meeting might."[43] Basil has been primed to perceive evidence of supernatural forms of memory by his friend and mentor, Pascoe, an Irish painter modeled on George Russell, who is "great on re-incarnation."[44] Wilmot, however, is inspired by the sight of the sudden, highly charged connection between her son and "Bride" to begin her own occult investigations, which brings her into contact with Pascoe, with whom she discusses the "evidences and uses of rebirth" with great enthusiasm.[45] Pascoe's occult studies have been recently reinvigorated, he tells Wilmot, by his contact with the mystical poet Benador Quested, a thinly veiled version of Yeats. Quested is a vegetarian, and he runs a donkey sanctuary in Devon. He is working doggedly, following his return from India, to get the world to recognize that "all life is one."[46] Had the novel been completed, Wilmot would presumably have continued her study of the occult under the direction of Quested, the subject of the manuscript's final sentence. The unfinished novel, then, reads as a genealogy of Gyles's occult beliefs, establishing the significance of Russell's and Yeats's influence and the centrality of reincarnation in her understanding of the world's operations.

Gyles's belief in rebirth fostered a blasé attitude toward warfare and death. If one's life and one's body are only a fraction of one's existence, and the self has the capacity to be reborn, to return and live again, martyrdom may be taken lightly. Seamus Deane argues that Yeats's belief in reincarnation similarly inflected his vision of blood sacrifice. He asserts that, in Yeats's thinking, "by virtue of [reincarnation], death was both contemplated and overcome."[47] The concept of reincarnation and the fundamental antimaterialism of most occult systems contributed to a disregard for the body and physical suffering, for material existence was considered within these systems too brief to be of importance. As William H. O'Donnell notes, many occultists practiced fasting to "demonstrate [their] scorn for material life."[48] In Yeats's unfinished semiautobiographical novel *The Speckled Bird*, the protagonist fasts to receive visions, and Gyles's neglect of her own bodily needs was notorious. After a quarrel with F. J. Dick, she returned to "bread and shell-cocoa," so Yeats brought her an offer for well-paid advertisement work, "but she said that to draw advertisements was to degrade art" and "returned to starvation with joy."[49] She also escaped a nursing home following her affair with Smithers, because she said that they gave her too much to eat.[50] According to Yeats, "starvation and misery had a large share in her ritual of worship."[51] The belief that one's material body represents only a tiny fragment of one's ongoing existence makes it far easier to disregard the safety and sanctity of that body. Yeats's and Gyles's attachment to the doctrine of reincarnation should be understood, then, as a necessary component of their shared idealized vision of martyrdom at the fin de siècle.

Yeats's and Gyles's enthusiasm for the concept of heroic sacrifice in the 1890s would have been similarly bolstered by the apocalyptic elements of occult discourse. As Alex Owen discusses in her recent work on the occult at the turn of the century, the coming Armageddon was treated as a commonplace by the Hermetic Order of the Golden Dawn.[52] Yeats captures this apocalyptic passion for violence in *The Speckled Bird* in the rousing speeches of Maclagan, a character modeled on MacGregor Mathers. When the protagonist first encounters Maclagan, the occultist proudly announces, "Things are going very quickly in the world in our times, and you and

I may see the streets and factories burning. Then we who have seen the truth will be listened to. We will reshape the world."[53] This rhetoric grows increasingly violent later in the text, as Maclagan proclaims, "There's going to be a great change, there are going to be great disturbances. You and I shall see the streets run with blood, for no great spiritual change comes without political change too. Everything happens suddenly."[54] Many occultists at the turn of the century acknowledged the necessity of violence in the process of revolutionary change. As Joy Dixon notes, "Theosophists saw the war as a final sweeping away of old forms that would usher in the New Age."[55] A new reality, a new world, could only develop once the previous world had been decisively destroyed and discarded.

The Secret Rose exhibits a marked preoccupation with apocalypse and self-sacrifice, an energy Gyles seems to have detected and drawn on in the images she designed for the book's cover. According to Yeats, Gyles had a "thorough understanding of the symbolism of [his] work."[56] Comprehending his meaning so clearly, she was able to collaborate with him in producing a "total book" that romanticizes loss of life and establishes violent change as unavoidable and even desirable. Because Gyles engaged so intensely with Yeats's apocalyptic vision and these ideas seem to have informed her later thinking concerning self-sacrifice, the content of *The Secret Rose* deserves consideration in an analysis of Gyles's work and career. Augustine Martin has argued that the central pattern of unity within *The Secret Rose* is the apocalyptic structure of each individual story in the collection: "Even in the few stories that are not overtly apocalyptic, which do not involve supernatural revelation or prophecy, the action resolves itself in a moment of visionary insight."[57] In addition, "the stories are so arranged that these moments of vision mark stages in the progress of history between one apocalyptic change and the next."[58] The collection opens with stories set in the pagan world, then moves into the monastic age, the medieval period, and the seventeenth and eighteenth centuries, and concludes with an occult tale set at the end of the nineteenth century. The moment of vision or apocalypse with which each story concludes allows a new age to be initiated, and the final story, "Rosa Alchemica," indicates that another moment of incredible violence and change is about to begin.

"Rosa Alchemica" brings the apocalyptic and sacrificial content in the collection to a head, speaking more forcefully about violent change and martyrdom than any of the previous tales. The story was first published in the *Savoy* in 1896, and this earlier version of the story began with the discussion of a massacre described explicitly as a "martyrdom": "A few years ago . . . a number of eccentric men and women . . . were surprised at prayer . . . and beaten to death with stones. . . . I first heard of these unfortunates, on whom the passion for universal ideas, which distinguishes the Celtic and Latin races, was to bring so dreadful a martyrdom, but a few weeks before the end."[59] Gyles almost certainly read "Rosa Alchemica," probably in its *Savoy* form, before beginning her designs, for, as Russell C. McDonald has noted, her design for the back cover for *The Secret Rose*, a rose "with many spears thrusting against it, but in vain, as was shown by the shattered points of those nearest to the petals," seems to have been derived directly from a passage in the story.[60] In any case, this opening reference to martyrdom, referred to as a "tragic end" in the revised version of the story, is but the first of many in the tale. The narrator speaks in this opening passage of the death of Michael Robartes, another character modeled on MacGregor Mathers. Robartes visits the narrator, a dabbler in the occult, not long before his demise to invite the timid novice to become an initiate of the "Order of the Alchemical Rose." The narrator resists, but, following a vision brought on by Robartes in which he "[passes] into that Death that is Beauty herself," he agrees to go wherever Robartes decrees and to do whatever he bids.[61] They travel to the western coast of Ireland to the Temple of the Alchemical Rose, the sight of which seems to itself portend apocalypse: "I was possessed with the phantasy that the sea, which kept covering it with showers of white foam, was claiming it as part of some indefinite and passionate life, which had begun to war upon our orderly and careful days, and was about to plunge the world into a night as obscure as that which followed the downfall of the classical world."[62] Landscape and architecture are saturated with mystical significance, communicating the coming of radical change. The peasants shout to them as they pass, "Idolaters, Idolaters, go down to Hell."[63] The narrator inquires of Robartes, "Are you not afraid . . . that these wild fishing people may do some desperate thing against you?" He replies by expressing an antimaterialist enthusiasm for martyrdom: "I and mine . . . are long past human hurt or help, being incorporate with immortal spirits, and when we die it shall be the consummation of the supreme work."[64] Once inside the temple, the narrator participates in a magical dance with an "immortal august woman" who "[drinks] up [his] soul as an ox drinks up a wayside pool," and then he falls into a faint.[65] He awakens surrounded by sleeping members of the Order of the Alchemical Rose and hears the sounds of "the tumult of angry men and women's voices."[66] The narrator retreats, leaving the members of the Order to their fate at the hands of the crowd, hearing as he runs "many voices of exultation and lamentation."[67] He continues, he notes in the story's conclusion, to be haunted at certain moments by these voices but takes comfort at those times in the rosary he wears about his neck. As John Wilson Foster notes, the story subtly critiques the narrator's lack of spiritual conviction.[68] In these final moments, abandoning his fellow initiates, retreating from the martyr's fate, he is represented as cowardly and weak, one who has withdrawn from the spiritual truths that he encountered at the temple into the comfort of traditional Christian faith. It is Robartes and his fellow martyrs who represent true passion and heroism, facing death with exultation, as the "consummation of the supreme work."[69] This story, which was so influential in Gyles's development of a design for the book's cover, would have also exposed her to a highly idealized representation of self-sacrifice.

Gyles's contact with Yeats during this period would have also exposed her to his developing ideas about Irish nationalism, which were at this time deeply integrated with his interest in the occult. Works like *The Secret Rose* demonstrate the extent to which these two elements of his thinking were intertwined during this period. His dedication of *The Secret Rose* to Æ notes that "so far . . . as this book is visionary it is Irish," and the apocalyptic history set forth in *The Secret Rose* revolves primarily around the great changes that happened in Ireland and ends by implying that an even greater change may soon occur within the country.[70] It is easy to see how occult apocalypticism might function effectively in tandem with Irish nationalist ideologies. Much like many occult systems of the fin de siècle, the Fenian cult of blood sacrifice promoted the idea that bloodshed would operate as a necessary foundation for the coming of a new age. Similarly, occult antimaterialism could operate as a useful foundation for the promotion of sacrificial ideals. As Susan Harris notes in her discussion of Irish nationalism and the concept of martyrdom, "the idea of regeneration through blood sacrifice privileges the intangible rewards of death over the actual living body. Making what Pearse calls 'the ultimate sacrifice' requires the victim to decide to value a larger, as yet illusory goal above the immediate needs and desires of his own body."[71] The suffering of the nationalist martyr is minimized by linking his sacrifice to a national tradition and the potential for a free future. The sacrificial victim passes away so that the new age may begin and in so doing enters the ranks of past soldiers and heroes who died for Ireland. Whereas Yeats might have balked at the material effects of the cult of blood sacrifice during the Easter Rising, he played a central role in propagating this sacrificial ideology in the decades preceding the rebellion, generating a series of ethereal and immortal figures inflected by his ties to occult antimaterialism and apocalypticism.

Yeats relied primarily on feminine figures to communicate his enthusiasm for nationalist self-sacrifice, a fact that must have impacted Gyles as she developed her own romanticized vision of martyrdom. Yeats's most well-known call to martyrdom, *Cathleen ni Houlihan*, was first performed in 1902, but his earlier Cathleen, *The Countess Cathleen*, who sacrifices her own soul to save the starving people of Ireland, appeared in the 1892 collection *The Countess Kathleen and Various Legends and Lyrics* as well as the 1899 *Poems* for which Gyles designed the cover. In allowing a woman to occupy the role of martyr, Yeats did violate certain codes of representation. According to Susan Harris, turn-of-the-century gender ideology exempted women from this position: "Blood, which in the martyr's case, marks his release from the limited corporeal world into the realm of ideal and abstraction, marks the menstruating woman as mortal, embodied, gendered, tied by her cycle to temporally bound existence. . . . Women are not symbolically eligible for the role of sacrificial victim."[72] Harris argues that Yeats's departure from the traditional gender dynamics of martyrdom caused Irish audiences to condemn the work. He corrected this mistake in his later play, *Cathleen ni Houlihan*, in which a female figure motivates male martyrdom but does not sacrifice herself. Gyles, however, would have had far more extended contact with the earlier text and its peculiar mythology of feminine martyrdom, and she must have found the fact that the earlier play allows a female figure to usurp the privileged masculine role of sacrificial victim singularly alluring.

I would argue, however, that Yeats is not the sole source of Gyles's interest in the concept of martyrdom. The appeal of self-sacrifice was reinforced through her friendship with Oscar Wilde. According to Eleanor Farjeon, Gyles first met Wilde in Paris: "Leonard Smithers wanted to publish a new edition of *Salome*; Althea was to decorate it, and Smithers sent her to France to make Oscar's acquaintance. They met for the first time in the Gare du Nord. She was hungry, and he led her from bistro to bistro, feeding her by colour scheme, calling for a green drink with a rose-pink sandwich here, a purple drink with a yellow sandwich there. They seemed to pass several days and nights of enthralling talk doing this."[73] Clifford Bax claims that on first encountering her "rustic surname," Wilde "paused a moment, then said, 'Ah! You must call yourself Althea Le Gys.'"[74] The two became fast friends, and, by all accounts, she spoke warmly of him for years after he died. She seems to have been deeply affected by Wilde's death. According to Yeats, on hearing of his death, she said, "He was so kind, nobody ever lived who was so kind."[75] Though the time they spent together was limited, Wilde made an enormous impact on Gyles, and he became a crucial reference point for her during her later years. Almost all accounts of Gyles after her affair with Smithers include some mention of a portrait of or presentation copy from Wilde in her whereabouts. Arthur Symons, for example, visited her in 1900 and found her "lying in bed in a room bare except for five books (one a presentation copy from Wilde) and the extravagant costume jewelry she used to wear."[76] These objects seemed to function for her, like Victoria's brooches and busts of Albert, as signifiers of her identity and links to a romantic and beautiful past.

Gyles's interest in Wilde, however, predated their acquaintance. Her unpublished novella *A Woman without a Soul* reads much like a revision of *The Picture of Dorian Gray*, a feminized retelling of one of Wilde's most significant works. The manuscript is not dated, but it was composed in Dublin, presumably not long before Gyles left for London, which was in late 1891 or 1892, not long after *Dorian Gray* first appeared in *Lippincott's* (1890).[77] As the story begins, Winifred Orwes, abandoned by Hubert Ledbury for another woman, contemplates suicide, but she cannot follow through for fear of harming Hubert. Eugene Carruthers, a magician, encounters her at this moment of crisis, and she calls him to help her, "to rid [her] of [her] soul if only for an instant that [she] may kill [herself]."[78] He agrees to help her if she will give up her soul, not for an instant, but for a full seven years. Once the spell is cast, Winifred awakens as cold and cruel and beautiful as Dorian:

> "I wanted to kill myself[,] didn't I? I recollect I wanted to kill myself because the man I loved threw me over for another woman! Oh what a fool I was! I will do better than that now." The scarlet lips parted in a laugh that sang through the air. . . . "Ah" she cried springing up "this is glorious! He shall come back again, he shall suffer as he made me suffer. I feel so strong" clenching her white hands "I feel as if I had some new power." "And so you have" he said "See!" & he pointed to a mirror at the end of the room & it reflected the same woman who had entered the room an hour before, then with wild eyes, white lips, & a quivering frame. Now the eyes gleamed with a light that held & fascinated. The lips, as scarlet as if the words that passed had bruised them, curved themselves into a mocking smile. On her cheeks between the whiteness of chin & brow glowed a rich deep colour like living flame. The light in her eyes & the smile round her lips deepened as she cried with a long drawn sigh of content, "I see my power. I am beautiful." "Yes" he replied "you have no soul, for 7 years you will remain thus."[79]

Winifred reclaims Hubert, who cannot resist her new beauty, and the two live a dissipated life together for seven years, building around themselves an "environment of evil."[80] However, when Winifred's soul returns, her beauty fades. In a moment her body "that for 7 years had been the home of evil passions & had grown inwardly hideous with sin, a seething mess of pollution & corruption" shows the signs of her soulless living.[81] She appears aged and worn, and Hubert begins to lose interest and seek affection elsewhere. She contemplates sacrificing her soul to Carruthers once more, but, in fear of further ruining Hubert through continued exposure to her sinfulness, she throws herself from a bridge.

A Woman without a Soul bears striking similarities to *Dorian Gray* in terms of both style and content. The exhilarated descriptions of Winifred's cold beauty as well as her commission of "sin after sin" while soulless echo Wilde's narration of Dorian's pleasure in dissolute behaviors once the portrait begins to absorb the consequences. The story of a beautiful body protected from the visible evidence of sin has been altered, however, so as to contemplate how gender might inflect this sort of supernatural experience. Whereas Dorian dies the moment that the portrait is destroyed and the spell is broken, Winifred must continue to live without her former beauty. Gyles stresses Winifred's desperation once she has lost her looks as well as Hubert's cruelty as he remarks on the change: "You've quite lost your complexion."[82] Dorian is freed immediately from the body that bears the mark of his sins. Winifred, conversely, must suffer the indignity of wearing the material evidence of her freedoms before a vituperative audience that speculates audibly concerning what has caused her to "go off so quickly as she has."[83] Whereas Dorian inadvertently takes his own life, Winifred does so willingly, a martyr for love, a reformed woman who has rejected her previous sinful ways. Dorian and Winifred's experiences are superficially identical, but Winifred's period of sin without visible consequence results in far more pain, tragedy, and regret. Gyles suggests there are greater punishments for feminine transgressions. The echoes of *Dorian Gray* in *A Woman without a Soul* indicate that Wilde was informing Gyles's thought well before their first meeting a decade later. From the earliest days of her career, his work influenced her own consideration of the concepts of sin and sexual freedom and the manner in which certain privileges are gendered.

Gyles's initial interest in Wilde must have been compounded by the events of 1895, as the discourse surrounding Wilde following his imprisonment would have held much attraction for an individual drawn to the concept of martyrdom. Richard Kaye has recently argued that "the playwright's devotees were eager to place a halo over Wilde immediately after his three-act trial," and his posthumous followers quickly began to develop a "sense of Wilde as risk-taking leader of a newly constituted breed of erotically dissident men."[84] Kaye notes that the term *martyr* began to be applied to Wilde as early as 1895, and this conception of Wilde as suffering saint gained credence in the early years of the twentieth century. Edith Lees Ellis, for example, declared in 1911 that Wilde represented a "martyr to unscientific legislation."[85] Kaye's work on the evolution of the discourse concerning Wilde's "martyrdom" demonstrates that a cosmopolitan confederacy of authors, including Hugo von Hofmannsthal, Octave Mirbeau, and Marcel Proust, collaborated in the development of this idea at the turn of the century, and his status as saintly hero had been widely disseminated by the teens.

Although the concept of martyrdom may operate as a powerful locus for community building and activism, a source of inspiration for nationalist energies or sexual minorities, sacrificial ideologies obviously tend to lead in dangerous directions. Kaye is careful to stress the extent to which the celebration of the concept of martyrdom can be limiting, "[duplicating] banal psychological conceptions" or "[becoming] entangled with conservative conceptions of homosexual desire, in which same-sex preferences must inevitably lead to self-willed isolation and morbidity."[86] The celebration of martyrdom also poses the threat of rendering masochistic and destructive behaviors alluring, a danger that becomes quite clear when Gyles's work and career are read in light of her sustained engagement with sacrificial ideologies as disseminated by Irish Decadents. In addition, these ideologies facilitate a disregard for human life, a dismissal of the material body in favor of loftier goals, another dangerous idea to which Gyles succumbs in the early years of the war. In the following section, I consider the impact of these ideologies on Gyles in the first decades of the twentieth century, the moment at which she "lost caste" and embraced the violent jingoism of the First World War.

II. The Century Turns: Gyles and the Post-Victorian Legacy of Irish Decadence

The impact of Gyles's extended contact with sacrificial ideologies and occult antimaterialism becomes highly visible once the century turns. It is in her later work that we can see Gyles contending with her Irish Decadent cultural inheritance. As I have argued here, Decadent aesthetic modes, such as detachment and irony, became useful to post-Victorian Decadents as they worked to resist the prevalent jingoism and belligerence of the World War I period. However, although Gyles, like Beerbohm and Lee, continued to create works in a late-Victorian Decadent aesthetic style well into the twentieth century, her persisting attachment to Decadence did not produce pacifist attitudes or cosmopolitan skepticism. Gyles's contact with Yeatsian occultism and mythologies of martyrdom inflected her particular mode of post-Victorian Decadence, which seems to have made it more difficult for her to maintain a sense of apartness from or skepticism of violent conflict. She was able to enter fully into the spirit of 1914, without concerns about violence and loss of life, in part because of her commitment to an occult understanding of death's impermanence and a belief in the martyr's immortality. In addition, her adoration of a vision of Wilde as saintly and tragic contributed to her enthusiasm for sacrificial ideologies, which in turn inflected her own tendency to conceive of herself as an outsider and fallen woman, a martyr for the cause of sexual freedom. In a discussion of the impact of Wilde's death on the members of the Tragic Generation, Warwick Gould argues that Althea Gyles was "made and destroyed by that counter-culture Wilde's fall had engendered."[87] She constructed her identity in relationship to a romantic vision of Wilde as sacrificial victim, and she was undone by her excessive investment in a vision of herself as similarly tragic and brave. Although Yeats and Wilde cannot be held responsible for her fate, she might not have been so easily seduced into celebrating war and sacrificing herself had she not been indoctrinated within a set of overlapping cults that celebrated martyrdom and linked destruction to rebirth.

Althea Gyles loudly pronounced her belief in her own right to sexual freedom when she began her affair with Leonard Smithers in 1899, a sin for which she, unlike Winifred Orwes, immediately suffered the consequences. The two seem to have begun their relationship while discussing Gyles's commissioned illustrations for "The Harlot's House." In 1898, she wrote to Yeats announcing the new project and speaking boldly of the scandalous quality of her work: "I hope the drawings won't shock Mr Symons."[88] They very well might have. The illustrations represent the dancing "strange mechanical grotesques" passing "shadows . . . across a blind," as described in Wilde's poem, but the figures behind the blinds in Gyles's images are clearly not clothed (Figure 4.3). Their nipples are visible. While the "slim silhouetted skeletons" in Wilde's poem dance quadrilles, Gyles's skeletons are locked in passionate embraces, kissing and caressing the naked bodies that surround them. Gyles has chosen to enlarge and inflame the erotic content of the poem. Many have remarked that these works reveal the operations of Smithers's influence. The images also announce the emergence of a newly sexualized persona, a young woman aggressively courting scandal, reveling in the representation of dangerous

Figure 4.3. Althea Gyles, illustration for *The Harlot's House* by Oscar Wilde, 1904. Reproduced courtesy of the Harry Ransom Center, University of Texas at Austin.

and illicit situations.[89] Her work for Smithers immediately caused consternation within her circle. She wrote to Yeats, "People are being horrid to me about it so please listen to this and don't say anything to any of my personal acquaintances about it such as the Coopers or Gore Booths etc. if you chance to come across them[.] They can do what they like when the book comes out but I cannot endure any more lectures on the subject."[90] She insisted that "nothing [would] alter her determination" to do the illustrations and that she had "two most excellent motives" for completing the work. (Ian Fletcher speculates that the "excellent motives" were "aesthetic hunger" and "her loyalty to Wilde."[91])

Once Gyles began her relationship with Smithers, Yeats himself became outraged. In a letter to Lady Gregory concerning the affair, he bristled with shock and disapproval. He informed Lady Gregory that Gyles, after years of despising Symons and Moore because of their loose morals, had "ostentatiously taken up with Smithers, a person of so immoral a life that people like Symons and Moore despise him."[92] He stated that he had forbidden her to bring Smithers along to his "at homes," acknowledging that this "probably [would] make her quarrel with [him] for which [he would] be sorry as [he imagined he was] about the only person [belonging] to the orderly world she [was] likely to meet from" that moment onward.[93] He stated that he believed it a "point of pride" for her to pronounce her feelings publicly, representing her relationship with Smithers as a headstrong form of self-sacrifice, an attempt to "[throw] off every remnant of respectability with an almost religious enthusiasm."[94] Yeats posited Gyles's affection for Smithers as a form of madness or zealotry and described her treatment of herself as destructive. This sense of Gyles as a possessed sacrificial victim is consistent with Yeats's assessment of Gyles in *The Trembling of the Veil*, in which he notes that Gyles "sacrificed herself [to her work] with Asiatic fanaticism."[95] Yeats's correspondence and comments concerning Gyles indicate that he played a prominent role in promoting a vision of Gyles as martyr.

Yeats's smug condemnation of the affair angered Gyles. She scolded him for his treatment of Smithers: "I have 'a few words' for both you and [Symons] which are that it is very wrong to slander so *excellent* a man as Mr Smithers."[96] Their friendship cooled almost immediately. On December 21, 1899, Yeats wrote to Lady Gregory, "I am afraid it will be some time before Althea Gyles does that bookplate. I have heard or seen nothing of her since I wrote her that letter, and expect, or rather Symons suspects, that Smithers has forbid her to come near me."[97] While Yeats believed that they might begin to collaborate once again after "Smithers [was] a lost illusion," the friendship seems to have been irreparably damaged.[98] Gyles is mentioned from time to time in his later correspondence, but they produced no further work together, and there is no record of contact between them in the twentieth century.

The affair with Smithers concluded not long after it began. According to James G. Nelson, "Smithers's approaching financial disaster may have played a role in cooling his ardor for Gyles, who, it would appear, failed to come to his rescue with money derived from her affluent family."[99] Gyles became extremely ill when the relationship ended. Most accounts represent her as destroyed by the "religious enthusiasm" with which she had "thrown off respectability." She apparently continued to write to Smithers, but he declined to reply. His bankruptcy became official in September 1900, and she wrote to him from her sickbed in the Hospital for Diseases of the Chest in the City Road: "Leonard dear[,] I heard yesterday that you had failed at last[.] I'm sorry from the bottom of my heart that I couldn[']t get the money from my people & that you should be in trouble[.] Perhaps you will laugh at my writing to you after your not answering my letter but perhaps you may see it as I mean it."[100] Smithers does not seem to have responded.

Once Yeats had abandoned her, Arthur Symons served as a temporary patron and protector. In a September 15, 1900, letter to Rhoda Bowser, Symons relayed "a sad little story" of a parcel of poems he had received from Gyles late at night along with a note "to say she was ill in bed, had been ill for a year, thought she was going to die, and was to be moved into a hospital on Monday, and before it was too late she wanted to put together a little book of her best poems."[101] She asked him to come to her, and when he arrived he found her with "chloral by her side," "very white with her red hair all over the pillow."[102] She looked over an article Symons had written on the recently deceased Ernest Dowson. "When I meet him, I'll tell him about it," she promised.[103] And then she said, "All my friends have deserted me: I've not seen a creature but the doctor ever since I've been ill. Look (she waved her hand towards the wall) I've taken down all their photographs: I've only left my own now. I don't know anybody else now."[104] Gyles felt keenly her abandonment by the Decadent circle that had made so much of her work in the 1890s. Symons wrote to Bowser that he felt "awfully sorry for her, though [he] found her rather a trying person when she was well, and she used to rather hate [him]."[105] According to Symons, even Lady Colin Campbell, whose notorious divorce case scandalized late-Victorian England, had "left her, like all the rest."[106]

However, Gyles did not die as promised, and Symons did introduce her to a publisher. According to Symons, the publisher was having the book set, "when he discovered that she absolutely insisted on dedicating it 'to the beautiful memory of Oscar Wilde.' He would have passed everything but the word 'beautiful,' but there he stuck, and she also, and the MS was returned."[107] Gyles held her ground, and the collection never appeared. The defiant dedication linked her own sacrifice to the most significant and tragic of 1890s martyrs. At each step along the way of her fall, she reiterated and reinforced the sense of her own tragedy as an echo of 1895. When Symons was poised to rescue her, she threw herself back into oblivion, emphasizing that the sacrifice was for Wilde and like Wilde's. She never published a collection of poems, though she lived for almost another half-century.

The destructive impact of Gyles's contact with sacrificial ideologies is also clear in her war poems, in which she transferred the passion for bloodshed and sacrifice that she had developed in conversation with Yeats's particular version of Irish Decadence to the service of a more generally British enterprise. Irish nationalism never became a significant cause for Gyles. In fact, in an unpublished poem in a folder labeled "probably all Althea Gyles" in the archive of the Shakespeare Centre in Stratford-upon-Avon, Gyles apologizes for her neglect of her birthplace. The first stanza of "To Ireland" asks the "lovely mother of [her] life" to "lay pardon and peace with tender hands / Upon a broken heart that loves / More dearly alien lands."[108] There is no account of Gyles's return to Ireland once she had departed for London in the 1890s. She did return to the topic of Ireland in, for example, the aforementioned unpublished play concerning reincarnation. Gyles shared with Yeats a sense that occult truths could be more easily accessed in their home country. In his dedication to *The Secret Rose*, Yeats advances the claim that Ireland "has preserved with some less excellent things a gift of vision, which has died out among more hurried and more successful nations," and Gyles's aforementioned unpublished play echoes this argument concerning Irish visionary qualities.[109] Doctor Aloysius Beauchamp states that he has accompanied the Cardinal to study obsession and "the causes of so much insanity in Ireland," because he believes that the tendency to "slip back" is more prevalent in that country.[110] The Irish, Gyles implies, are more open to contact with the memories and emotions of their past lives. Ireland did, then, have a certain appeal for Gyles, and the nation certainly operated as a source of inspiration. Some of her most well-known works, such as her image of Deirdre or her cover for *The Secret Rose*, draw on Irish folklore and mythology. However,

Irish politics do not seem to have held much interest for Gyles. Irish nationalism is significant in relationship to her work and career so far as her contact with Irish sacrificial ideologies inflamed her appetite for aggression and martyrdom. However, she disentangled these energies from the true project of Irish nationalism, reveling in the glorification of violence while neglecting the admirable aspirations of those committed to that violence.

At the beginning of World War I, Gyles contributed two poems, "The Farm Hand" and "The Holy War," to "a war anthology" titled *Lord God of Battles* (1914). The collection, edited by A. E. Manning Foster, begins with an epigraph from Shelley, "Poets are the trumpets which sing to battle," and includes original and republished works by Sir Arthur Conan Doyle, Thomas Hardy, Rudyard Kipling, and Gerard Manley Hopkins.[111] The tenor of the majority of the poems is righteous, jingoistic, and belligerent. The opening poem by Robert Bridges, "Thou Careless, Awake!," sets the tone of the collection, calling England to "stand . . . for honour" and God to "guard the Right!"[112] The English soldiers are referred to as "peacemakers," armed for the cause of "Freedom," and English warfare is at once aestheticized and purified:

> Much suffering shall cleanse thee;
> But thou through the flood
> Shalt win to salvation,
> To beauty through blood.[113]

As Noshee Khan notes, Bridges referred explicitly to the war as a battle between forces aligned with God and those aligned with the Powers of Darkness: "I hope that our people will see that it is primarily a holy war. It is manifestly a war declared between Christ and the Devil."[114] Gyles's contribution, "The Holy War," replicates this attitude, "[epitomizing] the sentiments which permeate much of the verse inspired by a belief in the righteousness of the English cause":

> We fight for Peace – not for Revenge or Hate,
> Forgetful of the names of Fame or Fate –
> Winning by war the Time when wars shall cease.
> Soldiers of Concord! Sentinels of Peace.[115]

As Khan argues, "Gyles's proclamation of the nation's justness in taking up arms, accentuated by strident capitals, assumes that the reader feels the antithesis between the opposing armies to be as spelled out by the Poet Laureate."[116] The violence performed by British forces is recast and reformulated as justice. The repetitive intoning of the term *peace*, which appears in both the first and last lines of the poem, obscures the work's argument, foregrounding a word whose meaning lies in direct contradiction with the poem's essential content.

Gyles's "The Farm Hand" also echoes Bridges's opening statement, which insists that English soldiers "die gladly" for their country.[117] In a similarly romanticized representation of martyrdom, Gyles relies on anti-materialism, mythological atemporality, and occult ideas concerning the impermanence of death to redeem and hallow the loss of a soldier's life. She generates an idealized vision of a heroic rural laborer leaving the "slow toil of peace for the sharp toil of war," a poetic figure of stoic strength and selflessness:

> Across the wold beneath the pale first star,
> Baring his wet brow to the evening wind,
> No thought of his own valour in his mind,
> To war he turns.
> To war he turns.[118]

The slow spondees of the repeated dimeter line, "To war he turns," isolate and freeze the moment in which the soldier departs for battle, expanding the interval before death and thus subtly eliding the violence of war. Invoking what Richard Kearney describes as "a 'sacred' tradition of death and renewal which provides justification for present acts of suffering by realigning them with recurring paradigms of the past," Gyles collapses the present suffering of the soldier with past heroism and thus minimizes (while at the same time inflating) his sacrifice.[119] The farm-hand "[turns to war]" as a "brother of warriors whose deeds outshine / Time's mists!"[120] "Their honour," the poem argues, "soared" from hearts just like his. He is, in turning to war, one with the sacred warriors of the past. The poem concludes with a series of ecstatic exclamations concerning the immortality of heroes past and present:

> God speed these Heroes as those Heroes sped!
> Victory! Home! Or life with the great dead!
> How Valour burns![121]

Should the farmhand die, his death, like the death of Oona and Costello, Deirdre and Naisi, or the lady beneath the grieving knight, will not be permanent. He will continue living, "life with the great dead," a martyr's immortality. "How Valour burns," the poem both begins and ends, and this burning is revealed to be not a destructive fire, an object of critique, but an alluring and perpetual flame of belligerent passion that promises its recipient the pleasures of sacred self-sacrifice and everlasting life.

Gyles did eventually reconsider this enthusiasm for battle. Her commitments diversified in the twentieth century, and she came to identify herself with socialist causes and vegetarianism. These ethical commitments, which express real concern for material bodies, counteracted her earlier disregard for present suffering. As she became increasingly engaged with discourses concerning workers' and animals' rights, it presumably became more difficult to hold these new ideals, which work to eradicate pain, in tension with the more belligerent energies of her earlier career. Her writing in the 1910s demonstrates her new links to socialist communities and her growing concern with the well-being of animals. In 1911, she contributed a story to the *Vineyard*, the publication associated with the Peasant Art Guild and connected with the John Ruskin school at Haslemere, and the Reading archive holds a set of unpublished essays presumably composed around the same time that advance Ruskinian arguments concerning the need for beauty and propose the founding of schools for impoverished city children where they might learn to garden and sketch. *Pilgrimage*, which was composed in the late 1910s, makes much of Benador Quested's vegetarianism, and the two lovers Esme and Raimond in the aforementioned unpublished play also refuse to eat meat. Gyles's thinking concerning these new causes became intertwined with her previous occult interests. *Letters to Children about Drawing, Painting, and Something More*, for example, published under the pseudonym John Meade in 1914, integrates the ideas of Ruskin and Morris with a concern for the natural world as well as the dryads and fauns: "Man has a right to build houses, but he has no right to build hideous ones. What can all the Dryads and Fauns and Fairies who tend the trees and flowers and grass think of man when he destroys their beautiful work in order to make the things he does?"[122]

Gyles often explored the relationship between her occult and political beliefs in works devoted to Christmas, a topic with which she seems to have been positively obsessed. She returns to this subject repeatedly in poems and short stories that demonstrate the interconnectedness of animal and human life and the ties between Christ and the spirits. After moving to Folkestone in 1910, she composed a series of Christmas carols that were printed for a group called "the Order of the Holy Mount." Many of these carols argue for the rights of beasts. They rely on the concept of "One Life," a Theosophical principle concerning the unity of all living things, to persuade readers to perceive the connections between Christ and the animals, to see him "in all things that live."[123] A number of the carols and stories also advance claims concerning the ties between the spirit world and the Christ child. "A Child's Christmas Carol," for example, represents the entire natural and spiritual world joined in rejoicing at the birth of Christ.[124] Gyles's Christmas works imagine a world in which Christian and occult forces as well as the human and animal worlds are understood as integrated and in sympathy.

In an unpublished essay titled "Winter," Gyles reveals why Christmas became such a useful concept to her as she theorized her own conception of One Life, a deeply unified and spiritual world in which ox and ass, dryad and faun, Christ and children perceive their connections to and alliances with one another. She notes that, while we are apt to think primarily of winter as a cold and uncomfortable season, it is during this time of year that we are most open to perceiving the spiritual truths that surround us. Evidence of this may be found in the Western child's joy at Christmas and in Christmas traditions of the past, when "mystery plays were acted and tales told, not only of Angelic beings, but also of a multitude of lesser elemental creatures, elves, gnomes, ouphens, or fairies."[125] The content of these plays reflects the fact that "the call of winter had evoked a deeper consciousness and with the awakening of this consciousness, a sympathy with these beings."[126] At Christmas the individual sees more clearly her connection with these other planes and thus feels less hostility toward that which is not entirely understood. It is a moment of spiritual vulnerability and perceptiveness, of ethical openness and engagement.

It makes sense, then, that Gyles's later recanting of her enthusiasm for war would occur in another piece devoted to the topic of Christmas. The aforementioned folder marked "probably all Althea Gyles" in the Shakespeare Centre's archive includes an unsigned, undated, and unpublished poem titled "How the Prince of Peace Came Back." The opening stanza of the poem establishes that it is Christ's habit to return to earth each year on Christmas Eve. However, "this year He comes again" to find an "angry glow lighting up the sky" and the sound of "the shouts of men who die."[127] Christ calls out to inquire why no one keeps his vigil. He is told they have all forgotten, for they "have all gone to the war to fight."[128] The discouraged Christ nevertheless resolves to stay and wait for the travelling kings. Three men with a kingly bearing finally appear, but when Christ asks where his gifts of myrrh and gold are, they respond, "All the gold has now been spent / To keep up our heavy armament."[129] He is told to return to heaven, for "the day of the Christmas Babe is past."[130] In the poem's final stanza, Christ's eyes grow dim as he realizes there is "no room for Him."[131] This is a marked departure from the romantic treatment of war on display in Gyles's poetry of 1914. She apparently rethought her enthusiasm for warfare in relationship to her growing commitment to a set of beliefs and practices that sought to alleviate rather than dismiss suffering.

However, the appeal of sacrificial ideologies does not seem to have dissipated entirely for Gyles. Although she did rethink her relationship to nationalist conceptions of martyrdom, the appeal of Wildean self-sacrifice and the notion that the destruction of brave individuals might initiate a new age of sexual and gender politics seem to have remained central to her worldview. Following her affair with Smithers, she continued to compose poetry celebrating feminine figures who are fallen, outcast, and willing to sacrifice themselves for love. In the wake of her own condemnation, she expressed a sense of affiliation with vilified women in works that contest conventional gender ideology. In 1901, for example, immediately after the affair ended, Gyles's "The Love-Child" appeared in the *Kensington*. This poem, in which the angels draw a dead baby buried by an "outcast mother" from the earth to lay him upon the Virgin Mary's breast, implicitly censures the culture that judged the mother so harshly.[132] In 1907, she published a poem titled "Mary Magdalene" in the *New Age*. The speaker expresses a sense of affinity with Mary, referring to her as "the most near unto the heart" and "the quickest to hear and understand" of "all the Saints in the calendar."[133] As a fallen woman, Mary Magdalene possesses a particular appeal for outsiders: "If Cain the Outcast prayed to her, / She would succor him with eager hand, / And tho' the passionate Lilith would not pray, / She would help and understand."[134] In the years following her own denunciation by the *Yellow Book* circle, Gyles continually revisited the theme of feminine rebellion and moral exile, articulating sympathy and admiration for those who chose to contest and violate boundaries.

Gyles also continued to consider the romantic allure of suicide, a theme taken up earlier in *A Woman without a Soul*. Death was, of course, one of the central preoccupations of Gyles's work. In a 1949 letter to Gyles's niece, Joyce Cazalet, Cecil French refers to the "many beautiful phrases" her aunt had made "about what is called 'death.'"[135] The tendency to romanticize death so evident in her work of the 1890s persists in her later poetry. Her preoccupation with this topic has much to do with her interest in the occult and reincarnation, certainly, but she also turns to the topic of death in those works concerned with romantic love and self-sacrifice. In "The Song of the Seine: To the Court of Kings" (1901), for example, the river promises relief to those in the throes of heartache.[136] In "From Rosamor Dead to Favonius for Whom She Died" (1906), Rosamor speaks from beyond the grave of her continuing love for Favonius, who never truly returned her affection.[137] If the idea of sacrificing one's life for a national cause finally lost its attraction for Gyles, her twentieth-century poems reveal a writer still very much drawn to the idea of romantic martyrdom, of destroying oneself for love, particularly love unreturned.

The most troubling elements of Gyles's career, her pro-war poetry, her "loss of caste," her abandonment on the grounds of sexual indiscretion by a supposedly bohemian circle, can be traced to her investment in sacrificial ideologies. In her post-Victorian works, it is possible to see a woman writer struggling with the impact of her contact with Irish Decadence, with Yeatsian occultism and the emerging cult surrounding Wilde. Gyles, of course, chose not to take her life. She lived for half a century with the consequences of the isolating choices that she made. However, because to a certain extent she remained invested in sacrificial ideologies, she rarely expressed regret concerning those choices or anger at the circle that had abandoned her. The task of critiquing the manner in which the apocalyptically minded 1890s had disappointed the men and women to whom it had promised great change was left to their twentieth-century successors.

III. "Poor Old Althea": Twentieth-Century Women Writers and the Ghostly Presence of the Naughty Nineties

Gyles's self-sacrifice never seemed entirely complete. It went on for decades, and those around her were continually confronted with the physical evidence of her ongoing dejection. She became highly dependent on the assistance of others in the years following the affair with Smithers. In a 1908 letter to Florence Farr, Yeats accused her of "[collecting] the necessities of life from her friends and [spending] her own money on flowers."[138] Clifford Bax, who published some of her poems in his Theosophical journal *Orpheus*, told Ian Fletcher in 1957, "She would lie on her grubby bed till noon . . . a born dependent, a parasite, emotional and mental."[139] Many who encountered her seemed to struggle with the corporeal evidence of her suffering, of her age, and the fact that she was no longer as young or as beautiful. In her discussion of martyrdom, Susan Harris argues that it is crucial for the sacrificial body to remain hidden.[140] The sight of the suffering body undermines the antimaterialist element of sacrificial ideologies. Gyles's body, however, remained stubbornly visible, a physical reminder of the plight of outcast women.

After the turn of the century, the task of caring for Gyles was handed over to a new generation of writers and bohemians, many of whom were drawn to Gyles's associations with the late-Victorian past yet repelled by the physical evidence of her age. In 1908, for example, Compton Mackenzie invited Gyles to stay with him and his wife, Faith, in Cornwall. Mackenzie's interest in the legacy of the 1890s is evident in his *Sinister Street* (1913–14), an Oxford novel that looks back to the Decadence of the fin de siècle, and he seemed to find Gyles intriguing on the grounds of her connections to that period. He is careful to note in his autobiography, *My Life and Times*, that Wilde admired her work and that she collaborated with Yeats. She was a living link to a most fascinating past moment. However, contact with the physical remains of that past was not as delightful as he might have hoped. His response to the sight of her on the train platform once she accepted his invitation resonates with disgust: "My immediate thought was that we had made a mistake in bringing her to Cornwall. She looked rather like a part of the decorations of a harvest festival which had been caught up unwittingly by one of the congregation and dragged outside."[141] He shuddered at the sight of her dress, which "hung upon her, not in graceful folds as it should, but in the depressions one may see in a field of hay-grass beaten down by heavy rains."[142] Although he notes that she was at the time "just forty," he also makes a point of stressing that "her cheeks, no doubt once rosy and bloomed with youth, were now pale; her hair, no doubt once autumn-gold, was now as dead as a faded rug; her pale blue eyes lacked lustre."[143] She appears in Mackenzie's narration as an undead corpse from a previous age. He eventually "banished" her from his home, exasperated with what an "intolerable nuisance" she proved to be.[144]

The women writers who encountered Gyles tended to exhibit a bit more reverence for her as well as patience with her eccentricity. Eleanor Farjeon, a member of the Dymock Poets circle, met Gyles in the 1910s. In her memoirs, Farjeon states that Clifford Bax, who was at the time publishing Gyles's poetry in *Orpheus*, told Farjeon, "I think, Eleanor, you should know Althea Gyles."[145] "What he told me," she states, "enlisted my sympathy and interest."[146] She went to visit Gyles in a "slum called Paradise, mounted a stair in a wretched house," and found her "sitting up in a rumpled bed in surroundings of unspeakable filth and disorder," "plates with last week's cutlets congealed on them, and other things one dared not investigate."[147] Gyles waved her forward "with the most exquisite hands [she had] ever seen, and the dirtiest."[148] While Farjeon, like Mackenzie, notes the more troubling elements of Gyles's appearance, her "witch-like" looks, her "mottled cheeks," she also writes that "there was a touch of humorous inspiration in the stream of chatter she let loose in her piping voice," and "she fascinated while she stirred compassion."[149] Farjeon was not immediately repulsed by Gyles's need. She fulfilled her commands, settled her feuds, took up her "cudgels."[150] She read her writing, typed her "charming fairy tales," and bought paintings from her. In return, Gyles served as a medium to the Yellow Nineties. According to Farjeon, their meetings were suffused with the aura of the fin de siècle. As they sat together and drank coffee that Gyles brewed "in a cracked jug with her perfect Botticellean hands," "she told tales of Oscar in Paris."[151] Wilde, in fact, seemed to oversee the proceedings: "A silver-framed photograph of him, his picturesque head rising out of a fur-collared coat, stood among the combings on her dressing table."[152] Farjeon acknowledges that she was drawn in by Gyles's post-Victorian Decadent "chatter about Aubrey and Bosie and Oscar (whom she adored)."[153] In her account, Gyles is at once romantic and pathetic, a figure with a wildly glamorous past and an intensely disappointing fate. Gyles's romantic appeal, however, Farjeon states, could be "one's undoing": "One ought to have fled at sight, for Althea Gyles was an Old Woman of the Sea. Sooner or later one had to shake her off one's shoulders."[154] Her mother begged her to discontinue assisting Gyles, but she continued to try to help her from a distance. She attempted to place her new works in journals such as *Form*, but she eventually concluded that "'Poor Old Althea' was too long out of date."[155] Farjeon herself led a somewhat unconventional life, carrying on long-term relationships with men she never married and writing two sets of sonnets for married men for whom she felt affection, and this must have contributed to her understanding of and compassion for Gyles's position. The demands "Althea Gyles of the Nineties" placed upon her were nevertheless finally too draining, and Gyles's anachronism became impossible rather than charming.

Faith Compton Mackenzie's attraction to Gyles seems to have arisen from a similar interest in her rebellion. Like Farjeon, Mackenzie led an unconventional life. According to her memoirs, she, in fact, made a vow to "run away from convention."[156] She worked for a time as an actress, traveling to New York and living in various boardinghouses in London. During this period, she lived in a flat with Mabel Beardsley, who was "still wearing black for Aubrey" and seemed "scarcely of this earth."[157] She met Compton Mackenzie in her brother's rooms at Oxford, and they married soon after in a secret ceremony with a road-sweeper as a witness. She credits her time on the stage as the "foundation for the peculiar structure of [her] future life": "I knew from the first that I didn't want a nice conventional marriage, and I was justifiably sure I had avoided this."[158] The two seem to have been content at first. However, when Compton left Faith alone in Capri during the war, she began an affair with Nini

Caracciolo, who was half her age, and became pregnant. She induced a miscarriage and consequently sank into depression. When Compton returned, she attempted to cut off relations with Caracciolo, and he waited outside in the cold hoping for a sight of her, fell ill, and died. Compton suffered acutely during the following weeks as he was forced to attend the funeral and watch Faith mourn.[159] In his autobiography, Compton states that the Swedish physician and psychiatrist Axel Munthe visited them at the time and made the following suggestion: "Why don't you both admit that marriage in the conventional sense is no longer possible? Why don't you give freedom to each to live his or her own life and yet agree to live together in friendship as man and wife?"[160] After some discussion, Faith agreed. The arrangement does seem to have been trying at times for Faith, but they operated according to this agreement until Faith passed away in 1960.

Faith composed three volumes of memoirs, *As Much As I Dare* (1938), *More Than I Should* (1940), and *Always Afternoon* (1943), and in each she carefully veils from view the troubles of her marriage. While the difficulties are implicitly acknowledged in the chapters detailing their lengthy separations, she tends on the whole to use only the most positive terms to describe Compton. However, she finally managed to articulate a critique of their marriage in a novel devoted to the topic of Althea Gyles. *Tatting* (1957) focuses on their early days in Cornwall, when Gyles stayed with the couple and Compton worked as a lay reader preaching in the local parishes. Compton was a writer when Faith first met him, and his decision to pursue work in the church came as something of a surprise. In her memoirs, she claims that she responded blithely to Compton's career change: "Should I after all be a clergyman's wife? . . . This totally unexpected development in Monty stunned me at first. But I decided that whether he were a priest or not he would always make life amusing."[161] In *Tatting*, conversely, her heroine, Laura, can be more frank about the fact that she had decided at an early age that she was decisively opposed to marrying into the church: "She had even 'gone on the stage' to avoid the possibility. . . . Laura desired to see the world, to avoid church work that would as obviously be her fate as the curate who would inevitably fall in love with her."[162] Her skeptical perception of her husband Guy's growing commitment to his parish duties, including the founding of a Sunday school, is intermingled with her apprehensions concerning reproduction: "Laura would muse as she watched [Guy pass with a child clinging to each hand], this was not propaganda, but obviously a delight in children that he was at last able to indulge. He will love youth to the end of his days and he will want a big family. This was a stunning thought. It's not what I want."[163] Laura's unease with Guy's new commitments is further acknowledged in a discussion with Ariadne Berden, an aging woman artist who is very clearly modeled on Althea Gyles. When Ariadne hears of Guy's new vocation, she is horrified and inquires if he had even told Laura of his faith before she married him. Laura must admit that he mentioned nothing during their short period of engagement. She is then candid with Ariadne, admitting, "I don't look forward to that sort of life. In fact, I thought I had avoided it."[164] It is in conversation with Ariadne that Laura is able to be truly honest about her concerns and fears about her marriage. Contact with a woman like Ariadne facilitates her capacity for critique.

The critique of gender politics is voiced subtly in *Tatting*, through Laura's timid criticisms of Guy and her more open acknowledgment of the cruelty of Ariadne's fate. Faith, like Farjeon, seems to have responded to Gyles with interest and compassion, and, in her final years, she seems to have found it fruitful to think through questions of gender and injustice by returning to a moment decades ago when she was confronted with an aging woman, disdained and discarded. Gyles functions for her as an illuminating instrument, a locus for an interrogation of the persisting inequalities that mar women's lives. While the novel allows that Ariadne is wildly strange, it also expresses a certain admiration for her willfulness as well as regret concerning her fall from grace following an affair with a "drunken scoundrel."[165] As *Tatting* opens, Laura brings groceries to "poor Ariadne," "lying there in that squalid Chelsea room neglected by the famous friends who had admired and praised her work in the 'nineties."[166] Her insistently visible corporeality and mortality are noted, her "blazing feverish eyes, that cavernous mouth, lacking teeth that she could not afford, that wild faded hair."[167] However, the tone of the cataloging of Ariadne's physical defects is markedly different here. She is to Laura an object of sympathy, a body full of wasted potential, slowly deteriorating, abandoned by the hypocritical circle that made much of her a few years earlier: "She had known them all; to her Oscar Wilde was poor Oscar, and when he died she had wept. . . . The small residue of that fascinating company now hardly remembered the existence of the child of promise, Ariadne."[168] Guy, conversely, responds to her appearance in a caustic and cruel manner. He refers to her as a "physical ruin" of "thirty-five if not forty" and speaks derisively of her "scarecrow haggard face."[169] In this novel, written only a few years before she died, Faith dwells with discomfort on a young man's harsh appraisal of an aging woman. Guy's dismissal of Ariadne as a physical ruin has an echo of Hubert's cruel assessment of Winifred once her soul has returned. Faith shared with Gyles an acute sense of the manner in which feminine bodies are evaluated, consumed, and rejected.

While the novel exposes the extent to which the male gaze limits feminine subjectivity, Faith also attends to the role sacrificial ideologies played in Ariadne's/Althea's downfall. Guy wonders whether Ariadne is a fraud and sends a set of inquiries to an old friend, Terence, whose father knew Ariadne when she was younger. The response he receives mimics Yeats's representation of Gyles as one devoted to the concept of self-sacrifice with "Asiatic fanaticism." According to Terence, Ariadne left her wealthy family to go to Dublin because she believed she was "called" to art, and she nearly starved to death in Dublin, refusing offers of advertising work, stating "she would rather die than degrade her art to that extent."[170] Ariadne continues to adhere to such destructive notions in the novel's present, as she "[fades] away in Chelsea, so proud and poor," musing upon her links to the fin de siècle while slowly and almost purposefully starving to death: "She lay on her camp-bed without even her pencil poised, gazing at her precious Beardsley, solitary on the whitewashed wall of her room. Aubrey himself had given it to her. . . . What drawing! What a mind! But oh! She had said that long ago. Now it didn't inspire. Aubrey was dead. Life was surely over. She was tired, she wished someone would do something for her."[171] Though she is "poor, . . . consumptive, starving," she is "still bursting with genius. But too – too tired. She would lie there until somebody came to rescue her."[172] Faith's Ariadne romanticizes the concept of her own passing, aiding and abetting the forces arrayed against her.

Faith, however, chose to alter the outcome of Gyles's story. After staying with Guy and Laura for a period, Ariadne receives a letter from Aunt Grizelda, the only survivor of her family, who has sold the big house and bought a little home in the neighborhood that she wishes to share with Ariadne. Ariadne is transformed by the news. She announces that this will be "a rebirth," that she will "be able to demolish the past."[173] The spectral remnant of the 1890s seems finally capable of entering the present, of disentangling herself from the disappointments she suffered at the fin de siècle and entering into a new age. Faith has revised Gyles's story, transforming it into a fantasy of wrongs righted, of an outcast woman reclaimed and reborn.

If an aunt ever did contact Gyles, the assistance she offered must have been temporary, for in the 1930s Eleanor Farjeon received a "sudden wild letter" from her in Brixton asking her to "come at once and rout some lodgers in the house against whom she had some incoherent grievance."[174] When Farjeon arrived, she found her "living in a Brixton basement in the same awful state as [she] had first found her in Chelsea" with a "big mongrel dog."[175] According to Ian Fletcher, she "refused all offers" of assistance from her family in her later years.[176] Her last address was 19 Tredown Road, Lewishman, where, Warwick Gould writes, "she lived in a room empty but for a chaise lounge, some bric-à-brac, and the manuscripts now in the University of Reading."[177] She died, her martyrdom complete, in a nursing home near the Crystal Palace in 1949.

While many of the post-Victorian Decadents on whom I focus in this project inspired in the young men and women of the twentieth century reverence, respect, at times even awe, Gyles operates in the work of early-twentieth-century women writers as an object of sympathy and concern and a figure for the extent to which the Yellow Nineties disappointed the men and women who had been promised a new age. She was in their eyes an abandoned casualty, exploited and discarded, a martyr who refused to die yet continued to suffer for a cause that would seemingly never be won. She serves here as a representative of post-Victorian Decadence's less pleasing legacies. The strain of Decadence to which she responded, a Yeatsian and somewhat Wildean strain that venerated sacrificial ideals, showed its destructive potential during the post-Victorian period of Gyles's career, rendering her susceptible to the passion for violence that circulated during the First World War, facilitating her construction of herself as a martyr for the cause of women's sexual freedom. The fallout of her entanglements with Irish Decadence indicates much about the darker side of fin-de-siècle utopianisms, the lust for violence these utopianisms often engendered, and the radical optimism they enabled, allowing vulnerable subjects to surrender themselves to political projects whose success was far from certain.

CHAPTER 5

Crusading Decadent

Beresford Egan, Global Dandyism, and Post-Victorian Decadent Feminism

A review of Beresford Egan's illustrated work *De Sade* (1929) published in the Philadelphia *Sunday Dispatch* notes that the markedly strange images in the text seem at the same time somewhat familiar: "Beardsley . . . gave to the world of the 'nineties a curious macabre quality in decorative illustration that stamped his work with extraordinary distinction. Mr. Egan has the same uncanny technical mastery of the single line, the same deft sense of balance between blacks and whites, the same elfin and elusive flights of fancy."[1] The reviewer also notes that Egan shares Beardsley's "gift for making his effects at once arresting and repellent."[2] His drawings are, according to the reviewer, "informed by a considerable dexterity in the use of a devastating order of irony," and, with his "subtle and saturnine and sardonic" manner, "he will recall to old-timers that young band of decadents and poseurs that made *The Yellow Book* back in the 'nineties and will recall with peculiar vividness the work of that unforgettable genius, Beardsley."[3]

While the reviewer insists that the illustrations are "bold" and "original," he also makes it clear that they might be categorized as pastiche.[4] They "recall" the work of the fin de siècle, of the Decadents of the Yellow Nineties. While Egan often railed against the comparison of his work to Beardsley's, arguing that Beardsley was a pen draftsman and his own use of a brush generated work of a fundamentally different order, the fact remains that he purposefully cultivated a Decadent persona, affiliating himself explicitly with Wilde and reviving Beardsley's style, and he peppered his works with nods to the Yellow Nineties. An Eganesque character in his novel *But the Sinners Triumph* (1934), for example, is described in the following manner: "An elegant, elongated young man, with a penchant for gold-tipped cigarettes and gaudy neckwear. He changes his raiment four times a day and never sits down more than he can help for fear of de-creasing his trousers. . . . When he talks, which is often and at great length, he puts one in mind of Oscar Wilde."[5] The illustrations for his novels and pamphlets often echoed and parodically repeated Beardsley's illustrations for *Salome*. He looked like Dorian Gray. He drew like Aubrey Beardsley. He talked like Oscar Wilde. More importantly, he drew from the works of his late-Victorian precursors what the reviewer for the *Sunday Dispatch* refers to as a "devastating order of irony," a Decadent brand of dandyish detachment that allowed him to remain aloof from yet critically engaged with England's cultural and political climate in the late 1920s and early 1930s. He brought Wildean wit and Beardsleyesque satire to bear upon the policing of gender roles during the interwar period and the suppression of "subversive" culture by the Obscene Publications Act. In linking himself with Wilde and Beardsley, he established himself as part of a transhistorical network of sexual dissidents, and his connections to this network and the particular set of aesthetic strategies with which the Decadent Movement is associated, including camp, parody, detachment, and erotic excess, allowed him to maintain a skeptical distance from an unsatisfactory present and generate an imagined alternative to the cultural restrictions of the early twentieth century.

In this chapter, I situate Egan's Beardsleyesque caricatures from the 1920s and 1930s within the political atmosphere of interwar England. It is often argued that England retreated into a fervidly middle-class, nostalgically regional form of isolated and conservative domesticity, "insular 'village England,'" following World War I.[6] Beresford Egan drew upon the tropes of Victorian Decadence to contest the reactionary sexual and gender politics of the interwar period. His illustrations for *The Sink of Solitude* (1928) (a satire of the controversy surrounding the publication of Radclyffe Hall's *The Well of Loneliness*) and *The Policeman of the Lord* (1929) (a satire of Home Secretary William Joynson-Hicks's campaign against obscene art, communists, and nightclubs) rely on Beardsley's model of extravagant perversity and parody to satirize desperate efforts to regulate the moral and sexual purity of the nation. Egan's illustrated novels, such as *Pollen* (1933) and *But the Sinners Triumph*, continue the subversive project of these earlier works by celebrating sexually adventurous female dandies. Egan's perverse illustrations for these texts recall the Decadents' use of pornographic excess to bait and (ideally) transform the Victorian middle class. Decadent models were crucial to Egan as he generated an alternative to the reactionary conservatism of the interwar period. Egan's post-Victorian Decadence was, however, inflected in significant ways by his national identity and by his marriage. This chapter places special emphasis on the role that Egan's childhood in South Africa and his marriage to his first wife, Caterina

Bower Alcock, played in his development of a uniquely transnational and feminist Decadent aesthetic.

Egan's capacity for detachment seems to have been compounded by his upbringing in South Africa. His intimate ties with another nation inhibited his ability and his desire to fully identify as English, and this cosmopolitan sensibility engendered a particularly detached brand of devastating irony. Coolly separate and apart from any one form of national identification, Egan remained skeptical of interwar discourses that tied sexual purity to national security and repeatedly intervened in conversations concerning sexual ideology in order to satirize gender policing conducted in the name of England. His hybrid national identity facilitated a uniquely detached and skeptical perception of nationalist sexual and gender ideologies during the interwar period.

Egan's fascinating collaboration with his wife, Caterina Bower Alcock, further inflected his understanding of gender politics. Alcock's feminism and her innovative thinking on the topic of same-sex desire had a profound influence on Egan's developing understanding of gender and sexual identity. The work he produced in cooperation with her and in the immediate aftermath of their relationship engages with modern discourses concerning "sexual inversion" in a highly original and sophisticated fashion.[7] Although the ambivalent gender politics of Egan's Decadent influences register very clearly in his works of the 1920s and 1930s, he also exhibits the capacity to exceed these models in his treatment of feminine sexuality and desire, an ability that I associate in this chapter with the persistent impact of Alcock on his thinking. In the years following their brief marriage, Egan wrote a series of texts that chronicle the evolution of a female dandy, a coolly detached feminine figure who emerges victorious over her every masculine adversary and the paralyzing effects of wartime trauma. In generating this striking figure, Egan demonstrated the capacity to build on yet move beyond his Decadent models in his thinking about femininity.

Beresford Egan is responsible for some of the most interesting and conflicted representations of femininity and same-sex desire produced during the interwar period. His work has, however, received almost no critical attention. The notable exception is *The Sink of Solitude*, which is mentioned frequently in criticism concerning *The Well of Loneliness* (1928).[8] The fact that critics have found *The Sink* so interesting is not surprising. In engaging with Hall, Egan enters into a conversation concerning "sexual inversion," and his satiric response to the novel offers unique insight into popular thinking concerning same-sex desire in the 1920s. However, critical understanding of interwar discourses concerning gender and sexuality would be rewarded by a more thorough consideration of Egan's larger body of work. The scant scholarship on Egan that does exist neglects the question of his national identity as well as the role Alcock played in the creation of many of his most important works. Much is missed when *The Sink* is read in isolation from Egan's other works and without attentiveness to Egan's cosmopolitanism or the role Alcock played in its composition. In this chapter, I investigate how Egan's transnational sensibility and his oft-overlooked collaboration with a woman writer inflected his peculiar brand of post-Victorian Decadent feminism.

I. Global Decadence and the Transnational Dandy

In a 1932 review of Egan's work, Seton Peacey argues that "Beardsley used continental methods, but his mind was considerably insular: Mr. Egan is continental both in mind and method."[9] Peacey implies that Egan compounds and extends a cosmopolitanism that is not fully formed in the Decadence of the 1890s. In reviving Beardsley's style and inflecting it with a particularly cosmopolitan form of detachment, Egan was able to parodically extend the reach of the subversions performed by Beardsley and Wilde. In her recent work on the global circulation of Decadence, Regenia Gagnier has encouraged us to attend to the manner in which Decadent principles were transformed and revised as they moved around the world.[10] To do this kind of work, we have to be willing to think outside conventional categories of periodization and be attentive to the manner in which Decadence persisted beyond the turn of the century as it was received, revised, and practiced by authors and artists across the globe. Egan operates here as a particularly rich case study in the transnational as well as transhistorical life of Decadent ideals, revealing that the Yellow Nineties thrived beyond the borders of the Victorian period and outside the boundaries of England. Attentiveness to Decadent networks in the twentieth century, when Decadence left Britain and circulated the globe, allows us to see how this aesthetic impacted imperial subjects and informed their practices and, in Egan's case, to understand how a globalized post-Victorian Decadent aesthetic functioned in cultural and political debates within the metropole. When late-Victorian Decadence is no longer understood as a purely Victorian or even a purely British phenomenon, we are able to see much more of its global and temporal reach and perceive the cultural work it continued to perform in the twentieth century as it traveled from London to Johannesburg and back again.

Egan was born in London, but before he was ten years old he had sailed with his family three times between England and South Africa. His family lived in Durban and Cape Town and then settled in Johannesburg, where Egan remained until his twenty-first birthday. The *Companion to South African Cartoonists* stresses the extent to which this extensive international travel engendered in Egan a highly cosmopolitan sensibility, noting that "these experiences broadened his view and made him conscious of the expanse of the world."[11] Although he did at times refer to himself as British, he just as often exhibited a suspicion of English patriotism and nationalism, and he was frequently quite withering about the place of his birth. He occupied during the 1920s and 1930s a liminal position first as a restless transplant to South Africa and then as a recent immigrant to England, a hybrid figure with his feet in two places.

The hybridity of Egan's aesthetic, however, extends beyond the boundaries of the two nations that might claim him as a citizen. In his autobiographical *Epitaph* (1943), Egan describes the moment when his "tastes took an upward curve" as he first began to forge transhistorical networks with the sexual dissidents of the nineteenth century.[12] He was working as a sports cartoonist at the *Rand Daily Mail* in Johannesburg when he discovered Félicien Rops, Hokusai, and Baudelaire and his "whole conception of Art was turned inside out."[13] This is, of course, a highly diverse set of national influences, drawing from Belgian, Japanese, and French sources, and Egan explicitly describes his interaction with these works as a form of global exploration. The avenue they opened to him felt incredibly vast, and though he was "momentarily hesitant," he was also "unafraid" and forged ahead: "What is the use of making a discovery if one turns one's back on it, as did the Portuguese shortly after the flukey voyage of Bartholomew Diaz around the Cape of Good Hope? Unlike the Portuguese, I proposed to follow up on my happy accident. I was going to use the 'Cape' of Félicien Rops as a permanent base on my voyage to the 'India' of plastic thought. Hokusai and Baudelaire, aided and abetted by Wilde and Rowlandson, were to be my pilots."[14] Egan's mode of Decadence was from the first, then, a highly cosmopolitan and transhistorical aesthetic, a network of affiliation that violated temporal and national boundaries, cobbled together from the French poetry, Japanese illustrations, and British epigrams of the previous century, a set of sympathies that allowed him to imagine himself out of the restrictions of the imperial periphery he occupied and, once he found his way to the metropole, remain skeptically distant from twentieth-century English patriotism, jingoism, and gender ideology.

Rops, Hokusai, Wilde, and Baudelaire, in "[turning] inside out" his "whole conception of Art," seemed to have simultaneously opened up alternative possibilities for identity formation, engendering in Egan a skepticism concerning conventional modes of masculinity. In *Epitaph*, he casts himself as one rescued from a highly gendered imperial periphery by cosmopolitan forms of Decadent masculinity, noting that Baudelaire "came to [him] as a cry in the wilderness of muscular christianity."[15] During his final years in Johannesburg, he cultivated a dandyish persona, designed to shock the attendants of the city's sports events. He wore "lavender suits, suede shoes, Churchillian hats and a gold-rimmed monocle."[16] He was "overdressed, ambitious and – dissatisfied," exhausted with the "unprogressive" task of "[following] the fortunes of muscular Christians."[17] Playing the part of the dandy, performing his taste, elitism, and detachment from his immediate surroundings, intensified his exasperation with Johannesburg's sporting community, and the transnational network Egan forged with his Decadent precursors presented him with a temporally and nationally hybrid alternative to the masculine models surrounding him.

The influence of Hokusai, Rops, and eventually Beardsley also altered the style in which Egan imagined the human face and body. The cartoons he drew for the *Rand Daily Mail* never depart very far from the fashion of the day. The caricatured figures possess enormous heads and tiny bodies. The representation of each face typically relies on the exaggeration of a single feature. Soon after his arrival in London, he began searching "musty bookshops for Beardsleyana with some success," and, as a result, as Adrian Woodhouse notes, he began "[developing] a luxuriant style of brush-work and subject-matter that looked back a generation to the 'Yellow' 1890s."[18] The newly sinister style engendered by his contact with Decadent influences abounds in detail, revels in the curves of lithesome frames, and troubles and threatens with ominous figures who confront the viewer with smoldering glares. The faces are at once hard and soft, angular and curved, alluring and threatening. The bodies are, as the *Sunday Dispatch* reviewer put it, "arresting and repellant."

Egan's network of affiliation with the Decadent past, his new manner, also seemed to allow him to reimagine the way he represented race. In his work at the *Rand Daily Mail*, he represented black South Africans in drastically caricatured, simian terms (Figure 5.1). After arriving in London, however, he began working on an ad campaign for the South African tourist board, completing a series of full-page advertisements that appeared in *Country Life*. These images are a striking departure from the cartoons that appeared in the *Rand Daily Mail*. They center on imposing,

Figure 5.1. Beresford Egan, "Safety First," *Rand Daily Mail*, September 23, 1925, 5. © Estate of Beresford Egan. Reproduced courtesy of the National Library of South Africa.

visually arresting forms. The features remain racialized, but the figures are also aestheticized in the style of Beardsley with a hint of Art Deco and an element of modernism's mode of primitivism (Figure 5.2). This is not to say that these images operate outside the logic of imperialism, but they do engage with a different set of racial codes drawn from a diverse set of late-Victorian and modernist influences, a network of modern and transnational thinking concerning the aesthetics of representing race. This code, this aesthetic, has its own set of limitations, certainly, but it should be noted that contact with this network broadened Egan's capacity for imagining racial otherness, elevating it from the contemptuous caricaturing that he conducted for the *Rand Daily Mail*. Beardsley's interest in androgyny has also been imported, inflecting these images with an aura of erotic intimidation. Exposed breasts curve beside muscular arms, much as delicate arms clash with hairy, masculine knees in Beardsley's illustrations for *Salome*.

Figure 5.2. Beresford Egan, detail from advertisement for South African Tourism Board, *Country Life*, October 6, 1928. © Estate of Beresford Egan.

Blackness is no longer a source of comedy or an object of derision. The subjects of Egan's South African tourism advertisements loom like Salome in voluminous draped clothing and contradictory gender signs, a source of sexual fascination and a certain degree of fear. Egan's South African tourism ads serve as a powerful example of the fascinating transformations Decadence underwent as it circulated globally in the twentieth century.

Contact with Decadence had an expansive impact on Egan's aesthetic in almost every way. It was, however, the Decadent interest in androgyny and gender trouble that seemed to have been most influential for him as he reimagined the face and the body in Yellow Nineties terms. For the sports cartoonist from Johannesburg, the Decadents' shockingly playful treatments of gender offered a method for conceiving of identity in a far more elastic manner. Egan was in his work of the late 1920s drawn persistently to images of effeminate, dandyish men and "inverted" women. Forging an aesthetic network of affiliation with French and English men of the latter half of the nineteenth century allowed Egan to imagine himself outside the boundaries of muscular Christianity and to envision the field of gender as a realm of ever-shifting inversions. According to Woodhouse, when Egan first arrived in London, he drew black-and-white illustrations for *The Picture of Dorian Gray*, and he dreamed of illustrating the works of Baudelaire, continuing to engage with the Decadent influences that lured him from his home.[19] The complexity of his treatment of sexual and gender identities was, however, further amplified during the next period of his career when he began to collaborate with a woman writer.

II. The Satirists: Interwar Sexual Politics and the Collaborative Work of Beresford Egan and C. Bower Alcock

Egan's best-known work, *The Sink of Solitude*, satirizes the scandal surrounding the publication of Radclyffe Hall's *The Well of Loneliness*. Egan's elaborate illustrations for *The Sink* subject the entire affair to a Beardsleyesque parodic treatment, and the work as a whole derides the efforts of Home Secretary William Joynson-Hicks to suppress the novel and cast the issue as a matter of national security. Egan's perception of the scandal was certainly inflected by his hybrid national status and the global set of aesthetic affiliations he established in the 1920s. The transhistorical and transnational networks Egan forged with Beardsley, Hokusai, Rops, Wilde, and Baudelaire, along with his own status as a national outsider, pulled him back and away from the kinds of patriotism and temporal rootedness that might have made him more likely to be swept up in contemporary national or moral enthusiasms, allowing him to intervene in a hysterical conversation concerning the national threat posed by gender and sexual transgressions with a devastating order of Decadent irony. The skeptical and cosmopolitan post-Victorian Decadent could look with detachment on the policing of gender and sexuality conducted in the name of England and perceive its foolishness as well as its malice.

However, as much as Egan's complex national affiliations informed his vision of sexual and gender politics in the 1920s, his capacity for critical thinking concerning these topics seems to have been expanded by his collaboration with his wife, Caterina Bower Alcock, an Oxford graduate whom he met soon after arriving in London. The relationship operated according to a progressive ethos of collaboration, with the two working as equal intellects and aesthetic producers. A colophon that appeared on the title page of their *Policeman of the Lord*, which they also used as letterhead in the late 1920s, highlights their comradeship and cooperation, showing them twinned in dark defiance (Figure 5.3). The manner in which Alcock's vision inflects works like *The Sink of Solitude* has gone almost wholly unnoted. Her name does not appear on the title page of many of their collaborations, so her role as collaborator has escaped critical attention. Acknowledging Alcock's part in these productions allows for a more nuanced reading of their strange gender and sexual politics to emerge. Whereas critics such as Ellen Rosenman and Laura Behling have read *The Sink of Solitude*, for example, as hostile to or entirely satirical in its treatment of Hall and her work, I argue that this pamphlet and the later works produced by Alcock and Egan represent a much more ambivalent and complex response to the shifting field of gender and sexual identities during the interwar period.[20] Although these works do not entirely endorse "sexual inversion," they do articulate a thoroughgoing dismissal of repression and the attempt to discipline and inhibit the expression of desire. Alcock's feminism inflects the dandyish spirit of these works and nuances their treatment of sexual and gender identity. In this 1920s collaboration, we get a vision of what it might have been like had the Decadent and the New Woman entered into cooperation with one another, had George Egerton and Beardsley coauthored political pamphlets.

The Sink treats the scandal surrounding Jonathan Cape's publication of Radclyffe Hall's *The Well of Loneliness* as fundamentally laughable and ridiculous. A few weeks after the novel first appeared, the editor of the *Sunday Express*, James Douglas, called on Home Secretary William Joynson-Hicks to suppress a text that threatened to spread the "leprosy" of "sexual inversion and perversion."[21] The intensely conservative Joynson-Hicks,

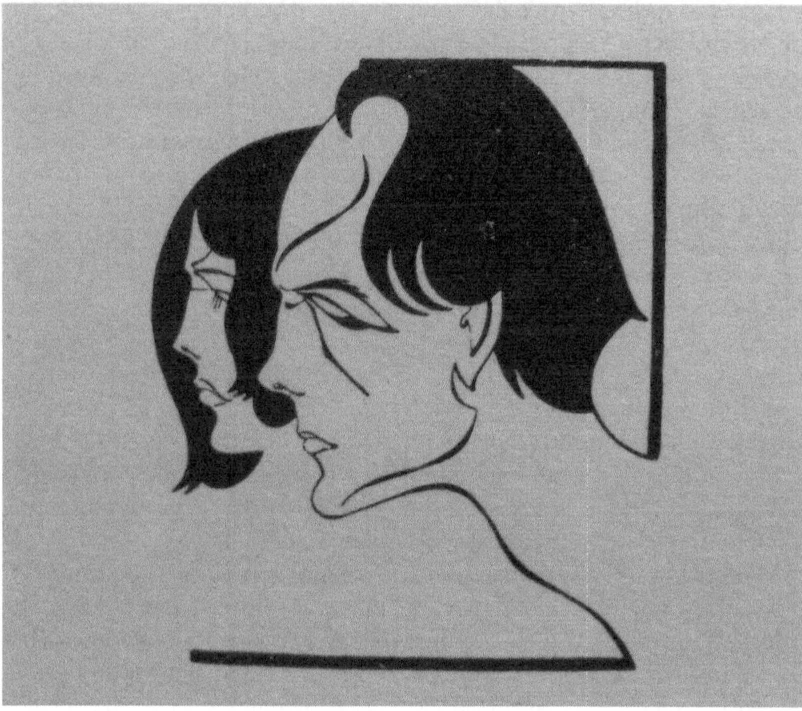

Figure 5.3. Beresford Egan, colophon from title page of *The Policeman of the Lord*, 1929. © Estate of Beresford Egan.

commonly referred to as "Jix," instructed Cape to withdraw the book from circulation, but Cape instead chose to continue printing the novel in Paris. Imported copies were seized, and the novel was prosecuted under the Obscene Publications Act. Egan and Alcock, along with their friend P. R. Stephensen, an Australian author and publisher, collaborated in the creation of an illustrated verse satire of the entire affair, which was published clothed in yellow paper "redolent of the Yellow Book of the 1890s."[22] Vera Brittain described the pamphlet as "a blow struck for liberty in the true Areopagitican tradition."[23] Nothing is immune to the work's consuming parodic energy. A product of collaboration between a transnational trio of detached dandies, an Australian writer, a South African illustrator, and his English wife, the modern broadside exhibits contempt for English prudishness and nationalist ideas concerning gender purity. Stephensen's preface warns that "newspapers are doping the coupon-clipping soul of England into imbecility," and the verse asserts that "English intellects have gone to seed."[24] "Merciless lampooning," Stephensen insists, "is the only defense against this kind of thick-headedness and humorlessness."[25] Egan's illustrations and the accompanying verse, which was composed by Stephensen, Egan, and Alcock, are quite merciless in their attacks on the self-selected defenders of English purity.[26] The drawings represent Jix as a simian fool. The verse derides Douglas's moral indignation: "Then at last JAMES DOUGLAS sees the work; — / . . . He girds his loins (if any) for the right / Exclaiming 'Onward-Christians-to-the-fight!' / Depress! Repress! Suppress! (Sunday Express)."[27] The poem focuses in particular on Jix and Douglas's belief in their patriotic responsibility to protect the innocence of the nation: "Two men now burst with holy indignation / To save the morals of the British nation. / . . . *Two* men can keep the British Empire clean."[28] The verse is rife with Wildean references, noting, for example, that "RADCLYFFE poisoned JIMMY with a book!," linking the events of 1928 to those of 1895 and thus equating Jix and Douglas with the persecutors of Wilde. The Home Secretary becomes here part of a larger tradition of sanctimonious cruelty and gender policing.

While the work was meant primarily to savage the self-righteousness of Jix and Douglas, Egan's merciless drawings also wounded Hall. In a mockery of Hall's earnest attempt to communicate the agony of the "female invert," Hall is represented in *The Sink*'s best known and most frequently reproduced illustration, *St. Stephen*, hanging from a cross. Hall's partner, Una Troubridge, notes in her memoirs that this "vile, obscene, and blasphemous caricature . . . caused [Hall] such deep spiritual pain that throughout the remaining years of her life she could scarcely bear to speak of it."[29] Egan's illustrations for *The Sink* express a certain degree of suspicion concerning the concept of sexual inversion in women. In *Similia Similibus*, for example, the inverted woman is exhibited in a much less flattering light than is the effeminate dandy on whom she gazes (Figure 5.4). According to Michael Baker, who corresponded with Egan while composing a biography of Hall, "Egan took the view that the anguished tone of *The Well* was totally unjustified given that lesbians, unlike male homosexuals, could not be charged with a criminal offence. But this seems to have been a rationalization of a more personal reaction, for he had once pushed to the ground a woman who made amorous advances to his wife. When she protested she was a woman, Egan countered: 'Why do you try to be like a man then?'"[30] The concept of the "inverted woman" seems to have troubled Egan. In her reading of the images in *The Sink*, Martha Vicinus notes that Egan takes particular pleasure in mocking the large breasts of masculine women, "reminding his largely male viewers that nothing could

Figure 5.4. Beresford Egan, *Similia Similibus*, from *The Sink of Solitude*, 1928. © Estate of Beresford Egan.

turn these women into true men."[31] It must be acknowledged that the illustrations do demonstrate a certain degree of hostility toward Hall and the types of desire and identity she represents. It is first and foremost those who condemned Hall who are castigated, but Egan is also cruel to Hall herself and to what Stephensen describes in his preface as the "postwar lesbians" and their "pathetic... mannish modes and poses."[32]

The work cannot simply be read, however, as a condemnation of same-sex desire. Its primary project remains the castigation of censorship and repression. The work is strange and conflicted, but it cannot be properly described as emerging from a conservative ethos. Its authors have chosen to concern themselves with Hall's freedom to represent same-sex desire, and they reserve their most unmitigated contempt for those persecuting the author. Though Egan's drawings do appear troubled by the notion of female masculinity, many of his works from this period simultaneously reflect a curiosity about and attraction to the concept of same-sex desire. According to Adrian Woodhouse, the image *Courtesan* (1930) pictures a Chelsea lesbian who made advances to Alcock (Figure 5.5). The heavy-lidded woman with her exposed breast seems to at once thrill and repel the artist as she reaches with threatening claws beyond the boundaries of the frame. In this, Egan's drawings of "inverted women" much resemble the works they so reverently pastiche, Beardsley's illustrations for *Salome*. The reviewer for *G. K.'s Weekly* notes the resemblance, asserting that in their desire to shock, the illustrations "[make] us cry 'The Beardsley touch!'"[33] However, it is not simply a stylistic resemblance or a similarly taunting relationship to audience that ties the two illustrators together. Beardsley's illustrations and Egan's menace the viewer with images of transgressive femininity while at the same time expressing a certain level of hysteria about the power of the castrating or masculine woman. This ambivalence about feminine sexual agency was common at the turn of the century. As Judith Walkowitz notes, fin-de-siècle male writers like Karl Pearson might "[champion] the sexual choices of the advanced New Woman in the abstract" while being "terrified and disoriented by any signs of female sexual agency in the flesh."[34] This conflict operates at the heart of Decadent art and literature. However, Beardsley's parodic response to the concept of female sexual agency, like Egan's, seems particularly split in its intentions and effects, at once and equally lampooning and further disseminating a new vision of feminine sexuality. As Dennis Denisoff argues in his discussion of sexual parody, parody does not always try to eradicate its object. Parodists are often wrestling with and engaging with the object of parody,

Figure 5.5. Beresford Egan, *Courtesan*, 1930. Private collection of Adrian Woodhouse. © Estate of Beresford Egan.

and their work often serves to further circulate and even promote the parodied object or concept.[35] Beardsley's work expresses uncertainty about as well as fascination with dissident forms of femininity, revealing a certain degree of dread about the threat that these women pose while forcing the British public into confrontation with shifting gender norms. Egan's pastiche of Beardsley allows him to signal a similar kind of ambivalence about the redrawing of the map of gender and sexual difference and to participate in that revision while sounding a note of anxiety about its implications.

Recent criticism on *The Well of Loneliness* and its parodies has endeavored to distinguish between *The Sink*'s attitudes toward Hall in particular and same-sex desire more generally. Laura Doan, for example, has argued that Egan's aversion to Hall arose primarily from suspicion of "the structure of Hall's ideology of Sapphic liberation."[36] Doan insists that, by drawing visual links between Hall and Jix, Egan implies that, in its "penchant for self-sacrifice, the righteous indignation, the zealousness of the true believer," Hall's vision of same-sex desire "resonated with a religious fervor similar to that embraced by her so-called attackers, and was thus incompatible with Sapphic modernity, which is of different stuff altogether."[37] According to Doan, "beneath Hall's highly fashionable 'look,' Egan discerned a conservatism that left her unsuited to become the earthly incarnation of the Sapphic spirit toward which, it would seem, he had no particular animosity."[38]

Egan's illustrations do seem to delineate a distinction between female masculinity and Sapphism. As Doan notes, the parodists represent Sappho herself in glowing terms. She emerges in the illustrations as the representative of a much more acceptable model of female same-sex desire. Although turn-of-the-century sexological discourse often equated same-sex desire with gender inversion, Egan separates the two concepts, splitting the "womanly" subject of same-sex desire from the masculine woman, celebrating one while denigrating the other.[39] Egan's Sappho is beautiful, graceful, thin, not at all masculine. She represents an attractive alternative to the enormous and masculine Hall. It is not Sapphism, then, that is made ridiculous. Female masculinity, as opposed to the concept of love between women, is represented by Egan as off-putting.

Other critics, however, have argued that it is earnestness, the anathema to the Decadent posture, that Egan condemned. Margaret Breen states that "Egan lampoons Hall's biblical earnestness," and Richard Dellamora similarly notes that the St. Stephen image "desublimates the novel's erotic earnestness."[40] Breen, Dellamora, and Doan argue that it is earnestness, zealotry, and religiosity that are most mercilessly mistreated by *The Sink*.

The illustrations target, not same-sex desire, but Hall's excessively earnest expression of sexual inversion and its attendant traumas, along with the pious attempts to delimit the expression of any form of desire by the likes of Jix and Douglas.

It is worth noting that very little attention has been paid to the verse that accompanies the illustrations. Knowing that this verse was composed in part by a woman writer, one who would go on to make more aggressively feminist claims and articulate a defense of same-sex desire in the later work *De Sade* (1929), should force us to slow down and take the verse into further consideration. The verse, like the illustrations, aims its primary rage at Hall's persecutors but similarly subjects Hall to a certain degree of critique. As Sonja Ruehl has argued, the lampoonists defend "glorious Sappho . . . [in order to] dismiss Hall by contrast as mundane, trivial and trite on the grounds of literary merit alone."[41] Hall writes, they state, with the inspiration of a "mundane muse."[42] Her works can only offend "souls suburban."[43] Sappho, conversely, "[burns] with a peculiar flame."[44] She writes "beauty obscenely sweetly amorous."[45] Ruehl insists that, "putting themselves forward as defenders of aesthetic standards," the lampoonists "use this stance to dismiss any serious consideration of lesbianism itself."[46] I would argue, however, that this is not necessarily the case. The verse does privilege Sappho's talent far above Hall's and makes a mockery of the plot of *The Well of Loneliness*, seemingly satirizing the very concept of sexual inversion ("For trousers love she feels, for knickers hate").[47] Yet a stanza devoted to Mary, the partner of the inverted main character, Stephen, indicates a certain degree of sympathy for the plight of inverted women as well as those involved in same-sex relationships: "The world insists that girls shall not be boys," and though "Mary find convention all absurd / She weakens from the pressure from the herd."[48] These lines contain a nascent form of the argument Alcock developed to a much greater extent in *De Sade*, in which she argues that the sadistic herd harasses and disciplines those who depart from the norm in the name of morality while, in fact, satisfying a lust for violence. "The Ballad of Reading Gaol" (1898) is then referenced, reinforcing the sense that this is a story of unnecessary tragedy and persecution:

> Now once upon a time 'twas pointed out
> By someone, who if he were still about
> Would take an interest in the present case,
> That with mankind it is a commonplace
> To find that all men kill the thing they love –
> No doubt he thinks so still, although above.[49]

This subtle signal of sympathy, the placing of Wilde in heaven, the suggestion that he looks with interest on a case with similarities to his own, indicates that the verse does not wish to dismiss love between women. The most painful plot point in the novel, Stephen's sacrifice of Mary to a relationship with a man in the belief that this is the only way she might find true happiness, is spared the satirical tone with which the rest of story is relayed: "She finds a man, and though it spoil her life / MARY shall be a mother and a wife."[50] The indeterminacy of the referent "her" allows the reader to wonder what is more thoroughly spoiled, the lonely existence of Stephen or the life of Mary, who must pass into the monotony of conventional domesticity and reproduction. Far from dismissing same-sex desire, the verse foregrounds the injustice of the persecution of sexual dissidents.

Intervening in a debate about sexual dissidence was an act of political dissidence during this period, an act of resistance to ideologies that linked moral health to national health and posited same-sex desire as a threat to national security. Events such as the "Cult of the Clitoris" trial, discussed in the introduction to this book, made explicit the belief that sexual and moral permissiveness might render the nation vulnerable to threats from abroad. These beliefs persisted during the interwar period and contributed to the controversy surrounding the publication of *The Well of Loneliness*. As Celia Marshik makes clear in her discussion of the censorship of the novel, the suppression of Hall's work was considered by both Jix and Douglas to be an issue of national significance.[51] In his initial angry review, Douglas concedes that the battle for morality has been lost in France and Germany, but he argues "it has not yet been lost in England, and I do not believe that it will be lost."[52] Jix told the Public Morality Council that works like Hall's endangered the nation. Marshik notes that another novel, *The Sleeveless Errand* (1929) by Norah James, was seized the following year, and she connects the suppression of this novel, which links women's promiscuity to the recent war, to the censorship of *The Well*, which represents new sexual freedoms for women as a symptom of their participation in the war effort. Both texts imply that World War I irrevocably transformed female sexuality, and their prosecution indicates that "even a decade after the armistice... Britain's literati were not free to represent the war in particular lights. It was still risky to write certain kinds of fiction about the conflict in the late 1920s; the prosecutions of these novels demonstrate that wartime ideologies and statutes lingered even as the war itself receded into the historical distance."[53]

Egan and Alcock were opposing a moral crusade that was cast by Jix and Douglas as a matter of national security. They were nevertheless relentless

Figure 5.6. Beresford Egan, *John Bull and the Muse*, 1931. © Estate of Beresford Egan.

in their treatment of the scandal as entirely ridiculous and in their insistence that repression in the name of patriotism would not stand. Egan's vision of this type of nationalist moralism emerges most clearly in an illustration completed two years later entitled *John Bull and the Muse* (1931) (Figure 5.6). Egan represents England's moralizing as cruel, vulgar, and violent. John Bull sadistically whips a young woman stripped to the waist after beheading another offender. Egan equates the moral policing of England with vicious brutality. Beauty and sexuality are victimized and bullied into submission, disciplined by a national politics that demands blind obedience. He characterizes moral campaigns in the name of national security as not simply wrongheaded but as malicious and disgusting. When R. A. Caton, the publisher of the Egans' *De Sade*, was prosecuted for obscenity in 1933, one of the original *De Sade* plates, titled *The Moralist*, was deemed offensive. Egan and Caton decided to replace the offending image with *John Bull and the Muse.* However, they preserved the title of the original plate, in effect renaming this image *The Moralist.* The altered title seems all the more appropriate as it is specifically nationalist campaigns for purity, England's moralizing in the name of national security, that Egan and his fellow satirists so vehemently opposed.

The work of this period is unified in its aversion to censorship and repression. Egan, Alcock, and Stephensen continued critiquing nationalist purity campaigns in their follow-up to *The Sink*, *The Policeman of the Lord*, which attacks the home secretary not simply for his crusade against Hall but in addition for his campaigns against nightclubs, communists, and prostitutes. Egan's illustrations for *The Policeman* highlight the rebelliousness of their project. *An Astral Body*, for example, pictures Egan standing beside what Adrian Woodhouse has identified as a "stylized, half-naked representation of Caterina [thumbing] her nose at the Home Secretary."[54] This image may be understood as a figure for the nature of their project as a whole. As Seton Peacey argues, Egan's pictures are "vigorous and necessary indictments of the pruderies of the formative years of this century, and as searchingly moral as the writings of Mr. Havelock Ellis were concerning the pruderies of the later years of the nineteenth century."[55] Alcock makes a similar claim in her discussion of Egan. Much as Peacey emphasizes the "searching morality" of Egan's work, she states that Egan is "a combination of two incompatibles," for he is a "crusading decadent."[56] Because his work exhibits Decadent stylistic characteristics, she argues, it is tempting to simply categorize him as an aesthete, but his work's "greatest claim on the attention lies in the disturbing and incongruous energy of the underlying thought."[57] Far from art for art's sake, Caterina argues, this is work with deep political and ethical commitments. However, the crusade to which Egan is devoted is a quintessentially Decadent one. In battling censorship and Jix's campaigns for purity, he aligns himself with an aestheticist tradition that insists upon art's right to play freely with any content it wishes.

The extent to which Egan and Alcock's parodic response to censorship should be understood as part of a Decadent tradition becomes clear in the preface to the illustrated translation of Baudelaire's *Flowers of Evil* (1929) on which the two collaborated during this period. Alcock, whose name appears on the title page of the text as "C. Bower Alcock," composed both the preface and the translations, and her preface celebrates Baudelaire as "the crystal essence of decadence."[58] Alcock employs Paterian and Swinburnian rhetoric to make a case for Baudelaire's right to speak of whatever he may choose so long as he does so in a beautiful form. She echoes the subjectivist note of Pater's conclusion to *Studies in the History of the Renaissance*, describing the "chill conviction that man can never pierce the veil of his own personality," which, when linked with Baudelaire's aversion to progress and utilitarianism, produces the belief that experience's sole virtue is "a susceptibility to the impress of the mind."[59] This point of view, Caterina asserts, "[comes] to flower in a theory of art untainted by alien considerations of truth and goodness and unshackled by that paralyzing heresy of the didactic."[60] Baudelaire, she concludes, no matter how perverse his outlook may seem, can only be approached as an artist who "held up to literature the loftiest ideal of form."[61] Moral considerations have no place in the analysis of his work. Egan's illustrations for Alcock's translations of the poems drive this point home, aestheticizing love between women and androgyny at a moment when such representations were coming under direct attack. The post-Victorian adoption of Decadent rhetoric plays a crucial role in Alcock's defense of art's freedom to represent all forms of desire. In an echo of Swinburne's essays and Wilde's preface to *Dorian Gray*, the moralizing audience's view of scandalous content is redirected to the beautiful forms through which that content is being relayed.

Of all Egan and Alcock's collaborations, *De Sade: Being a Series of Wounds, Inflicted with Brush and Pen upon Sadistic Wolves Garbed in Masochists' Wool* articulates most explicitly their political vision in the late 1920s, and it relies on the methods of post-Victorian Decadence to generate a response to the ills of the early twentieth century. The text is composed of fifteen illustrations by Egan in a Beardsleyesque style, images of beautiful dandies, menacing villains, and naked female bodies, along with a dark essay by Alcock concerning the nature of the sadistic impulse. Connecting the persecution of same-sex desire, the marriage market, moral policing, and modern warfare, it is a thoroughgoing critique of interwar modernity. The work is described in a prospectus by R. A. Caton of the Fortune Press as "a fearless exposure of a dark fibre of human character and an unsparing dissection of society, laying bare its ramifications throughout the body politic. . . . Lances are shivered against the state, the church and society, as sails of a mill which grinds the grain brought to it into a shapeless mass. . . . The fifteen drawings . . . cover a wide range of manifestations of 'sadism' from the church's sanction of war to the Wilde case."[62] A reviewer from the *Rand Daily Mail* notes the Decadent spirit of the entire production, stating that "Beardsley and Wilde must be turning in their graves at this volume, which is haunted by the ghosts of the naughty nineties."[63] The Egans imported the naughtiness of the 1890s into the 1920s in order to lay bare, with Decadent wit, morbidity, and detachment, the pervasive violence and sickness of the modern moment.

Alcock's sensibility emerges most clearly in this work, in the essay's clear distaste for the prostitution of young women on the marriage market and in the explicit condemnation of the persecution of same-sex desire. The prospectus, in fact, featured Alcock's name on the title page, where she was listed as C. Bower Alcock. This was altered to the pseudonym "Brian De Shane" once the text was issued, as it was decided that the text might be too transgressive to feature a woman's name on the title page. Nevertheless, this is still the work in which she can be seen most clearly. In her essay, Alcock moves from a more abstract discussion of human aggression to a more pointed critique of the oppression of women and sexual minorities. She argues that the sadistic instinct has not been eradicated in the modern age. It has simply found subtler ways to express itself. Sadism has become increasingly "confined to the mental sphere," where it "takes the forms of overt disapproval or ostracism."[64] While this form of cruelty may seem "shadowy and emasculate" as compared to physical torture, war, and execution, Alcock is careful to note that the torment and loneliness resulting from ostracism can be agonizing.[65] It is here that the essay begins to move in the direction of a statement concerning sexual and gender politics. This cruelty, the cruelty of disapproval or ostracism, can, Alcock argues, be enacted by one individual against another, but it tends to be enacted on individuals by the "herd," resulting in the "wanton smutching and destroying of that which is fair and vigorous," known commonly as "morality."[66] This type of sadism has been practiced most often to protect property, more specifically to protect women as property that men might exchange. Because woman is a type of property that might "of its own volition, [stray] out of the dominion of its possessor," a system had to be put in place to curtail this behavior: "Sin was instituted – an ominous spectre of eternal damnation, haunting both man and woman, but especially woman."[67] Christianity, she argues, has been a "powerful weapon in the hands of men against women," as morality has been used as a determinant of feminine value. Women's access to material comforts has been "at once the safeguard and the reward of chastity."[68] The woman who refuses to participate obediently in this system becomes the victim of malice, allowing for the indulgence of the sadistic passion, as she is persecuted by men and women alike. However, she notes, the persecution of "men addicted to love of their own sex" is "even bitterer": "The air is still vibrant with echoes of the Wilde case, in which not all the wealth of that natural endowment of brilliance, versatility, and artistic ability could save their possessor from being hounded to death. Those who were actively alive in 1895 can recall the wave of delighted sadism that surged through this country, where the name of Oscar became a term of scurrilous abuse in the gutter."[69]

Alcock's critiques are strengthened and extended by Egan's Beardsleyeque illustrations. In *Business as Usual*, two ghastly men paw the arms of a beautiful young woman, assessing her value, while an approving matriarch looks on from above. Women, it is implied, function as a form of private property to be passed between monstrous men, and women themselves condone and facilitate this villainy. In *The Pariahs*, three effeminate young men, all of whom seem to resemble Egan himself, gather beside a piano (Figure 5.7). One places his arm upon the other's shoulder and gazes kindly at the other's sorrowful face, while the third figure gazes sadly at the viewer. These are the men Alcock describes as bitterly persecuted, "who form an inner ring in society with a marked guild consciousness and loyalty" due to the "almost masonic" feeling such bitter persecution produces among its objects.[70] In the essays and the illustrations, Decadent masculinity is wedded with feminism, and this strange pair is accompanied by a withering critique of state- and church-sponsored violence, which is pilloried in the illustrations and revealed by the essay to emerge from a twisted impulse towards cruelty.

Alcock left Egan in 1931, though they did not divorce until 1940, when she wished to remarry. While their marriage was brief, much of Egan's most interesting work springs from this period in his career, and Alcock's sensibility continued to inform the work he produced in the 1930s. These works share with *The Sink* and *De Sade* an interest in freedom of expression and same-sex desire as well as an investment in contesting conventional gender ideology. These later works should be understood as an extension of the thinking he began in collaboration with Alcock, the post-Victorian New Woman who brought a feminist sensibility to his post-Victorian Decadence.

Figure 5.7. Beresford Egan, *The Pariahs*, from *De Sade*, 1929. © Estate of Beresford Egan.

III. Post-Victorian Decadent Feminism: Egan, Sapphism, and the Female Dandy

In the work Egan completed on his own in the late 1920s and early 1930s, he continued to engage with the interwar contestation of sexual and gender ideologies while relying on post-Victorian Decadent strategies, a markedly cosmopolitan sensibility, and the inspiration of Alcock's thinking to forge a complex and conflicted response to the sexual politics of the early twentieth century. Egan's conflicted relationship to sexual and gender ideologies emerges clearly in the series of illustrated editions of the works of the French Decadent Pierre Louÿs that he completed for the Fortune Press between 1929 and 1930. Egan populates Louÿs's Decadent stories of ancient Alexandria and his translations of the erotic works of Lucian with dapper modern men whose elongated limbs are hugged closely by their incredibly tight trousers and androgynous women with broad shoulders adorned in flapper bobs. The illustrations are deeply ambivalent, at once erotic and sinister, reflecting a sensibility that seems simultaneously aroused and alarmed by gender trouble. This ambivalence, however, seems to be partially resolved in Egan's illustrated novels *Pollen* and *But the Sinners Triumph*. In these later texts, Egan articulates a Decadent brand of feminism through the radically strange and striking character Anna Beryl Foster. Anna is a female dandy whose sexual adventurousness, same-sex relationships, and detachment are represented by Egan in wholly approving terms. Although less than half a decade separates *The Sink* and *But the Sinners Triumph*, the latter work reflects a dramatic shift and development in Egan's thinking on sexual and gender identity.

Egan's connection with Louÿs has a certain logic to it, and considering the representation of gender and sexuality in the works of the two in relationship to one another illuminates much about Egan's peculiar and ambivalent sexual and gender politics during the 1920s and 1930s. The treatment of femininity in Louÿs's works is highly conflicted, at times daring and rebellious, insisting on women's role as desiring subjects, while just as frequently subjecting women to an objectifying gaze. His approach to sexual identity is similarly conflicted. Louÿs was a close friend of Wilde's in the 1890s. However, he eventually broke with Wilde on moral grounds, demanding that Wilde choose between their friendship and his affiliation with Lord Alfred Douglas.[71] Catharine Brosman describes Louÿs as "wholly, and very actively, heterosexual" and "hostile to male homosexuality."[72] Nevertheless, his works exhibit a marked preoccupation with love between women. Brosman argues that "the emphasis on lesbian love [in his works] is connected to the writer's concern with moral and intellectual freedom."[73] Yet Louÿs's investment in moral and intellectual freedom does not engender a wholly radical or liberatory vision of sexual desire. As Gretchen Schultz notes, many of the writers responsible for the "male-authored depictions of lesbians" that "flooded the intellectual and artistic marketplace" during the second half of the nineteenth century have been accused of "representing lesbians for the lascivious pleasure of male readers."[74] Although Louÿs's representations of love between women might be understood as a Decadent form of resistance to censorship and repression, these representations frequently seem to pander to a heterosexual male audience. Like Egan's illustrations for *The Sink*, many of Louÿs's works carefully separate same-sex desire from its links with gender inversion, dwelling on "womanly" subjects of same-sex desire who retain their attraction for heterosexual male readers. The speech of Naukrates in Louÿs's *Aphrodite* (1896) reflects the aesthetic of many of his works: "There is something charming in the union of two young women, on condition that they both consent to remain feminine, keep their hair long, uncover their breasts, and refrain from arming themselves with adventitious instruments, as if they were illogically envious of the gross sex for which they profess such pretty contempt."[75] As much as Louÿs's works might fall short of progressive ideals in their treatment of female subjects of same-sex desire, according to Brosman, Louÿs did share with his friend André Gide "the conviction that moral standards should be challenged and barriers broken down if the potential of human beings was to be fulfilled in European society."[76] His representations of erotic contact between women insist upon the beauty of these encounters and place these acts beyond the realm of morality. If Louÿs shied from considering love between men and treated female same-sex desire as a source of pornographic titillation, his interest in love between women must be understood as, in some small way, destabilizing to ideologies governing the understanding of feminine desire. In his discussion of a later edition of Louÿs's translations of Lucian, David Earle notes that the work is, like many modernist and Decadent works, "both androgynous and patriarchal."[77] It seems that this characterization, androgynous yet patriarchal, could serve as an appropriate designation for much of Louÿs's conflicted and ambivalent oeuvre.

Egan's illustrations of Louÿs's works might also be characterized in a comparable fashion, as androgynous yet patriarchal. The topic of love between women clearly exercised a similarly intense draw on Egan's imagination, as evidenced by works such as *The Sink* along with the illustrations he completed for Caton. In fact, Egan discussed with Caton the possibility of completing additional illustrated works focusing on erotic contact between women, including an edition of Sappho's poems as well as *Songs of Bilitis* (1894), a collection of erotic poetry concerning female same-sex desire that Louÿs claimed to have translated from an ancient text.[78] Although his representations of same-sex desire were not at all times flattering, this was clearly a theme Egan felt compelled to revisit. Like Louÿs, he seems to have been at once drawn to and repelled by the concept of same-sex desire, the practitioner of a queer heterosexual aesthetic that revels in the undoing of fixed gender categories while retreating from certain forms of desire. However, as much as the two appear aesthetically and politically compatible, Egan himself seems to have eventually grown exasperated by Louÿs's efforts to titillate his readers, describing Louÿs's works in a letter to Caton as "smutty tales" and remarking in a satirical verse concerning Louÿs's writing that "A brave attempt he makes at Fornication / Succeeding only, though, in Masturbation."[79] His interest in Louÿs did not blind him to the fact that his works often blurred the boundary between erotic iconoclasm and pornography.

Egan's illustrations of Louÿs's works are nearly as ambivalent in their treatment of the concept of gender trouble as their clearest influence and precursor, Beardsley's illustrations for *Salome*. In his discussion of Beardsley's work, Chris Snodgrass emphasizes the potential "revolutionary force" of the representation of sexuality in Beardsley's works, the extent to which such representations can "[mount] a flamboyant challenge against bourgeois limitations on sexual expression."[80] Egan's images, like Beardsley's, introduce a chaotic and potentially threatening kind of eroticism, contesting many elements of conventional categories of gender and sexuality. However, I would argue that, in Beardsley's work as well as Egan's, just as many elements of the sexual and gender politics of the culture contested are preserved. These are not entirely utopian or liberatory visions of desire or the female body. They send elements of an audience's understanding of sexual identity into chaos while reifying conventional power imbalances and reinscribing troubling elements of gender ideology.

Many of Egan's illustrations for Caton's editions of the works of Louÿs allude explicitly to drawings by Beardsley. Egan's *Chrysis and the Flute Girls*, for example, which appeared in Caton's edition of Louÿs's *Aphrodite* (1929), echoes Beardsley's attentiveness to the operations of the gaze in the original, expurgated *Toilette of Salome* plate (Figures 5.8 and 5.9). In both illustrations, a seemingly endless circuit of looking takes place around the centerpiece of a beautiful woman. As Snodgrass notes in his reading of the Beardsley image, "Salome herself, proportionally larger than her

Figure 5.8. Beresford Egan, *Chrysis and the Flute Girls*, from *Aphrodite* by Pierre Louÿs, 1929. © Estate of Beresford Egan.

Figure 5.9. Aubrey Beardsley, *Toilette of Salome*, original version, 1894. First published in 1907 Bodley Head edition.

attendants and ostentatiously nude except for her loosely draped dressing gown, seems rapt in an erotic dream, her left hand curling between her thighs in onanistic manipulation," while the youths surrounding her, with their hands thrust in their laps, their gazes crisscrossing one another, create a web of looking, desire, and pleasure.[81] The clothed androgynous youth on the left peers at the naked youth beside her while he gazes either at Salome or her naked attendant. Egan arranges his figures in a similar scenario, Chrysis the courtesan onanistically contemplating her own beauty in a mirror while the dark-haired girl on the left watches the light-haired girl watch Chrysis. Like Beardsley's *Salome* illustrations, this work upends conventional categories of desire, represents feminine figures as both agents and objects of the gaze, and foregrounds the power and the politics of looking. Yet the aestheticized female figures also conform to the demands of Louÿs's Naukrates. They have "consented to remain feminine." They invite the scopophilic gaze while enjoying its power themselves. As is often the case in Beardsley's work, scopophilia is, in both images, simultaneously theorized, problematized, and indulged.

Louÿs and Beardsley, with their highly conflicted and ambivalent sexual politics, clearly serve as a highly useful framework for understanding Egan's brand of post-Victorian Decadent eroticism. However, he does at times exceed his Decadent influences in his ability to imagine unconventional forms of feminine sexuality and desire. In the striking image *Megilla*, which appeared in the Caton edition of *Cyprian Masques* (1929), a collection of translations of Lucian by Pierre Louÿs, Egan departs from the castigation of the inverted woman on display in earlier works like *The Sink* (Figure 5.10). He departs, too, from his textual source in imagining female masculinity as alluring, fascinating, even beguiling rather than simply puzzling and strange. The dialogue with which the image is paired, "The Lesbians," represents female masculinity as a curious aberration. Leaina is quizzed by her friend Clonarion about the nature of her relationship with the masculine Megilla: "What is this we hear about thee, Leaina; the rich Lesbian Megilla is in love with thee like a man, and you unite with one another, just how I know not?"[82] Leaina blushes at the question, states that she is "ashamed" by the nature of their relationship, which is "so strange," and acknowledges that Megilla "is so tremendously male."[83] Leaina shares the story of her seduction by Megilla, when Megilla removed her wig to reveal that her head was "shaved to the skin like the most male of athletes."[84] When Leaina laughed at Megilla's performance of masculinity and inquired if she might be a hermaphrodite, Megilla announced "I am a man completely" with "the tastes, desires and all the rest of a man" and

Figure 5.10. Beresford Egan, *Megilla*, from *Cyprian Masques*, translated by Pierre Louÿs, 1929. © Estate of Beresford Egan.

"something that resembles virility."[85] Leaina, Clonarion, and the text itself seem bewildered by Megilla's female masculinity. However, in direct violation of his source (and of Naukrates's prescriptive statements concerning appropriate forms of lesbian identity), Egan imagines the ancient invert Megilla as highly pleasing and not in any way an object of derision, humor, or scorn. Egan's Megilla is up-to-date with a vengeance. She is slender and striking in her fitted jacket and pencil skirt. Her angular features are hugged closely by the tendrils of her modern bob. Her expression is calm and cool. The text's Megilla is on the defensive, forced to explain her troublesome gender identity, but Egan's Megilla is poised and self-assured. A long cigarette holder dangles casually from her hands as she reclines against a mantel. Her elongated hands, which are tipped with pointy claws, are somewhat monstrous, but these features are sinister rather than repugnant, rendering her dangerous as opposed to laughable. Unlike Egan's caricatures of Hall, which represent the female invert as foolish and distasteful, and the dialogue, which treats female masculinity as absurd, even comical, Egan's representation of Megilla allows the female invert to emerge as highly contemporary, arresting, and attractive.

Egan's novels similarly shed some of the limitations of his Decadent influences in their capacity to imagine a feminine form of dandyism, a witty, liberated, and successfully independent form of femininity that emerges victorious over masculine dandyism. The novels clearly draw on Swinburne, Rossetti, Wilde, and Beardsley in their representation of femme fatales and vamps. However, Egan progresses beyond his male Aesthetic and Decadent precursors in his capacity to merge the finest points of Decadent masculinity (coolness, detachment, wry intelligence, and epigrammatic wit) with the most pleasing parts of Decadent femininity. This is not an altogether new or unique innovation. As Talia Schaffer has argued in her discussion of the crucial role Ouida played in the development of the genre of the aesthetic novel, Ouida introduced female dandies in novels such as *Princess Napraxine* (1884) and *Othmar* (1885).[86] Wilde, however, "masculinized Ouida's aestheticism" and minimized the role of the female wit.[87] Elegant, witty women appear in minor scenes in many of Wilde's works, but "in an aestheticism that centers around issues of male subjectivity and sexuality, these women's linguistic gifts are no longer necessary to the plot."[88] In a return to Ouidean aestheticism, Egan places a female dandy front and center. His Anna Beryl Foster, the heroine of his illustrated novels *Pollen* and *But the Sinners Triumph*, surpasses the minor feminine wits in Wilde's plays and the androgynes of Beardsley's illustrations in her centrality to the texts she occupies, her sovereignty, and her absolute appeal. She is not surpassed, silenced, or murdered by the men whose power she encounters and undermines, and she is not simultaneously attractive and repellent, a source of anxiety and arousal at once like both Wilde's and Beardsley's Salome. Most importantly, she is never reformed. Her dandyism is explicitly linked to her final victory. She never needs to sacrifice her humor or surrender her position beyond good and evil. Modeled clearly on Alcock, Anna is the outcome of Egan's extended consideration of sexual and gender politics in the 1920s and 1930s and the product of his extensive collaboration with a feminist intellectual.[89]

The later *But the Sinners Triumph* relates the making of Anna Beryl, but Egan's first novel, *Pollen,* introduces us to a fully formed female dandy. Anna's allure expands and overtakes a text that seemingly ought to focus on its Decadent anti-hero Lance Daurimer. The novel opens with the dandyish Lance seeking to let a studio in Anna Beryl's home. The reader is ushered into a Decadent interior, decorated with Japanese prints and yellowed buffalo horns, and presented with Anna, who instantly wrests attention away from her masculine counterpart: "On a little carved gilt chair before her dressing-table she sat, jet hair falling in shining waves about her shoulders, a pale piquant face half turned; a wound of scarlet smiled at him; she was over thirty – shadowed eyes told their story."[90] The early pages of the novel signal directly that we are not within a conventional Decadent narrative, one in which world-weary, absinthe-drinking men overcome young prostitutes and actresses. Anna is not a vulnerable ingénue. She is older and knowing. She has seen all sorts of fallen things, and she communicates those experiences with a glance. Lance's detached, dandyish air evaporates straightaway. He "[fumbles] the cushions nervously," acknowledging immediately that "she was too much for him; he was used to virgins, he was so horribly clever with virgins: she was horribly clever."[91] Her horrible cleverness undoes Lance. He decides she is "far too beautiful to be good, and too intelligent – an impossible creature," possessing "the face of a Madonna, the body of a snake."[92] Her superiority to Lance is established in the novel's first chapter and confirmed repeatedly as the text progresses. Unlike Lance, who spends the majority of the text struggling and striving, it is she who lounges carelessly like a true dandy, smoking, drinking Madeira, reading, "wrapped in the generous silkiness of her kimono" or lounging in black silk pyjamas with "a huge red beetle with wide-spread wings richly embroidered on the left breast, and one black slipper with a like design forming the toe-cap."[93] It is she who effortlessly emits epigrams in a "soft mellow" voice "charged with laughter," warning, "Babies . . . [keep] wives in all day and husbands out all night."[94] Anna is, then, all things Decadent, the cleverness, the beauty, the disregard for conventional morality, and she possesses all of these qualities rather than serving as a muse for poetry about them.

Pollen engages with a whole host of Aesthetic and Decadent models, but, in its emphasis on seduction and influence, it draws most heavily from *The Picture of Dorian Gray*. Like *Dorian Gray*, the novel preoccupies itself with influence, power struggles, corruption, and the sway experience might hold over innocence. The thematic of influence does not play out, however, between Lance and Anna. Lance conceives of their relationship as a "war," but the outcome of that conflict seems to be settled from the first draw.[95] He feels that when Anna simply looks at him "through those long spiky black lashes, a demon whispered in his ear."[96] Rather than engage with a horribly clever woman who might pose a legitimate threat to his sovereignty, Lance chooses to enact his influence on one of the virgins with whom he tends to be so clever. He encounters the wealthy and beautiful Lady Marylyn, "innocence incarnate," attractive "in a girlish way," who sees the world as a "misty dreamland . . . peopled with fairies conceived by Dulac."[97] Like the "passionate purity" of Dorian Gray, which so titillated and fascinated Lord Henry, Marylyn's innocence seems to invite desecration, and she is just as suggestible as Dorian, a malleable form, a clean canvas upon which Lance's terrible and clever influence might operate. He takes it upon himself to taint Marylyn's worldview with his Decadence, to bring "a fallen angel by Beardsley" and "a divinity from Baudelaire" into her "pastel vision."[98] He detects curiosity slumbering within her breast, and he decides to awaken it: "[H]e wanted to buzz around the stamens of her mind, to open her petals, call her to life. Yes! He would call her to life; open her eyes slowly to reality, a certain kind of reality, the interesting side."[99] Much as the trembling, vulnerable Dorian began to "[vibrate] and [throb] to curious pulses" while listening to Henry's dangerous words, Marylyn "easily . . . [succumbs] to his sophistries; . . . [sucking] in the putrid pollen of his experience, and [flaunting] the enraging pistil of her innocence beneath his laden tongue."[100] Dorian turns Henry's teaching outward, ruining countless men and women by enacting a sinister form of Henry's hedonist philosophy, and Lance hopes Marylyn will do the same, unleashing her frightening new appetites on the world. He happily predicts that Marylyn will "destroy others, distributing the pollen with which he had impregnated her" and be "his revenge, his sweet revenge on womanhood."[101]

After all Lance's careful scheming, his struggle to wreak vengeance on women, however, it is the women who are victorious at the novel's end. Lance's plans fall to pieces. The Dorian monster he has created enacts her primary destruction on Lance himself. Marylyn does, as Lance hoped, "[bud] into the most gracious flower that ever bloomed in the Garden of Sin," but she also gets pregnant, and Lance, who converts to Catholicism, decides it is his duty (and in his pecuniary interest) to do the honorable thing.[102] Anna correctly forecasts that the newly fallen Marylyn will provide the newly Catholic Lance with endless opportunities for forgiveness by "[joining] the ranks of wives who take their husbands for granted and a *friend* for amusement."[103] After torturing him with a few dalliances that occur beneath his nose, Marylyn departs with a wealthy man and says her good-byes to Lance in a taunting note.

Marylyn's sinister victory pales in comparison, however, to the triumph of the cool and detached Anna Beryl. As much as Lance endeavors to distract himself with other affairs, she remains his primary obsession, the center around which the novel and his desires rotate. His thoughts return to her throughout the text as he seduces her maid, as he gazes on Marylyn's face, as he reunites with the pregnant Marylyn, as he discovers that Marylyn has left him for another man. In the novel's final chapter, he encounters Anna once more, and she calmly lectures him on the tenets of dandyish detachment. She tells him he is too "awfully extreme," turning from thorough badness to ridiculously excessive goodness, and that he should give indifference a chance. It is indifference, she notes, that she has "backed . . . for years and won – for in life, it's not the one who laughs first or *last*, but the one who smiles all the time who wins."[104] Apartness is lauded as the ideal approach to existence. The dandy's wry humor and blasé indolence, Anna argues, will always result in triumph. When Lance agrees to try her approach, she offers that she might even love him now that he is indifferent. When Lance replies, "But that's a paradox!" Anna retorts, in the novel's final line, "But life itself is just a rosary of paradoxes."[105] Anna's cool wisdom and epigrammatic wit close the novel and contain its essence. In her willingness to dwell in paradox, to remain always curious yet indifferent, she exemplifies a successful brand of dandyish femininity that trumps every brand of power and seduction that she encounters. In a clear retelling of the most infamous Decadent fable, there is not a Sybil Vane on display. Departing from his every Decadent influence, Egan engenders a female dandy who heralds a new model of interwar femininity.

Anna's interest and appeal are compounded in *But the Sinners Triumph*, which focuses on the earlier years of her life and links the evolution of her persona to international conflict and international travel. As he does in earlier works, such as *The Sink*, Egan explores the connections between gender and national politics. He ties the emergence of the female dandy to the realities of World War I, and he allows her dandyish sensibility to blossom in an imperial outpost while freed from the constraints of English attitudes and mores. The text ties all sorts of malaise to the realities of interwar modernity. As the book jacket states, "it is a story dealing with the difficulties and diversions of the much-maligned War and post-War generations." Paul Allen notes in his description of the novel that the characters are "restless people caught between the wars. . . . They are all convinced, fashionably enough, that virtue is boring and sometimes ends in marriage, and they do not want a dull fate. They have seen the powers of higher compulsion than themselves in the deadly clashes of 1914–18, and in the imperatives of well-meaning Victorian parents. They conclude that 'the saints make very pretty stained-glass windows, but the sinners triumph.'"[106] The novel's characters are converted into amoral Decadents as a direct result of their wartime and postwar restlessness, and they reach their ultimate dandyish conclusions when they travel outside of England to Johannesburg. Although Egan himself never returned to South Africa, the nation serves a crucial function in his final novel, a separate space where his most interesting creation, the female dandy Anna Beryl Foster, can come into her own. Egan's textual return to South Africa serves as a reminder of his transnational sensibility, which underwrites the strident critique of international armed conflict in the text. The novel integrates Egan's Decadence, his strange brand of feminism, and his global sensibility, a fitting capstone to the most productive and interesting period in his career.

Like many novels of the interwar period, including *The Well of Loneliness* and *Sleeveless Errand*, *But the Sinners Triumph* argues that the war ushered in a new set of attitudes about and possibilities for sexual behavior and gender identity. Omnipresent violence and the imminent threat of death, it is implied, rendered traditional morality meaningless. The novel opens with Anna's brother Leonard and his friend Philip drunkenly invading Anna's bedroom. Philip clumsily kisses Anna, and she strikes him on the chin. The raucous events that open the novel are carefully linked to the fact of violence. The men's inebriation and their recklessness stem from their quickened sense of their own mortality. Leonard has just returned from France, and Philip is soon to depart. The following morning, Leonard muses to himself that he is very bad, but he is too tired and too old to reform, "and besides there was the war. . . . What time had he for a Victorian conscience?"[107] Philip's thoughts run similarly to his own mortality: "Haven't had a chance to live yet. I'm scared stiff. I don't want to die."[108] The nearness of death makes the pursuit of pleasure all the more pressing, forcing the younger generation into a Paterian approach to life and the present. Leonard decides to encourage Philip's wooing of his sister, telling him "he's no time to waste."[109] In his advice to Philip, he argues that courtship and sentimentality have no place on the wartime scene: "Cut out the first act – flowers, flattery and what not. Leave that to the martial grand-dads who'll be left behind.... Yesterday's methods are no use to you and me."[110] The claim that the war has ushered in a fundamentally new set of romantic practices is a refrain in the novel's first volume, "Fragments." While trying to seduce the beautiful Myra Cheriton, for example, Leonard claims the war has "swept [the principles] out of [him]."[111] Gender ideologies will also need to be revised. Leonard's father disapproves of Myra because she works as a secretary for the author Roy Massingham, but Anna predicts that "the jolly old war is going to jar quite a heap of his notions concerning the [female] *sex*."[112] Again and again, the novel insists that the world is entering into a new epoch, one that will have very little to do with the Victorian past and its principles.

This moral chaos and presentism produce the horribly clever Anna Beryl. When the novel begins, Anna is lying in bed in her "tremendously thrilling pyjamas" and daydreaming of returning to a store to purchase a Chinese kimono with an "embroidered riot of dragons, which had been just five and sixpence more than she had in her purse."[113] Here the text signals to the attentive reader that this is the dandy of *Pollen* in her nascent form, as Anna wears a kimono for much of the earlier novel. Her reading practices, we are told, are fostering her budding Decadence. She reads Ouida and Victoria Cross, "more than was good for her," ensuring her exposure to Ouidean dandyism and Cross's sexually adventurous New Women.[114] This early education has led her into temptation. She gazes into the mirror while applying lipstick and muses, "How romantic to be wicked; to eat all the forbidden fruit in the world and burn one's fingers a little."[115] Before Anna can take up the mantle of the fully formed female dandy, however, she must move through a set of hardening experiences that will cultivate her detachment and bring her to her final calm indifference. She has a fling with Myra and an affair with Philip, who is wounded in the war. After two years of visiting Philip in the hospital, she is "driven... into a nursing home for six months, to rave about the horrors of war and to plot, with imaginary conspirators, the assassination of Little Willie and Lloyd George."[116] When she emerges, she falls in with the notorious Roy Massingham, "nurtured on Wilde, on Pater, on Villon and Verlaine," and engages in an extended competition for his affections with the increasingly spiteful Myra. She grows progressively colder and more detached, evolving into a "Swinburne heroine" with a "*Mona Lisa* smile."[117] As the novel's second volume, "Kaleidoscope," concludes, she departs for South Africa with Roy, acknowledging almost immediately that she has already begun to tire of his kisses. When she realizes that he truly loves her, that she has tamed a notorious libertine, "all that [is] mean within her [arises] to gloat."[118] She has triumphed over her dandyish adversary. There is no question of her returning Roy's affections: "She couldn't love him because . . . he couldn't make her forget" Philip's agony, the sound of him calling her name as he suffered in the hospital. Forged by the terrors of the war, she seems beyond the reach of sentimentality and romance.

The novel's final volume, "Design," trails Anna and Roy to South Africa, with Myra and her suitor Cain Goshawk, a consumptive post-Victorian Pre-Raphaelite painter, in hot pursuit. The text mercilessly lampoons the ignorance of the English concerning the realities of the empire, laughing heartily at the characters' foolish response to Johannesburg. Egan takes careful pains to emphasize the exoticism of the locale for his characters, the ways in which it forces them to adapt and change, as well as the extent to which Johannesburg departs from their ignorant expectations. Anna expresses disappointment at the fact that the city resembles nothing more than "Manchester in summertime": "What had she expected – lions, antelopes, and *impies* of Zulu warriors? . . . No, not quite. But something more than a third-rate business centre."[119] Anna is outdone in her ignorance, however, by the ridiculous Cain Goshawk, who arrives outfitted for a safari in an "open-necked khaki shirt, riding-breeches and puttees, with topee complete."[120] His absurd costume elicits laughter and contempt from the people of the city. Like Anna, Goshawk is flabbergasted to see that the streets of Johannesburg are not teeming with giraffes, hyenas, and wildebeests. In this inversion of the standard British travel narrative, it is not the native population that emerges as ludicrous and strange. The transplanted Britons, arriving in a surprisingly modern imperial outpost, emerge as the primary source of peculiarity. In having their expectations upended, however, the travelers are primed for transformation.

As much as the trip to South Africa engenders the possibility for many comic errors, the novel takes very seriously the intellectual progress this radically different place allows its primary character to make toward dandyish perfection. As the final volume opens, Anna calls to Johannesburg, "What fresh illusions have you to offer a jaded soul, you metal-hearted city?"[121] The novel equates Johannesburg's merciless extraction of natural resources with Anna's Decadent approach to experience. Her dandyism seems to escalate during her time in South Africa. Her inner monologue becomes a factory for dismissive epigrams concerning marriage and domesticity:

"With the sounding of the nuptial bell Duty supplants Desire, the Rites of Love degenerate into Conjugal Rights, and the Kiss, once tender, becomes a drear formality, a constant reminder of the 'sacred' contract signed on the impulse of an evil moment."[122] Anna's final and most important moments of epiphanic development occur in the tender letters she writes to her deceased brother Leonard and to Cain Goshawk, who dies after the company has departed for Rhodesia. She has, she tells Leonard, lived religiously by Leonard's "romanceless principles," and she is now "the breathing epitome of selfishness; a creature loved, but unloving."[123] She intends, however, to throw off the shackles of Leonard's influence and develop her own approach to pleasure, one that allows for love. This is not, however, a capitulation to conventional morality and domestic ideology. She is still, she insists, "not the marrying sort."[124] She is "a dark-haired maiden *(?)*, with a pair of eyes and a private income."[125] As she speaks to Cain beyond the grave, she stresses the role that the war has played in altering her consciousness: "Whenever I think about the war, I want to do things – 'useful' things – I want to lop off the heads of Prime Ministers and potentates, I want to chop down military family trees, and chip the old blocks that sit so woodenly upon the shoulders of our club-easy Imperialists."[126] The war has produced in her a sharpened skepticism, a detached and critical perspective on nation, empire, and war, but her experiences, her affairs, her losses, witnessing the death of Cain himself, have also "taught [her] how to live – and how to *love*."[127] When Roy demands to know what it is she's scribbling, she announces that she is writing on the subject of her love for life drawn from the lessons she has learned from death. Anna's postwar Paterian dandyism draws on the experience of violence and cruelty in its keen perception of the foolishness of international conflict, but, like a true Paterian, she vows to remain open and vulnerable to beauty, experience, and pleasure. She will not wither under Leonard's romanceless principles or remain permanently wounded by the experience of war. Her enthusiasm for existence will operate as a counterpoint to the wounds that the war has inflicted. Anna's peculiar brand of dandyism will integrate detachment and indifference with a keen sense of delight. Refined by the suffering she has experienced, she will keep coolness and tenderness in play in her cultivated and thoughtful approach to existence.

These are Anna's books. They narrate Anna's development. However, they also end with Egan. In Johannesburg, the quartet encounters a young sports cartoonist, Pat Rix, who works for the *Rand Morning Leader*. He wears lavender suits. Acquaintances refer to him as "Dorian Gray." In her letter to Leonard, Anna notes that "he puts one in mind of an American comedian burlesquing Oscar Fingal O'Flahertie Wills Wilde."[128] He is "sick of [Johannesburg], sick of the people, sick of caricaturing 'phizogs' that were already caricatures."[129] He feels like "a salmon in a goldfish-bowl, set upon the window-sill of a suburban residence."[130] This restless Eganesque figure attaches himself to Anna's company and begins a romance with Myra. He departs Johannesburg, of which he has grown incredibly weary, to accompany them to Rhodesia and then on to London. A band of British aesthetes rescues him from an imperial outpost of muscular Christianity. The novel ends, then, where this chapter began, with Egan's tracing of the Decadent fiber that connects South Africa to England, his departure on that line of connection back to the metropole, where he can begin to articulate a detached critique of England's national and gender politics from its interior.

Although Egan lived until 1984, he produced much of his richest and most interesting work during the 1920s and 1930s. The onset of World War II did elicit some noteworthy satirical work on his part. He had by this time remarried, and his second wife, Felicity Devereux, was a committed pacifist. Egan seemed to share her commitments to a certain extent, and he produced a cartoon for *Peace News* that critiqued the exploitative behavior of the British government during wartime. When he was finally called to serve in the Royal Corps of Signals, he "in the words of his wife 'made himself unwell': he apparently had a nervous breakdown, received a shot from a rifle under mysterious circumstances and was discharged from the Army as unfit for service."[131] His *Epilogue* (1946), written during the war and published during the first months of peace, attempts to bring "the sovereign remedy of laughter" and the "purgative" of irony to bear upon the "general abasement of clarity" that occurred during the war.[132] This is clearly a work in the detached and Decadent tradition. However, the visual work of this period begins to appear more cartoonish, less sharp and striking, than the Beardlseyesque images of the earlier period. In addition, the treatment of gender politics becomes far less progressive. *Epilogue*, for example, devotes a great deal of energy to castigating the mannish and empowered women of the era. Although there is much that is fascinating about this period in his career, including his appearance in the Powell and Pressburger films *The Life and Death of Colonel Blimp* (1943) and *A Canterbury Tale* (1944), it is the work of the 1920s and 1930s that has the most to offer scholars of Decadence, modernism, and sexuality.

Beresford Egan is certainly not above reproach in his treatment of feminine desire and sexuality. However, his work from the 1920s and 1930s represents some of the richest and most interesting thinking on the topics of sexuality and female dandyism within the Decadent tradition. Generated at a moment when sexual dissidence was often read as political dissidence, his intervention into conversations concerning sexual inversion and feminine desire constitutes an act of resistance with wider ramifications. Situating his work within the context of interwar "village England" repression allows the radical valence of his manner of representing androgyny and same-sex desire to emerge. As an author and illustrator whose aesthetic was transnationally constituted, who responded to Decadent influences from a South African distance, Egan also allows for unique insight into the phenomenon of the global circulation of Decadence. Furthermore, rather than simply allowing us to see how an English aesthetic was reconstituted within an imperial periphery, Egan's career also allows us to see how a globally transmitted Decadence was practiced within the metropole, critiquing and opposing the politics of the imperial center from within. In addition, because much of his most important work was composed in collaboration with or under the influence of Caterina Bower Alcock, attentiveness to his work facilitates the consideration of a neglected woman writer and a clearer understanding of women's role in what is frequently understood as a masculine tradition. Acknowledging his part in early-twentieth-century aesthetic and political discourses will allow for a much fuller and more accurate vision of the interwar period to emerge, one that attends to the peculiar role aesthetic anachronism and cosmopolitanism played in progressive discourses concerning gender and sexuality.

Afterword
Notes on Post-Victorian Decadence after the Wars

On October 16, 1954, the Wilde centenary was celebrated with a plaque unveiling at Wilde's home at 34 Tite Street. The event seemed to mark a change in feeling about Wilde, his trials, and his imprisonment, and participants at the unveiling commented on these recent alterations in cultural attitudes toward same-sex desire. Compton Mackenzie's address heralded the emergence of more progressive attitudes and celebrated Wilde's impact: "If we are more civilised to-day than we were 60 years ago, we owe a lot of that to Oscar Wilde.... There was magic in Wilde; he was one of the greatest figures of a great decade.... Wilde helped to bring into our world more humanity and generosity."[1] A message from Laurence Housman expressed a similar sense of hopefulness about a new era of acceptance and advanced sexual politics: "I am very glad that this memorial meeting is being held for so good a purpose.... [Oscar Wilde's] unhappy fate has done the world a signal service in defeating the blind obscurantists; he has made people think. Far more people of intelligence think differently today because of him. And when he wrote his 'Ballad of Reading Gaol' he not only gave the world a beautiful poem, but a much-needed lesson in good will, pity, pardon, and understanding for the 'down-and-out.'"[2] Mackenzie and Housman insisted that things had changed, the world was markedly different than it was sixty years ago, and Wilde would never be treated in the same manner in this new, kinder cultural climate.

The use of the Wilde centenary as an opportunity to envision a more compassionate sexual politics is a representative example of the manner in which post-Victorian Decadence operated politically after the wars. Although post-Victorian Decadence was at its most visible and vital in the 1910s and 1920s, the figures of the fin de siècle continued to have a rich afterlife in conversations surrounding the politics of gender and sexuality throughout the latter half of the twentieth century. Furthermore, the thinking of Wilde and the post-Victorian dandies who adored him, such as Ronald Firbank, informed the development of queer theory and a modern queer aesthetic in the final decades of the twentieth century. Queer theorists and gay writers working to address the question of sexual politics in the modern era appropriated the strategies most essential to the Decadent aesthetic, such as camp, detachment, and irony, as models of political intervention. Post-Victorian Decadence haunted the postmodern moment, inflecting the tone and the practices of modern queer theory and modeling methods for negotiating trauma for contemporary writers engaging with the AIDS crisis.

Although Mackenzie and Housman imagined a burgeoning empathy and understanding of same-sex desire in 1954, such discourse hardly extended beyond academic and literary communities to the broader culture. Sympathetic critics and artists often implemented the memory of Wilde and Decadent aesthetic strategies in events and texts designed to generate new models of thinking about sexuality, but the turn to Wilde and the fin de siècle were just as often linked to moments that foregrounded the persistent persecution of sexual dissidence and the difficulties governing queer experience in the latter half of the twentieth century. As Ellen Crowell has recently noted, the Wilde centenary occurred at a moment "when the arrest and exposure of gay men for 'acts of gross indecency' was at a fever pitch; in 1953 alone, over two thousand men were arrested and half of these prosecuted for homosexual offenses."[3] Working with the Wilde collection at the William Andrews Clark Memorial Library in Los Angeles, Crowell has disinterred evidence concerning the relationship between the centenary events and a scandal involving John Gielgud, whom Max Beerbohm had suggested as a candidate to unveil the plaque at Tite Street. After accepting the invitation, Gielgud was arrested in a Chelsea public lavatory and charged with "persistently importuning for an immoral purpose."[4] Gielgud resigned from his role in the centenary event, and a series of other potential speakers, including T. S. Eliot, E. M. Forster, and Laurence Olivier, were invited and declined before Compton Mackenzie agreed to speak. Although, in a letter accepting the invitation to speak from Vyvyan Holland, Mackenzie described the centenary event as a "volte face," as Crowell argues, what occurred behind the scenes might be more properly described as a "déjà vu," undermining Housman's assertion that people had begun to "think differently."[5]

This midcentury upsurge in the prosecution of homosexual offenses, which had such unfortunate effects on the Wilde centenary, figures prominently in Alan Hollinghurst's *The Swimming-Pool Library* (1988), a novel that is linked to Wilde and to Decadence not simply through its preoccupation with the manner in which queer subjects have been disciplined and punished but also by its reliance on strategies drawn from a Decadent tradition to respond to the traumas besetting those subjects. The young, wealthy narrator, William Beckwith, befriends an older aristocratic man, Charles Nantwich, and comes to find out that his own grandfather, as director of public persecutions, had been the "driving force" behind the upswing in the legal persecution of gay men at midcentury, which had resulted in Charles's imprisonment.[6] Will's chilling revelation of the tragic effects that the "gay pogrom" conducted by his biological kin had on the life of his new friend overshadows the final chapters of the novel.[7] Shaken from his insouciance, Will takes on a new political sensibility as he decides to testify in court in support of his friend James, who has recently been entrapped for solicitation under a similar set of circumstances. Charles's and James's experiences resonate with one another, and with the déjà vu at the Wilde centenary, and thus undercut the promise of a new sexual freedom suggested by Will's rakish existence at the start of the novel. *The Swimming-Pool Library* joyously narrates sexual encounters between men but concludes with this memory of a past trauma. It is marked by an ambivalence about modernity and progress, proffering images of sexual liberation yet haunted by a certain melancholy about loss in the past, the present, and the future.

In its repeated turns to Oscar Wilde and Ronald Firbank, the novel emphasizes Decadence's connection with tragedy as well as the shrewdness and strength of its ironic manner. The references to Wilde in the novel remind the reader of the sadness that governed the lives of what Yeats referred to as the "Tragic Generation." As Joseph Bristow notes, the name of the hotel in Bloomsbury where Will meets up with a younger man named Phil for sexual liaisons is the Queensberry, and it was the Marquess of Queensberry, Lord Alfred Douglas's father, who persecuted Wilde and contributed to the circumstances that led to his trial for gross indecency.[8] Will consults Charles's journals as he considers writing a biography of his new friend, and the entries concerning his time in prison reverberate with the echoes of *De Profundis*, the posthumously published letter to Douglas that Wilde wrote while in prison, and "The Ballad of Reading Gaol." However, as much as the text underscores the traumas of Decadence's history, it also reminds us of aestheticism's hardness and its humor. As Will recovers from a violent, homophobic attack, he and James watch the 1952 film adaptation of *The Importance of Being Earnest* (1895) and take solace in the performances of Michael Redgrave and Michael Denison, "so brittle and yet resilient."[9] The references to Firbank also make note of tragedy, foregrounding his illness and his abbreviated life. When, for example, Firbank first appears in Charles's journals, he is represented as a figure of "harlequin melancholy."[10] He is beset by frequent attacks of coughing that leave him trembling and in tears, and he speaks often of his own impending death. However, when Will begins to read Firbank's *Valmouth* (1919), he is "surprised to find how difficult, witty, and relentless he was. The characters were flighty and extravagant in the extreme, but the novel itself was evidently as tough as nails."[11] The allusions to Wilde and Firbank in the text underscore the poignant elements of the Decadent tradition as well as the utility of humor, camp, and irony in responding to difficulty, the brittle resilience and toughness of aestheticism. As J. Stephen Murphy argues, "Hollinghurst's novel is about a history fraught with calamities, but it is ultimately about survival and survivors who have moved beyond the catastrophe through the work of not memory but irony."[12] This capacity for robust and resistant irony is traced to a Decadent tradition, a mode of humor and extravagance that finally refuses and deflects the tragedy that engendered it.

The Swimming-Pool Library engages in the same sort of nostalgia for a past aesthetic that was so central to post-Victorian Decadence, and Firbank, a temporally conflicted post-Victorian Decadent modernist, could be understood as the guiding spirit of the novel. The text opens with an epigraph from Firbank's *The Flower beneath the Foot* (1923), which emphasizes the temporal tensions in Firbank's works: "'She reads at such a pace,' she complained, 'and when I asked her *where* she had learnt to read so quickly, she replied, "On the screens at Cinemas."'" The novel begins, then, with a nod to Firbank's regretful engagement with the modern moment, a moment when literacy is garnered from the "screens," and the manner in which modernity causes him at once to laugh and to cringe. This sense of his temporal liminality is reinforced by the content of Charles's journals. Charles reports that when he first encountered Firbank, he appeared to be "of indeterminate age but clearly older than he wanted to be."[13] He is fundamentally out of sync with time. As Will presses Charles for more information at their next meeting, Charles states, "He belongs to another age – even then he belonged to another age."[14] In looking backward to Firbank as a figure who himself looked backward, the text stresses the importance of anachronistic aesthetic connections in the construction of queer identity. Much as Wilde turned to Greece, and Firbank turned to the fin de siècle, Will turns to Charles's past and finds in Charles's journals the "fore-echo" of his own life.[15] Immersing himself in Charles's life, Will embraces a post-Victorian Decadent strategy, a queer modernism that, as Heather Love has argued, relies on temporal inversion to negotiate modernity.[16]

In its frequent references to Firbank and Wilde, the novel highlights its own connections to a Decadent tradition, and it uses Decadent strategies to engage with the politics of the present. As Joseph Bristow notes, "the grief at the centre of *The Swimming-Pool Library* emerges only through its terrifying absence. . . . The historical framework of the novel depends on a knowledge about an epidemic that remains implicit, and whose presence can only be inferred through the most oblique hints. Nowhere at all does AIDS surface in a narrative that recalls 'the last summer of its kind there was ever to be.'"[17] Like Beerbohm's oblique treatment of the war in his caricatures of *Rossetti and His Circle* and his willfully detached radio broadcasts, Hollinghurst's novel refuses to come directly at the trauma with which it is preoccupied. In a recent interview, Hollinghurst stated, "I felt there was an expectation that I would write an AIDS novel, but I didn't want to write to meet anybody's expectations, and I also just didn't see an artistically satisfying way of doing it."[18] Much as Beerbohm insisted that he was incapable of truly getting at the horror of the war by addressing it explicitly, Hollinghurst carefully avoids the articulation of the coming doom that hovers around the borders of the text. And, just as Beerbohm retreated into the recent past to express his dissatisfaction with the war-torn present, Hollinghurst steps back a few paces from the catastrophe of AIDS, turning elegiacally to the moment that immediately preceded that trauma. In its obliqueness and indirection, its roundabout approach to horror and tragedy, the text embraces a Decadent model of critique. AIDS never arrives in the novel, but in the many losses Will experiences (losing Phil to another man, losing his beauty when he is attacked, the damage done to his relationship with his grandfather following the revelation of the "gay pogrom"), the novel gestures toward the more significant and widespread trauma that is to come.

As much as the novel refuses to speak about certain things, it is wonderfully explicit about others. Georges Letissier foregrounds the novel's treatment of sex in his discussion of Hollinghurst and Firbank's shared "aesthetic of the outrageous."[19] Hollinghurst's "outrageousness" in his treatment of sex might be seen as a method for expressing affiliation with Firbank's camp extravagance and the Decadent tendency to erotic excess. The pleasure the novel takes in sex flies in the face of the grief beneath its surface. As much as the novel attends to the pain that has been central to the Decadent tradition, to the traumas that impacted the lives of the members of the Tragic

Generation, it also revels in the aestheticist or epicurean approach to the pursuit of pleasure, the Decadent desire to shock, the wit of aestheticism, and the shared community created by camp taste.

Camp, which plays such a crucial role in post-Victorian Decadence as practiced by Beerbohm and Firbank, has also operated as one of the key concepts in modern queer theory. It is perhaps above all in discussions of camp that post-Victorian Decadence has remained visible and politically relevant. Late-Victorian and post-Victorian Decadence are central to Susan Sontag's attempts to theorize a "homosexual," "vanguard" taste.[20] Her "Notes on 'Camp'" (1964) are, in fact, "for Oscar Wilde"; she refers to camp as "a certain mode of aestheticism," and the essay is littered with Wilde's epigrams and references to Firbank, Beardsley, and Beerbohm.[21] Looking to Decadence allows her to envision queer modes of performance and consumption that "dethrone the serious," foster a vision of "life as theater," and create a sense of affiliation based in a set of shared tastes.[22] The political implications of an approach to existence that problematizes the concept of authenticity perhaps seem evident to us now, as do the political implications of a fundamentally subversive model of appreciation that generates communities of taste, but Sontag insisted that "the Camp sensibility is disengaged, depoliticized – or at least apolitical."[23] Subsequent theorists of camp, such as Judith Butler and Jack Halberstam, however, have called into question Sontag's vision of camp as apolitical and demonstrated the manner in which camp, particularly camp modes of drag performance, highlight the performativity of gender. In this sense, Wilde and Decadence can be understood as foundational to modern queer theory, as post-Victorian specters haunting late-twentieth-century discourses concerning gender and sexuality.

The presence of Decadence in modern queer theory is not, however, always spectral. Roger Luckhurst noted in 1995 how "crucial" Wilde was to many queer theorists, "because the new formation of the 'homosexual' as *type*, a personality, rather than merely a set of sexual *acts* that was encoded in the 1885 Criminal Amendment Bill is often argued to find its initial enforcement in the trial of Wilde in 1895."[24] Many of the most significant works of queer theory and queer studies published in the 1990s, such as Eve Sedgwick's *Epistemology of the Closet* (1990), Jonathan Dollimore's *Sexual Dissidence: Augustine to Wilde, Freud to Foucault* (1991), Ed Cohen's *Talk on the Wilde Side* (1993), and Alan Sinfield's *The Wilde Century: Effeminacy, Oscar Wilde, and the Queer Moment* (1994), relied heavily on Wilde to think through the history and politics of modern sexuality. This is not post-Victorian Decadence as pastiche, the reinvigoration of Decadent aesthetic modes as practiced by figures like Beresford Egan in the first half of the twentieth century. But this is, it seems, where the political energies of post-Victorian Decadence persist and thrive, in a tradition of critical discourse that is similarly playful, witty, and aloof. The tone of Decadence has inflected the tone of queer theory and queer studies and underwrites the models of reading and appreciation that are central to those traditions of thinking.

In modern theoretical discourses concerning queer aesthetics and in contemporary novels preoccupied with a queer literary tradition, Decadence continues to operate as a vital and effective political force, as a style of thought that engenders a dissident approach to the notion of sexual identity and as an oblique, indirect manner of negotiating trauma. Like each chapter that has preceded, the works and theories discussed here demonstrate that "art for art's sake" might be a misnomer and that Decadence far exceeds the boundaries of the period with which it is most associated. Authors and artists return to it again and again throughout the twentieth century as art for politics' sake, as a highly useful method for intervening in political debates while voicing an implicit critique of the present moment, a moment Decadence, even at the fin de siècle, always seems to be subtly eschewing. The "critical function" of Decadence remains in play more than a hundred years after the turn of the twentieth century, demonstrating that, though, as Holbrook Jackson argues, the 1890s are certainly a "distinctive epoch," the work of the decade and its thinkers spills far beyond its temporal boundaries, becoming more of a way of thinking than a moment in time.[25]

Notes

NOTES TO INTRODUCTION

1. *Catalogue of an Exhibition Entitled "Ghosts"* (London: E. Brown and Phillips, the Leicester Galleries, 1928), 7.
2. Ibid.
3. Ibid.
4. Ibid.
5. Ibid.
6. Max Beerbohm, *Observations* (London: W. Heinemann, 1925), plate 20.
7. Bernard Muddiman, *The Men of the Nineties* (London: H. Danielson, 1920), 19.
8. See Jonathan Freedman, *Professions of Taste: Henry James, British Aestheticism and Commodity Culture* (Stanford, CA: Stanford University Press, 1990), 202. For additional discussion of the definition of the term *Decadence*, see also Liz Constable, Dennis Denisoff, and Matthew Potolsky, eds., introduction to *Perennial Decay: On the Aesthetics and Politics of Decadence* (Philadelphia: University of Pennsylvania Press, 1998), 1–32, and Matthew Potolsky's introduction to his *The Decadent Republic: Taste, Politics, and Cosmopolitan Community from Baudelaire to Beardsley* (Philadelphia: University of Pennsylvania Press, 2012).

   The distinction between aestheticism and Decadence is also, of course, "fuzzy," and many of the figures under discussion here, such as Max Beerbohm or Vernon Lee, could be linked to both movements. I have found it useful here to use "Decadence" as a category of periodization to describe a later wave of aestheticism that flourished at the fin de siècle. Nevertheless, I will also highlight the manner in which fin-de-siècle figures like Beerbohm and Lee stressed the points of continuity between the Decadence of the 1890s and earlier forms of aestheticism as theorized and practiced by the Pre-Raphaelites and Walter Pater. In addition, the very nature of this project, which questions categories of periodization, works to undercut our understanding of Decadence as a movement that was restricted to the 1890s.

   For further discussion of the relationship between aestheticism and Decadence, see Dennis Denisoff, "Decadence and Aestheticism," in *The Cambridge Companion to the Fin de Siècle*, ed. Gail Marshall, 31–52 (New York: Cambridge University Press, 2007).
9. Potolsky, *Decadent Republic*, 4.

10. See Joseph Bristow, ed., introduction to *Oscar Wilde and Modern Culture: The Making of a Legend* (Athens: Ohio University Press, 2008), 26, 31.
11. "No One Found Who Saw Wilde Dead," *New York Times,* November 9, 1913, C4.
12. Jodie Medd, "'The Cult of the Clitoris': Anatomy of a National Scandal," *Modernism/Modernity* 9, no. 1 (2002): 24.
13. Ibid., 21.
14. Quoted in Charles Musser, "The Hidden and the Unspeakable: On Theatrical Culture, Oscar Wilde and Ernst Lubitsch's *Lady Windermere's Fan*," *Film Studies* 4 (2004): 21.
15. Ibid., 20.
16. Ibid., 22.
17. Quoted in Petra Dierkes-Thrun, *Salome's Modernity: Oscar Wilde and the Aesthetics of Transgression* (Ann Arbor: University of Michigan Press, 2011), 158; quoted in Patricia White, "Nazimova's Veils: Salome at the Intersections of Film History," in *A Feminist Reader in Early Cinema*, ed. Jennifer Bean and Diane Negra (Durham, NC: Duke University Press, 2002), 62.
18. For further discussion of Leverson's parodies of Wilde, see Margaret Debelius, "Countering a Counterpoetics," in *Women and British Aestheticism*, ed. Talia Schaffer and Kathy Psomiades, 192–210 (Charlottesville: University of Virginia Press, 1999).
19. Ada Leverson, *Tenterhooks* (New York: Mitchell Kennerley, 1912), 34.
20. Ibid., 55, 97–98.
21. Ibid., 107.
22. Ada Leverson, *Love at Second Sight* (London: Grant Richards, 1916), 121.
23. Ibid., 122.
24. Quoted in Eric Binnie, *The Theatrical Designs of Charles Ricketts* (Ann Arbor, MI: UMI Research Press, 1985), 1, 5.
25. From a synopsis of dresses Ricketts wrote for Robert Ross. Quoted in Margery Ross, ed., *Robert Ross: Friend of Friends* (London: Cape, 1952), 127.
26. Quoted in Binnie, *Theatrical Designs*, 41.
27. Martin Green, *Children of the Sun: A Narrative of "Decadence" in England after 1918* (New York: Basic Books, 1976), 140–41.
28. Ibid., 140.
29. Ibid., 78.
30. For Holland's description of this incident, see Vyvyan Holland, "Ronald Firbank," in *Ronald Firbank: A Memoir*, ed. Ifan Kyrle Fletcher, 109–11 (New York: Brentano's, 1932).
31. Brigid Brophy, *Prancing Novelist: A Defense of Fiction in the Form of a Critical Biography of Ronald Firbank* (New York: Macmillan, 1973), 280.
32. Ibid., 290, 282; Joseph Bristow, *Effeminate England: Homoerotic Writing after 1885* (New York: Columbia University Press, 1995), 105.
33. Richard Canning, ed., introduction to *Vainglory: With Inclinations and Caprice* (London: Penguin, 2012), xix.
34. E. M. Forster, *Abinger Harvest* (New York: Harcourt, Brace, 1936), 118.

35. Bristow, *Effeminate England*, 105.
36. For a discussion of the manner in which Firbank's style informed modernist practice, see Alex Murray, "Decadence Revisited: Evelyn Waugh and the Afterlife of the 1890s," *Modernism/Modernity* (forthcoming). Murray stresses the manner in which Waugh is representative of an early-twentieth-century tendency to continually revisit the 1890s.
37. Carl Van Vechten, *Excavations* (New York: Knopf, 1926), 172. Quoted in Kirsten MacLeod, "Making It New, Old School: Carl Van Vechten and Decadent Modernism," *Symbiosis* 16, no. 2 (2012): 220.
38. Alex Murray presented some of this work in a talk titled "'Venice, Sans Hope': Transatlantic Decadence and New York Writing" at the Birkbeck Forum for Nineteenth-Century Studies on May 30, 2013.
39. See the chapter on "The Decadent Revival" in David Weir's *Decadent Culture in the United States* (Albany: SUNY Press, 2008).
40. Weir, *Decadent Culture in the United States*, 152.
41. A. J. A. Symons, ed., preface to *An Anthology of "Nineties" Verse* (London: E. Matthews and Marrot, 1928), xvii.
42. Ibid., xx.
43. See Corvine Society, "A True Recital of the Procedure of the Second Banquet Held by the Corvine Society" (1929). Symons's brother Julian referred to Corvo as the "strangest artificial orchid of the nineties" in his biography of his brother. See Julian Symons, *A. J. A. Symons: His Life and Speculations* (London: Eyre and Spottiswoode, 1950), 117.
44. Corvine Society, "Second Banquet," 1.
45. Beerbohm's visitors' books from his home at Rapallo are in the Max Beerbohm Collection at Merton College, Oxford. Ezra Pound and T. S. Eliot visited Beerbohm's home on December 23, 1925, and Pound visited with his wife repeatedly over the years after they themselves settled in Rapallo. Hemingway visited in 1922. Visitors' books, Max Beerbohm Collection, Merton College Library, Oxford University.
46. Elizabeth Robins Pennell, *Nights: Rome and Venice in the Aesthetic Eighties, London and Paris in the Fighting Nineties* (Philadelphia: J. B. Lippincott, 1916), 118, 120.
47. Richard Le Gallienne, *The Romantic Nineties* (New York: Doubleday, 1925), 270–71.
48. Walter Pater, *Studies in the History of the Renaissance* (London: Macmillan, 1873), 211.
49. Osbert Burdett, *The Beardsley Period: An Essay in Perspective* (London: John Lane, 1925), 290.
50. Ibid., 7.
51. For further discussion of aestheticism's interest in the concept of detachment, see Andrew Eastham's *Aesthetic Afterlives: Irony, Literary Modernity, and the Ends of Beauty* (New York: Continuum, 2011).
52. Amanda Anderson, *The Powers of Distance: Cosmopolitanism and the Cultivation of Detachment* (Princeton, NJ: Princeton University Press, 2001), 153.

53. Pater, *Studies in the History of the Renaissance*, 210.
54. Quoted in Lawrence Danson, *Max Beerbohm and the Act of Writing* (New York: Oxford University Press, 1989), 230.
55. Vincent Sherry, *Modernism and the Reinvention of Decadence* (New York: Cambridge University Press, 2014), 153.
56. Many recent scholars have focused on the high modernists' need to repress or deny the significance of Victorian aesthetic strategies in their attempts to establish their own practices as vital, radical, and "new." See, e.g., Jessica Feldman, "Modernism's Victorian Bric-a-Brac," *Modernism/Modernity* 8, no. 3 (2001): 453–70. Feldman argues that "when modernist writers insist upon radical discontinuity, we should not take them at their word. We should examine those words and the resulting works of art carefully, because Victorian practices often vitally inform modernists works" (454). In *The Victorians in the Rearview Mirror* (Athens: Ohio University Press, 2007), Simon Joyce demonstrates that, though the members of the Bloomsbury group endeavored to represent themselves as firmly in revolt against the Victorians, their engagement with the Victorian past was sustained and complex. Feldman's and Joyce's work is part of a larger movement that works to blur the boundary between Victorian and modernist art and literature. This line of scholarship has allowed us to see that the modernists often borrowed and revised Victorian tropes, styles, and strategies. See, e.g., David Weir, *Decadence and the Making of Modernism* (Amherst: University of Massachusetts Press, 1995), and Eastham, *Aesthetic Afterlives*. My work is very much a part of this recent attempt to rethink the Victorian/modern divide. However, rather than establishing the roots of modernism in the Victorian period, I would like to look at figures who remain defiantly Victorian in the early twentieth century.

    For further discussion of the Victorian/modern divide, see, e.g., Cassandra Laity, *H.D. and the Victorian Fin de Siècle: Gender, Modernism, Decadence* (New York: Cambridge University Press, 1996); Anne Elizabeth Jamison, *Poetics en Passant: Redefining the Relationship between Victorian and Modern Poetry* (New York: Palgrave Macmillan, 2009); and Rachel Teukolsky, *The Literate Eye: Victorian Art Writing and Modernist Aesthetics* (New York: Oxford University Press, 2009).
57. Within the field of new modernist studies, critics have enriched our understanding of the modernist period by attending to works that would not typically be understood as high modernist. As Douglas Mao and Rebecca Walkowitz note, "were one seeking a single word to sum up transformations in modernist literary scholarship over the past decade or two, one could do worse than light on *expansion*." Douglas Mao and Rebecca Walkowitz, "The New Modernist Studies," *PMLA* 123, no. 3 (2008): 737.
58. Many critiques of aestheticism as apolitical, including Peter Bürger's characterization of the emergence of aestheticism as the moment when "the distance from the praxis of life" became the content of the work of art, drew on Theodor Adorno's characterization of Wilde as a "[prelude] to the culture industry." Adorno, *Aesthetic Theory* (Minneapolis: University of Minnesota Press, 1997),

239; Peter Bürger, *Theory of the Avant-Garde* (Minneapolis: University of Minnesota Press, 1984), 49. Recent work in Victorian studies has worked to trouble this vision of aestheticism by foregrounding the fact that Victorian aesthetes and Decadents often expressed earnest commitments to political ideals while at the same time espousing the motto "art for art's sake."

59. My work is in conversation with work by scholars, such as Diana Maltz and Ruth Livesey, who foreground aestheticism's political investments. See, e.g., Ruth Livesey, *Socialism, Sex, and the Culture of Aestheticism in Britain, 1880–1914* (New York: Oxford University Press for the British Academy, 2007), and Diana Maltz, *British Aestheticism and the Urban Working Classes, 1870–1900: Beauty for the People* (New York: Palgrave Macmillan, 2005). This recent work has allowed us to see how aestheticism was put to highly political use at the turn of the century in Britain by socialist artists and social reformers.
60. Pater, *Studies in the History of the Renaissance*, 211.
61. Bristow, *Effeminate England*, 110.
62. Bristow, for example, notes that Firbank "despised" the empire. Bristow, *Effeminate England*, 123. Christopher Lane describes Firbank as marked by a "national ambivalence" that "oscillates between Anglophilia and Anglophobia." Lane, *The Ruling Passion: British Colonial Allegory and the Paradox of Homosexual Desire* (Durham, NC: Duke University Press, 1995), 182.
63. Georges Letissier, "Alan Hollinghurst/Ronald Firbank: Camp Filiation as an Aesthetic of the Outrageous," *Études britanniques contemporaines* 45 (2013), http://ebc.revues.org/742.
64. In tying the Decadent posture to cosmopolitanism, I am also in conversation with recent work, by, for example, Tanya Agathocleous and Matthew Potolsky, that has noted the interplay between aestheticism or Decadence and cosmopolitanism at the fin de siècle. Agathocleous, for example, argues that "cosmopolitanism, like aestheticism, requires an attention to form – a self-consciousness about the medium and means through which any kind of unification is represented." Agathocleous, "London Mysteries and International Conspiracies: James, Doyle, and the Aesthetics of Cosmopolitanism," *Nineteenth-Century Contexts* 26, no. 2 (2004): 127. Matthew Potolsky argues that "Huysmans and Pater criticize the nationalist insistence on a unified canon founded on a vernacular language, promoting instead an international canon based on linguistic, cultural, and formal hybridity. Most suggestively, the decadent canons in Huysmans and Pater answer nationalist canons by imagining new forms of dispersed, cosmopolitan, and self-selected community bound only by taste, not by race, geography, or language." Potolsky, "Decadence, Nationalism, and the Logic of Canon Formation," *Modern Language Quarterly* 67, no. 2 (2006): 216. I am similarly interested in the manner in which Decadence seems to enable forms of resistance to the lure of nationalist or patriotic discourse.
65. George Bernard Shaw, "A Political Contrast," *The Nation*, September 18, 1920, 759.

66. Quoted in S. N. Behrman, *Portrait of Max* (New York: Random House, 1960), 265.
67. Beresford Egan, *Epitaph* (London: Fortune Press, 1943), 25.
68. This is not to say that nostalgia itself cannot operate in complex political ways. For a rich discussion of the politics of nostalgia for the Victorian past in the early twentieth century, see Chapter 2, "The Politics of Nostalgia: Conservative Modernism, Victorian Kitsch, and the English Country House," in Simon Joyce's *The Victorians in the Rearview Mirror*.
69. Linda Hutcheon, *A Poetics of Postmodernism: History, Theory, Fiction* (London: Routledge, 1988), 4.
70. Critics such as Marie-Luise Kohlke and Stephen Mills have used the term *post-Victorian* to refer to the era immediately following the Victorian period, but other critics, such as John Kucich, Diane Sadoff, and Andrea Kirchknopf, have used the term to describe neo-Victorian texts or postmodern texts preoccupied with the Victorian period. In this work, I reserve the use of this term to describe works composed in the early decades of the twentieth century that continue and extend late-Victorian aesthetic practices. See Marie-Luise Kohlke, "Introduction: Speculations in and on the Neo-Victorian Encounter," *Neo-Victorian Studies* 1, no. 1 (2008): 1–18; Stephen Mills, introduction to *Victorianism in the United States: Its Era and Its Legacy*, ed. Steve Ickingrill and Stephen Mills (Amsterdam: VU University Press, 1992), ix–xxi; John Kucich and Dianne F. Sadoff, *Victorian Afterlife: Postmodern Culture Rewrites the Nineteenth Century* (Minneapolis: University of Minnesota Press, 2000); Dianne F. Sadoff, *Victorian Vogue: British Novels on Screen* (Minneapolis: University of Minnesota Press, 2010); and Andrea Kirchknopf, *Rewriting the Victorians: Modes of Literary Engagement with the 19th Century* (Jefferson, NC: McFarland, 2013).
71. Rohan McWilliam, "Victorian Sensations, Neo-Victorian Romance: Response," *Victorian Studies* 52, no. 1 (2009): 107.

    For a discussion of Neo-Victorianism's particular affinity for the fin de siècle, see Margaret Stetz, "The Afterlives of Aestheticism and Decadence in the Twenty-First Century," *Victorian Literature and Culture* 38, no. 1 (2010): 306–11.
72. Mark Llewellyn, "What Is Neo-Victorian Studies," *Journal of Neo-Victorian Studies* 1, no. 1 (2008): 172.

NOTES TO CHAPTER ONE

1. Max Beerbohm, *Rossetti and His Circle* (London: William Heinemann, 1922), frontispiece.
2. Ibid., vi.
3. Ibid.
4. Ibid.
5. Max Beerbohm, *The Works of Max Beerbohm* (London: John Lane/The Bodley Head, 1896), 160.
6. Max Beerbohm, *Mainly on the Air* (New York: Knopf, 1946), 31.

7. Moray McLaren to Max Beerbohm, October 28, 1935, BBC Written Archive, Reading, UK.
8. Linda Hutcheon, "Irony, Nostalgia, and the Postmodern," in *Methods for the Study of Literature as Cultural Memory*, ed. Raymond Vervliet and Annemarie Estor (Amsterdam: Rodopi, 1998), 191.
9. Beerbohm, *Mainly on the Air*, 33.
10. Max Beerbohm, manuscript of "Prefatory Note" to *Mainly on the Air*, Mark Samuels Lasner Collection, on loan to the University of Delaware, Newark, 2.
11. Quoted in S. N. Behrman, *Portrait of Max* (New York: Random House, 1960), 265.
12. Quoted in Lawrence Danson, "Max Beerbohm and the Mirror of the Past," *Princeton University Library Chronicle* 43, no. 2 (1982): 92.
13. Gary McMahon, *Camp in Literature* (Jefferson, NC: McFarland, 2006), 9.
14. Susan Sontag, "Notes on Camp," in *A Susan Sontag Reader* (New York: Farrar, Straus, Giroux, 1982), 106, 107.
15. Dennis Denisoff, *Aestheticism and Sexual Parody 1840–1940* (New York: Cambridge University Press, 2006), 127.
16. Sontag asserts that "camp sees everything in quotation marks." Sontag, "Notes on Camp," 109.
17. Hutcheon, "Irony, Nostalgia, and the Postmodern," 205.
18. Danson, *Act of Writing*, 35.
19. Max Beerbohm, "A Defence of Cosmetics," *The Yellow Book* I (1894): 65, 68.
20. Max Beerbohm, "A Letter to the Editor," *The Yellow Book* II (1894): 281.
21. Ibid., 284.
22. N. John Hall, *Max Beerbohm: A Kind of Life* (New Haven, CT: Yale University Press, 2002), 31.
23. Ibid., 28.
24. Max Beerbohm to Reggie Turner, May 3, 1895, in *Letters to Reggie Turner*, ed. Rupert Hart-Davis (London: R. Hart-Davis, 1964), 102.
25. Oscar Wilde to Max Beerbohm, circa May 28, 1897, in *The Complete Letters of Oscar Wilde*, ed. Merlin Holland and Rupert Hart-Davis (New York: Henry Holt, 2000), 856.
26. Max Beerbohm, *A Peep into the Past* (New York: M. Harzof, 1923), 11.
27. Behrman, *Portrait of Max*, 48.
28. David Cecil, *Max: A Biography* (London: Constable, 1964), 180.
29. Max Beerbohm, *The Second Childhood of John Bull* (London: Stephen Swift, 1911), plates 2, 8, and 9.
30. Ibid., plate 11.
31. Ibid., plate 13.
32. Danson, *Act of Writing*, 169.
33. Max Beerbohm to Holbrook Jackson, October 30, 1913, in *Letters of Max Beerbohm, 1892–1956*, ed. Rupert Hart-Davis (New York: W. W. Norton, 1989), 94.
34. Quoted in N. John Hall, *Max Beerbohm Caricatures* (New Haven, CT: Yale University Press, 1997), 35.

35. Max Beerbohm, *A Christmas Garland* (London: William Heinemann, 1912), 17.
36. Ibid., 19.
37. Ibid.
38. Hall, *Max Beerbohm: A Kind of Life*, 146.
39. Max Beerbohm to Reggie Turner, December 27, 1914, in *Letters to Reggie Turner*, 239.
40. Cecil, *Max*, 334.
41. In a 1914 letter to Reggie Turner, Beerbohm writes, "The spirit of England is beautiful. Ever since I have lived away from England I have been growing more and more fond and proud of England as an *idea*." Max Beerbohm to Reggie Turner, September 6, 1914, in *Letters to Reggie Turner*, 236.
42. Ibid., 234.
43. Ibid., 235.
44. Cecil, *Max*, 339.
45. Christopher Morley to Louis Kronenberger, June 24, 1947, Mark Samuels Lasner Collection.
46. Bohun Lynch, *Max Beerbohm in Perspective* (London: William Heinemann, 1921), 130.
47. Ibid.
48. Beerbohm, *Works of Max Beerbohm*, 12.
49. Beerbohm, *Rossetti and His Circle*, vi.
50. R. E. F., "Lady Lilith by Dante Gabriel Rossetti," *Bulletin of the Metropolitan Museum of Art* 3, no. 7 (1908): 144.
51. *Christian Science Monitor*, "Rossetti, Laszlo, Zorn, and Sargent: Four Great Names," April 28, 1916, 8.
52. Roger Fry, "Rossetti's Water Colours of 1857," *The Burlington Magazine for Connoisseurs* 29, no. 159 (1916): 100.
53. Danson, *Act of Writing*, 241.
54. Ibid.
55. Beerbohm, *Rossetti and His Circle*.
56. Ibid.
57. Ibid.
58. Ibid.
59. Advertising pamphlet for *Rossetti and His Circle*, Mark Samuels Lasner Collection.
60. Edmund Wilson, *Classics and Commercials: A Literary Chronicle of the Forties* (New York: Farrar, Strauss, 1950), 433.
61. Ibid., 82.
62. Ibid.
63. Ibid., 84.
64. Danson, "Max Beerbohm and the Mirror of the Past," 88.
65. Danson, *Act of Writing*, 235.
66. Behrman, *Portrait of Max*, 41.
67. Max Beerbohm, *Seven Men* (London: William Heinemann, 1919), 8

68. Ibid. 6, 7.
69. Quoted in Cecil, *Max,* 336. N. John Hall does note, "Max was exhibited during the war, but not by his own doing. The Rossetti drawings were purchased by Mrs. Charles Hunter. . . . In November 1917 she lent fifteen of the drawings to Grosvenor Gallery for its Modern Loan Exhibition." Hall, *Max Beerbohm: A Kind of Life*, 153.
70. Cecil, *Max*, 337.
71. Ibid., 338.
72. Ibid., 336.
73. Max Beerbohm to Arnold Bennett, December 1, 1915, quoted in Arnold Bennett, *Letters of Arnold Bennett*, Vol. III, ed. James Hepburn (New York: Oxford University Press, 1970), 58.
74. Evelyn Waugh, "Lesson of the Master," *The Sunday Times*, May 27, 1956, 8.
75. Quoted in Hall, *A Kind of Life*, 154.
76. Henry McBride, "Max Beerbohm's Rossetti," *Dial* 74 (February 1923): 206.
77. Lloyd Goodrich, "*Rossetti and His Circle* by Max Beerbohm," *The Arts* 5 (1924): 294.
78. "Anonymous review of 'A Survey' and 'Rossetti and His Circle' by Max Beerbohm," *The Connoisseur: An Illustrated Magazine for Collectors* 64 (1922): 255.
79. Yvonne Cloud, "Max Beerbohm," *The Graphic*, April 18, 1925, 610.
80. Lynch, *Max Beerbohm in Perspective*, 74–75.
81. Ibid., 153.
82. Ibid., 158.
83. Ibid.
84. Stephen Gwynn, *Experiences of a Literary Man* (London: Thornton Butterworth, 1926), 142.
85. Max Beerbohm, *A Survey* (London: William Heinemann, 1921), Plate 34.
86. Ibid.
87. Ibid.
88. Max Beerbohm, *And Even Now* (London: William Heinemann, 1920), 185.
89. Danson, *Max Beerbohm and the Act of Writing*, 148.
90. Ibid.
91. Roger Fry to Max Beerbohm, May 11, 1917, in *Letters of Roger Fry*, Vol. II, ed. Denys Sutton (London: Chatto and Windus, 1972), 411.
92. Visitors' books, Max Beerbohm Collection.
93. Lytton Strachey to Max Beerbohm, August 1, 1918, Max Beerbohm Collection.
94. Ibid.
95. Virginia Woolf, "The Modern Essay," in *The Common Reader* (London: Hogarth, 1925), 275.
96. Max Beerbohm to Virginia Woolf, December 30, 1927, in *Letters of Max Beerbohm*, 164.
97. Ibid., 165.
98. Ibid.
99. Ibid.

100. Ibid., 166.
101. Virginia Woolf to Max Beerbohm, January 29, 1928, in *Letters of Max Beerbohm*, 166.
102. Ibid.
103. Ibid., 167.
104. Ibid.
105. Ibid.
106. Ibid.
107. Max Beerbohm to Miss Peyton, February 19, 1928, Mark Samuels Lasner Collection.
108. Moray McLaren to Max Beerbohm, October 28, 1935, BBC Written Archive.
109. Max Beerbohm to Moray McLaren, October, 30, 1935, BBC Written Archive.
110. Moray McLaren to Max Beerbohm, November 19, 1935, BBC Written Archive.
111. Moray McLaren, BBC Internal Circulating Memo, November 1, 1935, BBC Written Archive.
112. Ibid.
113. Ibid.
114. Ibid.
115. Beerbohm, *Mainly on the Air*, 65.
116. Ibid., 4.
117. Ibid.
118. Ibid., 7.
119. Ibid., 8–9.
120. Ibid., 10.
121. Ibid., 11.
122. Ibid.
123. Max Beerbohm to C. V. Salmon, July 3, 1942, BBC Written Archive.
124. C. V. Salmon to Max Beerbohm, July 8, 1942, BBC Written Archive.
125. Max Beerbohm to C. V. Salmon, July 24, 1942, BBC Written Archive.
126. Ibid.
127. G. R. Barnes, BBC Internal Circulating Memo, October 2, 1942, BBC Written Archive.
128. Beerbohm, *Mainly on the Air*, 21–22.
129. Ibid., 22.
130. Hutcheon, "Irony, Nostalgia, and the Postmodern," 207.
131. BBC Broadcasting Corporation, "An Audience Research Report: W.B. Yeats, December 26, 1954," Mark Samuels Lasner Collection.
132. Ibid.
133. Ibid.
134. Max Beerbohm, Manuscript of "W.B. Yeats," Mark Samuels Lasner Collection, 2.
135. Ibid., 5.
136. Ibid.
137. Ibid.

138. Claire Price, "The Last of the Exquisites," *New York Times Magazine*, September 10, 1939, 14.
139. Anthony Victor Cookman, "Max: An Enduring Cult," *Times Literary Supplement*, September 7, 1946, 426.
140. Ibid.
141. Kathleen Bruce to Max Beerbohm, January 19, 1942, Mark Samuels Lasner Collection.
142. Siegfried Sassoon to Max Beerbohm, December 29, 1935, in *Siegfried Sassoon: Letters to Max Beerbohm with a Few Answers*, ed. Rupert Hart Davis (London: Faber and Faber, 1986), 26.
143. Louis Kronenberger, "The Perfect Trifler," *The Saturday Review of Literature*, June 21, 1947, 9.
144. Frances Winwar, "Max Beerbohm at the Microphone," *New York Times*, January 26, 1947, BR4.
145. Price, "Last of the Exquisites," 14.
146. William Borst to Max Beerbohm, July 8, 1939, Mark Samuels Lasner Collection.
147. Harold Hobson, *The Devil in Woodford Wells: A Fantastic Novel* (London: Longmans, 1946).
148. Birthday book, Max Beerbohm Collection 1.13. Quotation from Augustus John appears courtesy of the estate of Augustus Edwin John/Bridgeman Images.
149. Ibid. Quoted in Hall, *A Kind of Life*, 217.
150. Price, "Last of the Exquisites," 14.
151. Bertrand Russell, "The Faultless Max at 80," *New York Times Magazine*, August 24, 1952, 18.
152. Ibid.
153. Ibid.
154. E. H. J., "A Posy for Rapallo," *Christian World*, August 28, 1952, 4.
155. Ibid.
156. Max Beerbohm, *Lytton Strachey* (New York: Alfred A. Knopf, 1943), 13.
157. Ibid.

NOTES TO CHAPTER TWO

1. Vernon Lee to Logan Pearsall Smith, October 23, 1919, in Mandy Gagel, ed., "Selected Letters of Vernon Lee (1856–1935)" (PhD diss., Boston University, 2008), 705.
2. Ibid.
3. Lee published *Satan the Waster: A Philosophic War Trilogy* in 1920, *Proteus, or The Future of Intelligence* in 1925, *The Golden Keys* in 1925, *The Poet's Eye* in 1926, *For Maurice: Five Unlikely Stories* in 1927, and *Music and Its Lovers* in 1932.
4. Floyd N. House, "Review of the Today and Tomorrow Series," *American Journal of Sociology* 31, no. 2 (1925): 271.

5. Quotation from Dr. James F. Clarke used in advertisements for the Today and Tomorrow series that appeared in periodicals including the *Bookman* and the *New York Evening Post*. See, e.g., Today and Tomorrow series, advertisement, *New York Evening Post*, November 16, 1925, 11.
6. Simeon Strunsky, "About Books, More or Less: Here Are Babies," *New York Times*, January 25, 1925, BR4; quotation from *Commercial Tribune* review that appeared on the book jacket of Lee's *Proteus* as well as in advertisements for the Today and Tomorrow series published in periodicals including the *New York Times* and the *Saturday Review of Literature*. See, e.g., Today and Tomorrow series, advertisement, *Saturday Review of Literature*, April 14, 1928, 766.
7. George Bernard Shaw, "A Political Contrast," *The Nation*, no. 27 (September 18, 1920): 759.
8. Vernon Lee's relationship to Decadence was extremely complicated, and the question of how to categorize that relationship continues to trouble critics today. In "Vernon Lee: Decadent Woman?," Ruth Robbins acknowledges that the term *Decadent* is more frequently applied to works by male writers and that Lee's "relationship to Decadent thought is not clear-cut," but she nevertheless insists that Lee's works exhibit Decadent characteristics. Robbins, "Vernon Lee: Decadent Woman?," in *Fin de Siècle/Fin du Globe*, ed. John Stokes (New York: St. Martin's Press, 1992), 157. Matthew Potolsky's discussion of Lee in relationship to "decadent cosmopolitanism," the inclusion of Lee's work in the *Daughters of Decadence* collection, and Catherine Maxwell and Patricia Pulham's decision to title their recent edited collection *Vernon Lee: Decadence, Ethics, Aesthetics* indicate that Lee and her work continue to be linked with the Decadent Movement. Matthew Potolsky, *The Decadent Republic of Letters: Taste, Politics, and Cosmopolitan Community from Baudelaire to Beardsley* (Philadelphia: University of Pennsylvania Press, 2012), 135–43. However, it is also the case that works such as *Miss Brown* (1884) articulate a caustic critique of aestheticism. The most useful approach to describing Lee's complicated relationship to both aestheticism and Decadence might be to think of her as, like Beerbohm, critiquing both movements from an insider's perspective.
9. Vernon Lee, *Renaissance Fancies and Studies* (London: Smith, Elder, 1895), 256.
10. Mario Praz identified Pater as "the forerunner to the Decadent Movement in England." Praz, *The Romantic Agony*, 1933, trans. Angus Davidson (Oxford: Oxford University Press, 1985), 355. As Betsy Winakur Tontiplapho notes, "the Decadents adopted the Conclusion of Pater's *Renaissance*, which ostensibly advocates living through the eyes, ears, nose, mouth, and skin, as their unofficial manifesto." Tontiplapho, *Poetics of Luxury in the Nineteenth Century: Keats, Tennyson, and Hopkins* (Burlington, VT: Ashgate, 2011), 187. In her emphasis on Paterian ideas about beauty, pleasure, and detachment, then, Lee may be seen as channeling an earlier form of aestheticism or as expressing the central Paterian sentiments of Decadence.
11. Vernon Lee, *Proteus, or the Future of Intelligence* (London: Kegan Paul, 1925), 58.
12. Ibid., 59.

13. Ibid., 11.
14. Walter Pater, *Marius the Epicurean*, vol. 2 (London: Macmillan, 1885), 353.
15. Oscar Wilde, *The Complete Works of Oscar Wilde*, vol. 4 (New York: Oxford University Press, 2007), 85.
16. Lee, *Proteus*, 14.
17. Lee has begun to receive significantly more critical attention in the past ten years. However, not enough attention has been paid to Lee's pacifist and post-World War I writings. Notable exceptions include Gillian Beer's essay "The Dissidence of Vernon Lee: *Satan the Waster* and the Will to Believe," in *Women's Fiction and the Great War*, ed. Suzanne Raitt and Trudi Tate, 107–31 (New York: Oxford University Press, 1997); Patricia Pulham's "Violence and the Pacifist Body in Vernon Lee's *The Ballet of the Nations*," in *Conflict, Nationhood, and Corporeality in Modern Literature: Bodies-at-War*, ed. Petra Rau, 46–63 (New York: Palgrave Macmillan, 2010); and Grace Brockington, "Performing Pacifism: The Battle Between Artist and Author in *The Ballet of the Nations*," in *Vernon Lee: Decadence, Ethics, Aesthetics*, ed. Catherine Maxwell and Patricia Pulham, 143–59 (New York: Palgrave Macmillan, 2006). Lee's pacifism also plays a prominent role in Patrick Wright's *Iron Curtain: From Stage to Cold War* (New York: Oxford University Press, 2007), and in Sondeep Kandola's *Vernon Lee* (Devon, UK: Northcote House, 2010).
18. Vernon Lee to Leo Stein, April 24, 1920, in "Selected Letters of Vernon Lee," 718.
19. Ibid.
20. Ibid., 719.
21. Ibid.
22. Ibid.
23. Hilary Fraser, "Writing in the Margins and Reading between the Lines in Vernon Lee's Library," in *Dalla Stanza Accanto: Vernon Lee e Firenze Settant'Anni Dopo: Atti del Convegno Internazionale di Studi Firenze*, ed. Serena Cenni and Elisa Bizzotto (Florence, Italy: University of Florence, 2006), 233.
24. This note appears on p. 463 of Lee's copy of George Bernard Shaw's *Intelligent Woman's Guide to Socialism and Capitalism* (London: Constable, 1928), Vernon Lee Collection, British Institute of Florence, Florence, Italy.
25. Vernon Lee, *Gospels of Anarchy and Other Contemporary Studies* (London: T. Fisher Unwin, 1908), 359.
26. H. J. Jackson, "Writing in Books and Other Marginal Activities," *University of Toronto Quarterly* 62, no. 2 (1992): 218–19.
27. Paul Crook, *Darwinism, War and History: The Debate over the Biology of War from the "Origin of Species" to the First World War* (Cambridge: Cambridge University Press, 1994), 130.
28. Beer, "Dissidence of Vernon Lee," 115.
29. Wilfred Trotter, *Instincts of the Herd in Peace and War* (London: T. Fisher Unwin, 1917), 173. *Instincts of the Herd* was first published in 1916, but the edition in the Vernon Lee Collection in the British Institute of Florence is from 1917. All citations here refer to the 1917 edition of the text.

30. Ibid., 157.
31. This note appears on p. 111 of Lee's copy of *Instincts of the Herd in Peace and War*, Vernon Lee Collection.
32. Trotter, *Instincts*, 171.
33. This note appears on p. 170 of Lee's copy of *Instincts of the Herd in Peace and War.*
34. Vernon Lee, "Bismarck Towers," *New Statesman,* February 20, 1915, 483.
35. Ibid.
36. Trotter, *Instincts*, 178.
37. This note appears on p. 178 of Lee's copy of *Instincts of the Herd in Peace and War.*
38. Caroline Playne, *The Neuroses of the Nations* (London: G. Allen and Unwin, 1925), 8; Sybil Oldfield, "Playne, Caroline Elizabeth (1857–1948)," in *Oxford Dictionary of National Biography* (New York: Oxford University Press, 2004), http://www.oxforddnb.com/view/article/38530.
39. The Union of Democratic Control was founded in 1914 to express dissent concerning Great Britain's foreign policy. They published books, pamphlets, and a journal. Lee published in the UDC's journal, and she contributed *Peace with Honour* (1915) to the UDC's pamphlet series.
40. Vineta Colby, *Vernon Lee: A Literary Biography* (Charlottesville: University of Virginia Press, 2003), 301.
41. Playne, *Neuroses*, 6.
42. Ibid.
43. Ibid., 15.
44. Max Nordau, *Degeneration* (London: William Heinemann, 1895), 42.
45. Vernon Lee, "Deterioration of the Soul," *Fortnightly Review* 59 (1896): 931.
46. See Richard Dellamora, "Productive Decadence: 'The Queer Comradeship of Outlawed Thought': Vernon Lee, Max Nordau, and Oscar Wilde," *New Literary History* 35 (2005): 529–46.
47. Playne, *Neuroses*, 8.
48. This note appears on p. 97 of Lee's copy of *The Neuroses of the Nations*, Vernon Lee Collection.
49. Playne, *Neuroses*, 136.
50. Ibid., 59.
51. This note appears on p. 59 of Lee's copy of *Neuroses of the Nations.*
52. Ibid., 60.
53. Ibid., 64.
54. Ibid.
55. This note appears on p. 64 of Lee's copy of *Neuroses of the Nations.*
56. This note appears on p. 97 of Lee's copy of *Neuroses of the Nations.*
57. Paul Crook, "Nature's Pruning Hook? War and Evolution, 1890–1918," *Australian Journal of Politics and History* 33, no. 3 (1987): 249.
58. The edition of *The Biology of War* in the Vernon Lee Collection in the British Institute of Florence is from 1919. All citations here refer to the 1919 edition of the text.

59. Constance Grande and Julian Grande, "Translator's Preface," in *The Biology of War* (London: J. M. Dent, 1919), viii.
60. L. L. Bernard, "Review (*The Biology of War*)," *The American Journal of Sociology* 25, no. 1 (1919): 97.
61. Jackson, "Writing in Books and Other Marginal Activities," 219.
62. G. F. Nicolai, *The Biology of War* (London: J. M. Dent, 1919), 173.
63. Ibid., 4.
64. Ibid.
65. Ibid., 10.
66. Ibid., 8.
67. Ibid., 18.
68. Ibid., 66.
69. This note appears on p. 66 of Lee's copy of *The Biology of War*, Vernon Lee Collection.
70. Ibid., 68.
71. Ibid., 36.
72. Ibid., 38.
73. This note appears on p. 38 of Lee's copy of *The Biology of War.*
74. Ibid., 56.
75. Ibid., 63.
76. Ibid., 15, 63.
77. In 1897, Vernon Lee and Kit Anstruther Thomson published the two-part essay "Beauty and Ugliness" in the *Contemporary Review*. The essay recounts Kit's physical responses to objects and artworks, which are in turn interpreted by Lee. The two concluded together that the pleasure one experiences when contemplating a thing of beauty arises from one's unconscious, bodily imitation of the balance or symmetry in a work of art. This experience results in increased vitality and a sensation of harmony.
78. Walter Pater, *Studies in the History of the Renaissance* (London: Macmillan, 1873), 213.
79. Vernon Lee, *Belcaro: Being Essays on Sundry Aesthetical Questions* (London: T. Fisher Unwin, 1887), 210.
80. Ibid., 227.
81. Lee, *Gospels*, 54.
82. Ibid., 38.
83. Ibid.
84. Ibid., 53.
85. Vernon Lee, *Satan the Waster: A Philosophic War Trilogy* (London: The Bodley Head, 1920), 236–37.
86. Vernon Lee, *Laurus Nobilis: Chapters on Art and Life* (London: John Lane/The Bodley Head, 1909), 57.
87. This argument is developed in my essay "Haunted Collections: Vernon Lee and Ethical Consumption," *Criticism: A Quarterly for Literature and the Arts* 48, no. 1 (2006): 39–67.
88. Vernon Lee, "The Sense of Nationality," *The Nation,* October 12, 1912, 96.

89. Ibid., 96, 97.
90. Ibid., 96.
91. Jonathan Freedman, *Professions of Taste: Henry James, British Aestheticism and Commodity Culture* (Stanford, CA: Stanford University Press, 1990), 69.
92. Pater, *Studies in the History of the Renaissance*, 211.
93. Ibid., 212.
94. Lee, *Satan*, 239.
95. Ibid., xvii.
96. Vernon Lee, "The Heart of a Neutral," *Atlantic Monthly* 116 (1915): 687.
97. Ibid.
98. Ibid.
99. Lee, *Satan*, vxii.
100. Ibid., xviii.
101. See Amanda Anderson, *The Powers of Distance: Cosmopolitanism and the Cultivation of Detachment* (Princeton, NJ: Princeton University Press, 2001).
102. Rebecca Walkowitz, *Cosmopolitan Style: Modernism beyond the Nation* (New York: Columbia University Press, 2006), 10.
103. For further discussion of Lee's cosmopolitanism, see Francesca Billiani and Stefano Evangelista, "Carlo Placci and Vernon Lee: The Aesthetics and Ethics of Cosmopolitanism in Fin de Siècle Florence," *Comparative Critical Studies* 10, no. 2 (2013): 141–61. In their discussion of Lee's relationship to Placci, Billiani and Evangelista stress Lee's skepticism concerning what she saw as a tendency to excessive detachment from social concerns and the treatment of the world as a source of pleasure in certain strands of cosmopolitanism. However, they also acknowledge that "Lee's negative critique of cosmopolitanism needs to be read against the positive cosmopolitan practice she adopts in her own work on art and aesthetics" (156).
104. Lee, *Satan*, xxxii.
105. Ibid.
106. Ibid.
107. Ibid., xxxiii.
108. In the conclusion to *Studies in the History of the Renaissance*, Pater asks, "How can we pass most swiftly from point to point, and be present always at the focus where the greatest number of vital forces unite in their purest energy?" See Pater, *Studies in the History of the Renaissance,* 210. He argues that to maintain this type of alert and engaged ecstasy is success, whereas failure is to form habits that render the eye rough and insensitive to difference.
109. Lee, *Satan*, xxxiv.
110. Ibid.
111. Ibid., xxxvii–xxxviii.
112. Portions of the project were published in the periodical press before 1932. An essay titled "Varieties of Musical Experience," for example, appeared in the *North American* in 1918.
113. This essay is cited by Patrick Wright as the first instance in which the "iron curtain" was taken from the theater and converted into a political metaphor. Lee refers in the essay to "War's monstrous iron curtain," which cuts nations

off entirely from one another. See Vernon Lee, "Bach's Christmas Music in England and Germany," *Jus Suffragii*, January 1, 1915, 218.

114. Lee, "Bach's Christmas Music in England and Germany," 218.
115. Ibid.
116. Vernon Lee, *Music and Its Lovers: An Empirical Study of Emotion and Imaginative Response to Music* (London: George Allen and Unwin, 1932), 34.
117. In "The School of Giorgione," Pater argues that "all art constantly aspires towards the condition of music." Pater, "The School of Giorgione," *The Fortnightly Review* 22 (October 1877): 528; Lee, *Music and Its Lovers*, 23.
118. Lee, *Music and Its Lovers*, 23.
119. Ibid., 56, 64.
120. Ibid., 515.
121. Ibid., 102.
122. Ibid., 98.
123. Ibid., 490.
124. Ibid., 559.
125. Ibid., 560.
126. Ibid., 561.
127. Evangelista and Billiani, "Carlo Placci and Vernon Lee," 161.
128. Richard Dellamora, "Vernon Lee's Moment," *Nineteenth-Century Gender Studies* 2, no. 2 (2006), http://www.ncgsjournal.com/issue22/dellamora.htm.
129. Ibid.
130. Shaw, "A Political Contrast," 758.
131. Quoted in Richard Cary, "Shaw Reviews *Satan the Waster*," *Colby Quarterly* 9, no. 6 (1971): 341.
132. Anonymous review of *Satan the Waster* by Vernon Lee, *Spectator*, May 9, 1930, 26.
133. "New Books," *The Manchester Guardian*, June 23, 1920, 7.
134. "The Decay of Satire," *Times Literary Supplement*, June 24, 1920, 389.
135. For further discussion of Lee and Wells's debate concerning the war in the pages of the *Labour Leader* and the *Nation*, see Colby, *Vernon Lee*, 289–90.
136. See Martha S. Vogeler, *Austin Harrison and the* English Review (Columbia: University of Missouri Press, 2008), 243.
137. See Damon Franke, *Modernist Heresies: British Literary History, 1883–1924* (Columbus: Ohio State University Press, 2008).
138. Anonymous review of *Proteus, or the Future of Intelligence* by Vernon Lee, *The Living Age* 326, no. 4232 (1925): 386.
139. Carroll Mason Sparrow, "Phoebus, or the Future of Prophecy," *The Virginia Quarterly Review* 2, no. 2 (1926): 282.

NOTES TO CHAPTER THREE

1. Mary Butts, "Baron Corvo," *London Mercury* 30, no. 175 (1934): 619.
2. Rolfe wrote under many pseudonyms during his career, including "Prospero," "Frank English," "Frederick Austin," and "Fr. Rolfe." I have chosen to refer

to him as Corvo throughout the chapter because my primary focus is on works and phenomena that use that name, such as Symons's *The Quest for Corvo* and the Corvine Society.

3. A. J. A. Symons, *The Quest for Corvo: An Experiment in Biography* (New York: Macmillan, 1934), 70.
4. Julian Symons, *A. J. A. Symons: His Life and Speculations* (London: Eyre and Spottiswoode, 1950), 117.
5. Symons, *Quest for Corvo*, 163.
6. Ibid., 283.
7. Butts, "Baron Corvo," 619.
8. Ibid., 620.
9. Ibid.
10. Ibid.
11. Ibid., 622.
12. Symons, *Quest for Corvo*, 13.
13. Butts, "Baron Corvo," 624.
14. Pamela Johnson, "The Fascination of the Paranoid Personality: Baron Corvo," *Essays and Studies* 16 (1963): 12–15.
15. Regenia Gagnier, *The Insatiability of Human Wants: Economics and Aesthetics in Market Society* (Chicago: University of Chicago Press, 2000), 152, 147–48.
16. Ibid., 152.
17. For further discussion of the history of the literary cult surrounding Corvo and his work, see Robert Scoble, *The Corvo Cult: The History of an Obsession* (London: Strange Attractor Press, 2014). Scoble's work traces the emergence of this cult in the years immediately following Corvo's death and follows the fluctuation in his fan base and reputation to the end of the twentieth century.
18. Frederick Rolfe, *The Desire and Pursuit of the Whole: A Romance of Modern Venice* (London: Cassell, 1934), 238.
19. Frederick Rolfe, *Hadrian the Seventh* (London: Chatto and Windus, 1904), 5–6.
20. Ibid., 2.
21. Ibid., 180.
22. Ibid., 181.
23. Ibid.
24. Ibid., 181–82.
25. Ibid., 181.
26. Ibid.
27. Ibid., 172.
28. Ibid., 365.
29. Ibid., 329.
30. "About San Pietro and San Paulo" and "About the Lilies of San Luigi" appeared in *The Yellow Book* VII (October 1895). "A Caprice of the Cherubim" and "About Beata Beatrice and the Mamma of San Pietro" appeared in *The Yellow Book* IX (April 1896).

31. Rolfe, *Desire and Pursuit of the Whole*, 238.
32. Ibid.
33. Alan Harding, *England in the Thirteenth Century* (New York: Cambridge, 1993), 279.
34. Frederick Rolfe, *Hubert's Arthur* (London: Cassell, 1935), 33.
35. Ibid., 56.
36. Donald Rosenthal, *The Photographs of Frederick Rolfe* (Hanover, NH: Elysium Press, 2008), 19.
37. Thomas Waugh, *Hard to Imagine: Gay Male Eroticism in Photography and Film from Their Beginnings to Stonewall* (New York: Columbia University Press, 1996), 86.
38. Rosenthal, *Photographs of Frederick Rolfe*, 51.
39. Richard Dellamora, *Friendship's Bonds: Democracy and the Novel in Victorian England* (Philadelphia: University of Pennsylvania Press, 2004), 21. Dellamora draws here on Foucault's discussion of Athenian pederasty in Michel Foucault, *The History of Sexuality: Vol. II. The Use of Pleasure* (New York: Random House Trade, 1985).
40. Ibid.
41. As I discuss later in the chapter, the Venice letters circulated privately between collectors in the early decades of the twentieth century. The first print edition of selections from the letters appeared in 1966, edited by Cecil Woolf, in a run of only twenty-five copies. I quote here from the more widely circulated 1974 edition. Frederick Rolfe to Charles Masson Fox, December 11, 1909, in *The Venice Letters*, ed. Cecil Woolf (London: Cecil and Amelia Woolf, 1974), 37.
42. Frederick Rolfe to Charles Masson Fox, n.d., in *Venice Letters*, 15.
43. Frederick Rolfe to Charles Masson Fox, Thursday [probably toward the end of 1909], in *Venice Letters*, 25; Frederick Rolfe to Charles Masson Fox, July 11, 1910, in *Venice Letters*, 66.
44. Frederick Rolfe to Charles Masson Fox, July 11, 1910, in *Venice Letters*, 66.
45. Frederick Rolfe to Charles Masson Fox, December 28, 1909, in *Venice Letters*, 41.
46. Letter Book, David Roth collection of Frederick William Rolfe Papers, Columbia University Rare Books and Manuscript Library, New York.
47. Ibid.
48. Ibid.
49. David Roth, "A Corvo Collection," *Desiderata* 4 (February 1955): 4.
50. Miriam J. Benkovitz, *Frederick Rolfe, Baron Corvo: A Biography* (London: Hamilton, 1977), 228.
51. Symons, *Quest for Corvo*, 233.
52. Frederick Rolfe to Charles Masson Fox, October 25, 1909, in *Venice Letters*, 17.
53. Frederick Rolfe to Charles Masson Fox, July 11, 1910, in *Venice Letters*, 67–68.
54. Gagnier, *Insatiability of Human Wants*, 147.
55. Ibid., 151.
56. Rolfe, *Desire and Pursuit of the Whole*, 126.

57. Frederick Rolfe to James Walsh, May 4, 1903, in *Letters to James Walsh*, ed. Donald Weeks (London: Bertram Rota, 1972), 13.
58. Rolfe, *Hadrian the Seventh*, 12–13.
59. Ibid., 16.
60. Ibid., 54.
61. Ibid., 164, 165.
62. Oscar Wilde, "The Soul of Man under Socialism," *Fortnightly Review*, February 1891, 316. For further discussion of the tension between individualism and socialism at the fin de siècle, see Regenia Gagnier, *Individualism, Decadence and Globalization: On the Relationship of Part to Whole, 1859–1920* (New York: Palgrave Macmillan, 2010).
63. See Henry Pelling, "Baron Corvo and Labour," *Labour Review* V (1960): 35–36, and Henry Pelling, "Corvo and Labour Politics," *Times Literary Supplement*, February 6, 1969, 137.
64. Pelling, "Corvo and Labour Politics," 137.
65. Pelling, "Baron Corvo and Labour," 36.
66. Benkovitz, *Frederick Rolfe*, 67.
67. Donald Weeks, *Frederick William Rolfe and Artists' Models* (Edinburgh: Tragara Press, 1981), 13; Donald Weeks, *Corvo* (London: Michael Joseph, 1971), 106.
68. Benkovitz, *Frederick Rolfe*, 69. See Frederick Rolfe, "An Unforgettable Experience," *To-Day*, April 21, 1894, 324–26.
69. Benkovitz, *Frederick Rolfe*, 69.
70. Pelling, "Corvo and Labour Politics," 137.
71. Rolfe, *Hadrian the Seventh*, 191.
72. Ibid., 179.
73. Quoted in Benkovitz, *Frederick Rolfe*, 68.
74. Corvo dedicated *In His Own Image*, a collection of Toto stories published by John Lane in 1901, to "*Divo Amico Desideratissimo*," and *Nicholas Crabbe* details his search for this friend. *The Desire and Pursuit of the Whole* imagines him eventually finding this divine friend.
75. Frederick Rolfe, *Nicholas Crabbe; or the One and the Many: A Romance* (London: Chatto and Windus, 1958), 218.
76. For a discussion of the Sette of Odd Volumes, see Ellen Crowell, "'We Are Odd!': Ye Archive of Ye Sette of Odd Volumes," *The Center and Clark Newsletter* (Fall 2011): 9–10.
77. Symons, *A. J. A. Symons*, 56.
78. Crowell, "We Are Odd," 9; Symons, *A. J. A. Symons*, 56.
79. For a discussion of the borrowing of practices from the Sette by the Rhymers' Club, see Norman Alford, *The Rhymers' Club: Poets of the Tragic Generation* (New York: St. Martin's Press, 1996), 8–9.
80. Symons, *A. J. A. Symons*, 56.
81. Ibid., 34.
82. Ibid., 26.
83. Ibid., 115, 31.

84. Ibid., 31.
85. Ibid., 34.
86. Ibid., 59–60.
87. A. J. A. Symons, *Frederick Baron Corvo* (London: Curwen Press, 1927), 5.
88. Ibid., 5.
89. Ibid., 30.
90. Ibid., 8.
91. Ibid., 11.
92. Ibid.
93. Ibid.
94. Ibid., 39.
95. Ibid., 40.
96. Ibid.
97. Ibid., 19.
98. Ibid., 18, 20.
99. Ibid., 23.
100. Arthur Symons, "The Decadent Movement in Literature," *Harper's New Monthly* 87 (1893): 859.
101. Symons, *A. J. A. Symons*, 58.
102. A. J. A. Symons, *A. J. A. Symons to Wyndham Lewis: Twenty-Four Letters*, ed. Julian Symons (Edinburgh: Tragara Press, 1982), 3.
103. Ibid.
104. The manuscript of Symons's unfinished biography of Wilde is in the William Andrews Clark Memorial Library along with Douglas's letters to Symons.
105. Symons, *A. J. A. Symons*, 217.
106. Quoted in Gagnier, *Insatiability of Human Wants*, 168.
107. Pater, *Studies in the History of the Renaissance*, 212.
108. Symons, *A. J. A. Symons*, 143.
109. Ibid.
110. Quoted in Symons, *A. J. A. Symons*, 144.
111. A. J. A. Symons, "Editorial Notes," *The Book Collector's Quarterly* I (1930): vi.
112. From an advertising circular sent out at the time. Quoted in Symons, *A. J. A. Symons*, 218.
113. Symons, *A. J. A. Symons*, 220.
114. Ibid., 122.
115. Robert Scoble, "The Corvine Banquets of 1929," *The Book Collector* 56, no. 1 (2007): 66.
116. From the menu of the first banquet, printed in Corvine Society, "A True Recital of the Procedure of the First Banquet Held by the Corvine Society" (1929).
117. Corvine Society, "First Banquet," 2.
118. Corvine Society, "A True Recital of the Procedure of the Second Banquet Held by the Corvine Society" (1929), 3.

119. Ibid.
120. For a full list of attendees, see the proceedings for the first and second banquets.
121. Tom A. Cullen, *A Playful Panther: The Story of J. Maundy Gregory, Con-Man* (Boston: Houghton Mifflin, 1975), 15.
122. Ibid., 21.
123. Ibid., 16.
124. Ibid., 22.
125. Ibid., 24.
126. Symons, *Quest for Corvo,* 269.
127. Ibid., 270.
128. Ibid., 274.
129. Ibid., 272–73.
130. Ibid., 73.
131. Ibid., 274.
132. Ibid., 273.
133. Quoted in Cullen, *A Playful Panther*, 81.
134. Ibid., 100.
135. Quoted in ibid.
136. Quoted in ibid., 126.
137. Ibid., 102.
138. Geoff Tibballs, *The World's Greatest Hoaxes* (New York: Barnes and Noble, 2006), 300.
139. Quoted in *Propriety and Honours: Interim Findings, Fourth Report of Session 2005–06* (London: Stationery Office, 2006), 4.
140. Ibid.
141. Cullen, *A Playful Panther*, 126.
142. Corvine Society, "First Banquet," 6.
143. Ibid., 7.
144. Ibid., 3.
145. Ibid.
146. Corvine Society, "Second Banquet," 14.
147. For a discussion of *The Quest* in relationship to experimentation within the genre of biography in the early twentieth century, see Laura Marcus, "The Newness of the 'New Biography': Biographical Theory and Practice in the Early Twentieth Century," in *Mapping Lives: The Uses of Biography*, ed. Peter France and William St. Clair, 193–218 (New York: Oxford University Press, 2002).
148. Symons states that his "hair began to rise" as he read the letters. Symons, *Quest for Corvo*, 12.
149. Ibid., 2, 3.
150. Ibid., 2.
151. Ibid., 3.
152. Symons, *A. J. A. Symons*, 116–17.
153. Ibid., 12.

154. Ibid.
155. Ibid.
156. Ibid.
157. Ibid., 14.
158. Ibid.
159. Ibid.
160. Ibid.
161. Ibid.
162. Ibid., 279.

NOTES TO CHAPTER FOUR

1. Aleister Crowley, "At the Fork of the Roads," *Equinox* 1, no. 1 (1909): 101.
2. Ibid., 102.
3. Ibid., 105.
4. Ibid., 107.
5. Ibid., 108.
6. Ibid., 104.
7. Ibid., 108.
8. Oscar Wilde to Frank Harris, November 21, 1900, in *The Complete Letters of Oscar Wilde*, ed. Merlin Holland and Rupert Hart-Davis (New York: Henry Holt, 2000), 1207.
9. Bernard Muddiman, *The Men of the Nineties* (London: Henry Danielson, 1920), 120; Robert Sherard, *The Real Oscar Wilde* (London: T. Werner Laurie, 1916), 427.
10. From Smithers's "Prefatory Note" to the edition. Oscar Wilde, *The Harlot's House: A Poem by Oscar Wilde with Five Illustrations by Althea Gyles* (London: Mathurin, 1904), 8.
11. In Mackenzie's novel, Ariadne Berden, a character modeled on Gyles, is said to have "lost caste" following an affair with "an abominable creature of high intelligence." Faith Compton Mackenzie, *Tatting: A Novel* (London: Jonathan Cape, 1957), 12.
12. Yeats's relationship to Decadence was complicated. His writing in the 1890s was highly influenced by his contact with Wilde and other members of the Decadent Movement. Working with the *Savoy* and the Rhymers' Club brought him into extended contact with the Decadent aesthetic, and the impress of this contact is clear in the work he produced during this period. However, as Linda Dowling notes, "Yeats's long career as a poet was . . . continually to swerve between attraction toward and revulsion from the stylistic elaborations of literary Decadence." Dowling, *Language and Decadence in the Victorian Fin de Siècle* (Princeton, NJ: Princeton University Press, 1986), 248. He continued to struggle with his connections to the movement long after the century had turned. Although, as Dowling notes, he did portray himself as "the culminating figure of fin de siècle Decadence" in the second volume of his autobiography, *The Trembling of the Veil* (1922), he also

represented himself as a "survivor of the wreck" that was the "Tragic Generation" (244). Sheryl Denise Hoffer nevertheless insists that "Yeats remains to some degree a Decadent throughout his career, though by no means is the 20th century poet as purely and extremely Decadent as he was in the 1890s." See Hoffer, "The *Savoy* Poems of William Butler Yeats," *Language and Literature* 16 (1991): 75–76.

13. W. B. Yeats, *The Autobiography of William Butler Yeats* (New York: Collier Books, 1965), 160.
14. As Barbara A. Suess notes, "most of the plays Yeats wrote in the 1890s and early 1900s . . . partook in the centripetal motion of race identity formation" and focused on the "Irish hero-martyr types of bard, soldier, and lover willing to fight and die for the respective and honored traditions of the imaginative arts, love of country, and love itself." Suess, *Progress and Identity in the Plays of W. B. Yeats* (New York: Routledge, 2003), 53. Although Conor Cruise O'Brien has described early works such as *Cathleen ni Houlihan* as expressing a "manic nationalism," most critics have argued that in the 1910s, Yeats grew increasingly ambivalent about Irish nationalist violence. O'Brien, *Ancestral Voices: Religion and Nationalism in Ireland* (Chicago: University of Chicago Press, 1994), 124. However, as Jonathan Allison argues, although the later Yeats often "[questioned] the wisdom of self-sacrificial martyrdom," poems like "The Rose Tree" do offer "a stark celebration of the blood sacrifice associated with Pearse's brand of political martyrology." Allison, "Yeats and Politics," in *The Cambridge Companion to W. B. Yeats*, ed. Marjorie Howes and John Kelly (New York: Cambridge University Press, 2006), 193. For a discussion of Yeats's complex ideas about nationalist sacrifice in his later work, see Terry Eagleton's reading of "Easter 1916" in "History and Myth in 'Easter 1916,'" *Essays in Criticism* 21, no. 3 (1971): 248–60.
15. Simon Nowell-Smith, "The Turn of the Century," *The Saturday Book* 25 (1965): 12.
16. Matthew Beaumont, "Socialism and Occultism at the Fin de Siècle: Elective Affinities," *Victorian Review* 36, no. 1 (2010): 223.
17. Ibid.
18. Richard Kearney, *Myth and Motherland* (Derry, UK: Field Day Theatre Co., 1984), 9–10.
19. Yeats, *Autobiography*, 160.
20. Ibid.
21. Ian Fletcher, "Poet and Designer: W. B. Yeats and Althea Gyles," *Yeats Studies* 1 (1971): 43.
22. Ibid., 159.
23. Ibid., 168.
24. W. B. Yeats, "A Symbolic Artist and the Coming of Symbolic Art," *The Dome* 1 (1898): 232.
25. Fletcher, "Poet and Designer," 46.
26. L. W. Fennelly, "W. B. Yeats and S. L. Macgregor Mathers," in *Yeats and the Occult*, ed. George Hills Harper (New York: Macmillan, 1975), 288.

27. See Warwick Gould, "Margaret Alethea Gyles [known as Althea Gyles] (1868–1949), Artist and Poet," in *Oxford Dictionary of National Biography*, online ed., ed. Lawrence Goldman (Oxford: Oxford University Press, 2004), http://www.oxforddnb.com/view/article/59193.
28. Fletcher, "Poet and Designer," 46.
29. A. R. Grossman, *Poetic Knowledge in the Early Yeats: A Study of the Wind among the Reeds* (Charlottesville: University Press of Virginia, 1969), 47.
30. Ibid., 48.
31. For a discussion of the role of the concept of the symbol in the collaboration between Yeats and Gyles, see Arianna Antonielli, "Althea Gyles's Symbolic (De)Codification of William Butler Yeats's Rose and Wind Poetry," *Studi Irlandesi: A Journal of Irish Studies* 1, no. 1 (2011): 217–47, and Fletcher, "Poet and Designer." For a discussion of Gyles's covers for Yeats in light of his interest in collaboration with women, see R. C. McDonald, "Modernism and Cross-Gender Collaboration: W. B. Yeats, Marianne Moore, and D. H. Lawrence," PhD diss., University of Michigan, 2007. Grossman discusses Yeats's desire to generate a talismanic book in his *Poetic Knowledge in the Early Yeats*.
32. Declan Kiely, "Partnerships in Symbolic Book Craft: W. B. Yeats and His Cover Designers," *Biblion: The Bulletin of the New York Public Library* 8, no. 2 (2000): 55.
33. W. B. Yeats, *The Secret Rose, Stories by W. B. Yeats: A Variorum Edition*, ed. Philip Marcus (Ithaca, NY: Cornell University Press, 1981), 139.
34. Yeats, "A Symbolic Artist," 237.
35. Ibid., 236.
36. Quoted in Fletcher, "Poet and Designer," 54.
37. Althea Gyles, untitled and undated play, Papers of Althea Gyles, University of Reading Special Collections, Reading, UK, act I, scene I, 5.
38. Ibid., act II, scene II, 8.
39. Ibid., act II, scene II, 17.
40. Ibid., act I, scene II, 23.
41. According to Warwick Gould, the novel was written in 1919, after Grant Richards encouraged Gyles to write her memoir of the 1890s. Richards rejected the manuscript in 1921. Gould, "Margaret Alethea Gyles."
42. Althea Gyles, manuscript of unpublished novel, *Pilgrimage*, Papers of Althea Gyles, 75.
43. Ibid., 78.
44. Ibid., 38.
45. Ibid., 216.
46. Ibid., 210.
47. Seamus Deane, "Yeats, Ireland and Revolution," *The Crane Bag* 1, no. 2 (1977): 58.
48. W. H. O'Donnell, "Yeats as Adept and Artist," in *Yeats and the Occult*, ed. George Mills Harper (Toronto: Macmillan, 1975), 65.
49. Yeats, *Autobiography*, 160–61.

50. Ian Fletcher, "A Note on Althea Gyles," collection description, Papers of Althea Gyles.
51. Yeats, *Autobiography*, 161.
52. See Chapter 7, "After Armageddon," in Alex Owen, *The Place of Enchantment: British Occultism and the Culture of the Modern* (Chicago: University of Chicago Press, 2007).
53. W. B. Yeats, *The Speckled Bird*, ed. William H. O'Donnell (Toronto: McClelland and Stewart, 1976), 22.
54. Ibid., 58.
55. Joy Dixon, *Divine Feminine: Theosophy and Feminism in England* (Baltimore: Johns Hopkins University Press, 2001), 87.
56. W. B. Yeats to T. Fisher Unwin, February 1, 1899, in *The Collected Letters of W. B. Yeats, 1896–1900*, ed. Warwick Gould, John Kelly, and Deirdre Toomey (New York: Oxford University Press, 1998), 2:352.
57. Augustine Martin, "Apocalyptic Structure in Yeats's *Secret Rose*," *Studies: An Irish Quarterly Review* 64 (1975): 24.
58. Ibid., 28.
59. Yeats, *Secret Rose*, 126.
60. Ibid., 141.
61. Ibid., 136.
62. Ibid., 138.
63. Ibid., 139.
64. Ibid.
65. Ibid., 147–48.
66. Ibid., 148.
67. Ibid., 149.
68. John Wilson Foster, *Fictions of the Irish Literary Revival: A Changeling Art* (Syracuse, NY: Syracuse University Press, 1987), 76.
69. Yeats, *Secret Rose*, 139.
70. Ibid., 233.
71. Susan Harris, *Gender and Modern Irish Drama* (Bloomington: Indiana University Press, 2002), 23.
72. Ibid., 2.
73. Eleanor Farjeon, *Edward Thomas: The Last Four Years* (London: Oxford University Press, 1979), 186.
74. Clifford Bax to Mrs. Joyce Cazalet, February 24, 1949, Papers of Althea Gyles.
75. W. B. Yeats to Lady Gregory, December 12, 1900, in *Collected Letters of W. B. Yeats*, 2:603.
76. Jad Adams, *Madder Music, Stronger Wine: The Life of Ernest Dowson, Poet and Decadent* (New York: I. B. Tauris, 2001), 170.
77. Warwick Gould states that Gyles left Dublin for London in late 1891 or early in 1892. Gould, "Margaret Alethea Gyles."
78. Althea Gyles, autographed manuscript of a short novel titled *A Woman without a Soul*, Department of Manuscripts, National Library of Ireland.
79. Ibid.

80. Ibid.
81. Ibid.
82. Ibid.
83. Ibid.
84. Richard Kaye, "Oscar Wilde and the Politics of Posthumous Sainthood: Hofmannsthal, Mirbeau, Proust," in *Oscar Wilde and Modern Culture: The Making of a Legend*, ed. Joseph Bristow (Athens: Ohio University Press, 2008), 117.
85. Quoted in ibid., 111.
86. Ibid., 129–30.
87. Warwick Gould, "The Crucifixion of the Outcasts: Yeats and Wilde in the Nineties," in *Rediscovering Oscar Wilde*, ed. C. George Sandulescu (Gerrards Cross, UK: C. Smythe, 1994), 168.
88. Quoted in Fletcher, "Poet and Designer," 73.
89. Bonnie Robinson similarly notes that with the illustrations for "The Harlot's House," she began to "[reflect] her now uninhibited lifestyle in her uninhibited drawings." See Robinson, "Althea Gyles: A Black and White Artist," *Turn-of-the-Century Women* 5 (1990): 23.
90. Quoted in Fletcher, "Poet and Designer," 73.
91. Ibid.
92. W. B. Yeats to Lady Gregory, November 28–29, 1899, in *Collected Letters of W. B. Yeats,* 2:473.
93. Ibid., 473–74.
94. Ibid., 474.
95. Yeats, *Autobiography*, 160.
96. Quoted in Fletcher, "Poet and Designer," 62.
97. W. B. Yeats to Lady Gregory, December 21–22, 1899, in *Collected Letters of W. B. Yeats,* 2:480.
98. Ibid.
99. J. G. Nelson, *Publisher to the Decadents: Leonard Smithers in the Careers of Beardsley, Wilde, and Dowson* (State College: Pennsylvania State University Press, 2000), 273.
100. Quoted in ibid.
101. Arthur Symons to Rhoda Bowser, September 15, 1900, in *Arthur Symons: Selected Letters, 1880–1935*, ed. Karl Beckson and John Munro (New York: Macmillan, 1989), 162.
102. Ibid.
103. Ibid.
104. Ibid.
105. Ibid., 163.
106. Ibid.
107. Arthur Symons to Thomas B. Mosher, July 5, 1904, in ibid., 172.
108. Althea Gyles, "To Ireland," Edith Lister Papers, A. H. Bullen Collection, Shakespeare Centre Library and Archive, Stratford-upon-Avon, UK.
109. Yeats, *Secret Rose,* 233.

110. Althea Gyles, untitled and undated play, Papers of Althea Gyles, act I, scene II, 23.
111. A. E. Manning Foster, ed., *Lord God of Battles: A War Anthology* (London: Cope, 1914), 4.
112. Robert Bridges, "Thou Careless Awake," in ibid., 7.
113. Ibid., 8.
114. Quoted in Noshee Khan, *Women's Poetry of the First World War* (Lexington: University Press of Kentucky, 1988), 39.
115. Althea Gyles, "The Holy War," in Foster, *Lord God of Battles*, 46.
116. Khan, *Women's Poetry of the First World War,* 40.
117. Bridges, "Thou Careless Awake," 7.
118. Althea Gyles, "The Farm Hand," in Foster, *Lord God of Battles*, 32.
119. Kearney, *Myth and Motherland*, 9–10.
120. Gyles, "Farm Hand," 32.
121. Ibid.
122. John Meade [Althea Gyles], *Letters to Children about Drawing, Painting, and Something More* (London: Mills and Boon, 1914), 105.
123. Althea Gyles, "A Child's Christmas Carol: The Ox and the Ass," Papers of Althea Gyles.
124. Ibid.
125. Althea Gyles, "Winter," Papers of Althea Gyles.
126. Ibid.
127. Althea Gyles, "How the Prince of Peace Came Back," Edith Lister Papers, 2.
128. Ibid.
129. Ibid., 6.
130. Ibid.
131. Ibid., 7.
132. Althea Gyles, "The Love-Child," *Kensington* 1, no. 5 (1901): 174.
133. Althea Gyles, "Mary Magdalen," *New Age* 1, no. 18 (1907): 281.
134. Ibid.
135. Cecil French to Mrs. Joyce Cazalet, February 24, 1949, Papers of Althea Gyles.
136. Althea Gyles, "The Song of the Seine: To the Court of Kings," *Candid Friend* 1, no. 1 (1901): 13.
137. Althea Gyles, "From Rosamor Dead to Favonius for Whom She Died," *Academy* 71 (1906): 549.
138. W. B. Yeats to Florence Farr, September ?, 1908, in *Letters of W. B. Yeats*, ed. Allan Wade (New York: Macmillan, 1955), 511.
139. Fletcher, "Poet and Designer," 77.
140. Harris, *Gender and Modern Irish Drama*, 9.
141. Compton Mackenzie, *My Life and Times: Octave Four, 1907–1915* (London: Chatto and Windus, 1965), 38.
142. Ibid.
143. Ibid.
144. Ibid.

145. Farjeon, *Edward Thomas*, 185.
146. Ibid.
147. Ibid.
148. Ibid.
149. Ibid.
150. Ibid.
151. Ibid.
152. Ibid., 186.
153. Ibid.
154. Ibid.
155. Ibid., 187.
156. Faith Compton Mackenzie, *As Much As I Dare* (London: Collins, 1938), 129.
157. Ibid., 123.
158. Ibid., 188.
159. For further discussion of the relationship between Faith and Compton Mackenzie, see Andro Linklater, *Compton Mackenzie: A Life* (London: Chatto and Windus, 1987).
160. Faith Compton Mackenzie, *My Life and Times: Octave Five* (London: Chatto and Windus, 1971), 131.
161. Faith Compton Mackenzie, *As Much As I Dare*, 198.
162. Faith Compton Mackenzie, *Tatting*, 21.
163. Ibid., 79.
164. Ibid., 28.
165. Ibid., 34.
166. Ibid., 8.
167. Ibid.
168. Ibid., 9.
169. Ibid., 14.
170. Ibid., 31, 33.
171. Ibid., 97–98.
172. Ibid., 99.
173. Ibid., 154.
174. Eleanor Farjeon to Mrs. Joyce Cazalet, May 16, 1951, Papers of Althea Gyles.
175. Ibid.
176. Fletcher, "Poet and Designer," 79.
177. Gould, "Margaret Alethea Gyles."

NOTES TO CHAPTER FIVE

1. Quoted in Beresford Egan, *Epitaph* (London: Fortune Press, 1943), 9.
2. Ibid.
3. Ibid., 10.
4. Ibid., 9.
5. Beresford Egan, *But the Sinners Triumph: A Drypoint* (London: Fortune Press, 1934), 276.

6. Patrick Deer, *Culture in Camouflage: War, Empire, and Modern British Literature* (Oxford: Oxford University Press, 2009), 5.
7. Because Egan and Alcock's thinking on the topic of same-sex desire developed in relationship to their reading of Radclyffe Hall's *The Well of Loneliness*, I use the term *sexual inversion*, a term Hall draws from Havelock Ellis and relies on heavily, in this chapter. However, this term could at times conflate sexual object choice with gender identity, and, as I argue, Egan endeavors to disentangle these two elements of the concept of female sexual inversion from one another. This term is parsed and complicated in later sections of the chapter.
8. See, e.g., Laura Doan, "Sappho's Apotheosis? Radclyffe Hall's Queer Kinship with the Watchdogs of the Lord," *Sexuality and Culture* 8, no. 2 (2004): 80–106; Sonja Ruehl, "Inverts and Experts: Radclyffe Hall and the Lesbian Identity," in *Feminist Criticism and Social Change: Sex, Class and Race in Literature*, ed. Judith Newton and Deborah Rosenfelt, 165–80 (New York: Methuen, 1985); Martha Vicinus, *Intimate Friends: Women Who Loved Women, 1778–1928* (Chicago: University of Chicago Press, 2004), 22–23; Richard Dellamora, *Radclyffe Hall: A Life in the Writing* (Philadelphia: University of Pennsylvania Press, 2011).
9. Seton Peacey, unpublished proof of essay "Beresford Egan: Artist and Thinker," *The Preface* (May 1932): 12, Adrian Woodhouse Collection, UK.
10. See, e.g., Regenia Gagnier, "The Global Circulation of the Literatures of Decadence," *Literature Compass* 10, no. 1 (2013): 70–81.
11. Murray Schoonraad and Elzabé Schoonraad, *Companion to South African Cartoonists* (Johannesburg: Donker, 1989), 118.
12. Egan, *Epitaph*, 23.
13. Ibid.
14. Ibid., 24.
15. Ibid., 25.
16. Ibid., 13.
17. Ibid., 23.
18. Adrian Woodhouse, *Beresford Egan* (Leyburn: Tartarus Press, 2005), 8.
19. See ibid.
20. As Laura Doan notes, when critics discuss parodies of *The Well of Loneliness* such as *The Sink of Solitude*, they "have tended to read such works as an excoriation of Hall, her sexuality, and/or her novel." Doan, "Sappho's Apotheosis," 82. See, e.g., Ellen Bayuk Rosenman, "Sexual Identity and *A Room of One's Own*: 'Secret Economies' in Virginia Woolf's Feminist Discourse," *Signs* 14, no. 3 (1989): 640, and Laura L. Behling, *The Masculine Woman in America 1890–1935* (Urbana: University of Illinois Press, 2001), 133.
21. James Douglas, "A Book That Must Be Suppressed," *Sunday Express*, August 19, 1928, 10.
22. Woodhouse, *Beresford Egan*, 11. For further discussion of the career of P. R. Stephensen, see Craig Munro, *Inky Stephensen: Wild Man of Letters* (St. Lucia, Australia: University of Queensland Press, 1992).

23. Vera Brittain, *Radclyffe Hall: A Case of Obscenity* (South Brunswick, NJ: A. S. Barnes, 1969), 95.
24. Beresford Egan and P. R. Stephensen, *The Sink of Solitude* (London: Hermes Press, 1928).
25. Ibid.
26. I am highly indebted to Adrian Woodhouse throughout this chapter and in particular in my discussion of the composition of the verse that accompanied *The Sink of Solitude* and *The Policeman of the Lord.* During an interview at his home in summer 2010, Woodhouse shared with me his knowledge about how the collaborators divided the responsibilities for the composition of each work.
27. Egan and Stephensen, *Sink of Solitude.*
28. Ibid.
29. Una Troubridge, *The Life and Death of Radclyffe Hall* (London: Hammond, 1961), 104.
30. Michael Baker, *Our Three Selves: The Life of Radclyffe Hall* (New York: Morrow, 1985), 257.
31. Vicinus, *Intimate Friends*, 222.
32. Egan and Stephensen, *Sink of Solitude.*
33. Quoted in Woodhouse, *Beresford Egan*, 13.
34. Judith R. Walkowitz, *City of Dreadful Delight: Narratives of Sexual Danger in Late-Victorian London* (Chicago: University of Chicago Press, 1992), 139.
35. Dennis Denisoff, *Aestheticism and Sexual Parody 1840–1940* (New York: Cambridge University Press, 2006).
36. Doan, "Sappho's Apotheosis," 90.
37. Ibid. Doan notes, "With both a halo and a heart hovering above his head, Egan appears to be offering viewers a curious and potentially confusing message: is Jix competing for sainthood with the crucified St. Stephen/Hall or are the pair somehow linked?" (86).
38. Ibid., 90.
39. As Judith (Jack) Halberstam notes, "inversion as a theory of homosexuality folded gender variance and sexual preference into one economical package and attempted to explain all deviant behavior in terms of a firm and almost intuitive belief in a binary system of sexual stratification in which the stability of the terms 'male' and 'female' depended on the stability of the homosexual-heterosexual binary." Halberstam, *Female Masculinity* (Durham, NC: Duke University Press, 1998), 82. For further discussion of the link between same-sex sexuality and gender inversion in sexological discourse, see Gert Hekma, "'A Female Soul in a Male Body': Sexual Inversion as Gender Inversion in Nineteenth-Century Sexology," in *Third Sex, Third Gender: Beyond Sexual Dimorphism in Culture and History*, ed. Gilbert Herdt, 213–39 (New York: Zone Books, 1994).
40. Margaret Breen, "Narrative Inversion: The Biblical Heritage of *The Well of Loneliness* and *Desert of the Heart*," in *Reclaiming the Sacred: The Bible in Gay*

and Lesbian Culture (New York: Harrington Park Press, 1997), 195; Dellamora, *Radclyffe Hall*, 205.

41. Ruehl, "Inverts and Experts," 33.
42. Egan and Stephensen, *Sink of Solitude*.
43. Ibid.
44. Ibid.
45. Ibid.
46. Ruehl, "Inverts and Experts," 33.
47. Egan and Stephensen, *Sink of Solitude*.
48. Ibid.
49. Ibid.
50. Ibid.
51. See Celia Marshik, "History's 'Abrupt Revenges': Censoring War's Perversions in *The Well of Loneliness* and *Sleeveless Errand*," *Journal of Modern Literature* 26, no. 2 (2002): 145–59.
52. Douglas, "A Book That Must Be Suppressed," 10.
53. Marshik, "History's 'Abrupt Revenges,'" 147.
54. Woodhouse, *Beresford Egan*, 16.
55. Peacey, "Beresford Egan," 12.
56. Caterina Bower Alcock, "A Satirist among Us," *Arts and Crafts* 2, no. 2 (1928): 67.
57. Ibid.
58. Beresford Egan and C. Bower Alcock, *Baudelaire: Fleurs Du Mal in Pattern and Prose* (London: Sophistocles Press, 1929), 7.
59. Ibid., 8.
60. Ibid.
61. Ibid., 10.
62. R. A. Caton, prospectus for *De Sade: Being a Series of Wounds, Inflicted with Brush and Pen upon Sadistic Wolves Garbed in Masochists' Wool*, Adrian Woodhouse Collection.
63. Quoted in Woodhouse, *Beresford Egan*, 20.
64. Beresford Egan and Brian DeShane [Caterina Bower Alcock], *De Sade: Being a Series of Wounds Inflicted with Brush and Pen, upon Sadistic Wolves Garbed in Masochists' Wool* (London: Fortune Press, 1929).
65. Ibid.
66. Ibid.
67. Ibid.
68. Ibid.
69. Ibid.
70. Ibid.
71. See H. P. Clive, "Pierre Louÿs and Oscar Wilde: A Chronicle of Their Friendship," *Revue de Littérature Comparée* 43 (1969): 353–84.
72. Catharine Savage Brosman, "Pierre Louÿs," in *Nineteenth-Century French Fiction Writers: Naturalism and Beyond, 1860–1900* (Detroit, MI: Gale Research Incorporated, 1992), 175.

73. Ibid., 178.
74. Gretchen Schultz, "Terms of Estrangement: Renée Vivien's Construction of the Lesbian Subject," in *The Rhetoric of the Other: Lesbian and Gay Strategies of Resistance in French and Francophone Contexts* (New Orleans, LA: University Press of the South, 2002), 79, 90.
75. Pierre Louÿs, *Aphrodite: A Novel of Ancient Morals* (London: Fortune Press, 1928), 108.
76. Brosman, "Pierre Louÿs," 179.
77. David M. Earle, *Re-Covering Modernism: Pulps, Paperbacks, and the Prejudice of Form* (Burlington, VT: Ashgate, 2009), 187.
78. Beresford Egan to R. A. Caton, February 14, 1929, Beresford Egan Correspondence, Proofs, and Receipts, 1929, Rare Books and Manuscripts Special Collections Library, Pennsylvania State University, University Park.
79. Beresford Egan to R. A. Caton, June 2, 1929, Beresford Egan Correspondence, Proofs, and Receipts.
80. Chris Snodgrass, *Aubrey Beardsley: Dandy of the Grotesque* (Oxford: Oxford University Press, 1995), 88.
81. Ibid., 65.
82. Lucian and Pierre Louÿs, *Cyprian Masques* (London: Fortune Press, 1929), 15.
83. Ibid., 15–16.
84. Ibid., 17.
85. Ibid., 18–19.
86. See Talia Schaffer, *The Forgotten Female Aesthetes: Literary Culture in Late-Victorian England* (Charlottesville: University of Virginia Press, 2000), 122–58.
87. Ibid., 151.
88. Ibid.
89. Woodhouse states, "Anna Beryl . . . was clearly based on Caterina." Woodhouse, *Beresford Egan*, 26.
90. Beresford Egan, *Pollen: A Novel in Black and White* (London: Denis Archer, 1933), 4.
91. Ibid.
92. Ibid., 10.
93. Ibid., 26, 42.
94. Ibid., 132.
95. Ibid., 11.
96. Ibid., 10.
97. Ibid., 43.
98. Ibid.
99. Ibid., 47.
100. Oscar Wilde, *The Picture of Dorian Gray* (London: Ward, Lock, 1891), 28; Egan, *Pollen*, 167.
101. Ibid., 168.
102. Ibid., 274.

103. Ibid., 275.
104. Ibid., 311.
105. Ibid., 312.
106. Paul Allen, *Beresford Egan: An Introduction to His Work* (Lowestoft, UK: Scorpion Press, 1966), 26.
107. Egan, *But the Sinners Triumph*, 21.
108. Ibid., 23.
109. Ibid.
110. Ibid., 32–33.
111. Ibid., 41.
112. Ibid., 51.
113. Ibid., 11.
114. Ibid., 19.
115. Ibid., 19, 20.
116. Ibid., 116.
117. Ibid., 166.
118. Ibid., 199.
119. Ibid., 192.
120. Ibid., 200.
121. Ibid., 191.
122. Ibid., 234.
123. Ibid., 268.
124. Ibid., 275.
125. Ibid.
126. Ibid., 285.
127. Ibid.
128. Ibid., 276.
129. Ibid., 239.
130. Ibid., 240.
131. Woodhouse, *Beresford Egan*, 37.
132. Beresford Egan, *Epilogue* (London: Fortune Press, 1945).

NOTES TO AFTERWORD

1. "Wilde Centenary Tribute," *The Stage*, October 21, 1954, 1, 11.
2. Ibid., 11.
3. Ellen Crowell, "Mr. Gielgud Regrets: Panic at the Wilde Centenary," *The Center and Clark Newsletter* 50 (Fall 2009): 12.
4. Ibid., 14.
5. Ibid., 15.
6. Alan Hollinghurst, *The Swimming-Pool Library* (New York: Random House, 1989), 310.
7. Ibid., 325.
8. Joseph Bristow, "Being Gay: Politics, Identity, Pleasure," *New Formations* 9 (Winter 1989): 76.

9. Hollinghurst, *Swimming-Pool Library*, 207.
10. Ibid., 178.
11. Ibid., 62.
12. J. Stephen Murphy, "Past Irony: Trauma and the Historical Turn in *Fragments* and *The Swimming-Pool Library*," *Literature and History* 13, no. 1 (2004): 66.
13. Hollinghurst, *Swimming-Pool Library*, 178.
14. Ibid., 196.
15. Ibid., 150.
16. See Heather Love, *Loss and the Politics of Queer History* (Boston: Harvard University Press, 2007).
17. Joseph Bristow, *Effeminate England: Homoerotic Writing after 1885* (New York: Columbia University Press, 1995), 172. Richard Dellamora similarly notes that, although the coming catastrophe of AIDS is "never named, it is everywhere implied" in the novel. Dellamora, *Apocalyptic Overtures* (New Brunswick, NJ: Rutgers University Press, 1994), 173.
18. Peter Terzian, "Alan Hollinghurst, the Art of Fiction No. 214," *Paris Review* 199 (Winter 2011), http://www.theparisreview.org/interviews/6116/the-art-of-fiction-no-214-alan-hollinghurst.
19. Georges Letissier, "Alan Hollinghurst/Ronald Firbank," *Études britanniques contemporaines* 45 (2013), http://ebc.revues.org/742.
20. Susan Sontag, "Notes on Camp," in *A Susan Sontag Reader* (New York: Farrar, Straus, Giroux, 1982), 118.
21. Ibid., 105.
22. Ibid., 116, 118.
23. Ibid., 107.
24. Roger Luckhurst, "Queer Theory (and Oscar Wilde)," *Journal of Gender Studies* 4, no. 3 (1995): 336.
25. Bernard Muddiman, *The Men of the Nineties* (London: Henry Danielson, 1920), 19; Holbrook Jackson, *The Eighteen Nineties: A Review of Art and Ideas at the Close of the Nineteenth Century* (London: G. Richards, 1913), 12.

Bibliography

PRIMARY SOURCES

Archives Consulted

Adrian Woodhouse Collection, Teversal, UK.

Beresford Egan Correspondence, Proofs, and Receipts Collection, Pennsylvania State University's Eberly Family Special Collections Library, University Park.

BBC Written Archive, Reading, UK.

David Roth Collection of Frederick William Rolfe Papers, Columbia University's Rare Book and Manuscript Library, New York, NY.

Department of Manuscripts, National Library of Ireland, Dublin.

Edith Lister Papers, A. H. Bullen Archive, Shakespeare Centre Library and Archive, Stratford-upon-Avon, UK.

Helen Farr Sloan Library and Archive, Delaware Art Museum, Wilmington, DE.

Mark Samuels Lasner Collection, on loan to the University of Delaware Library, Newark, DE.

Max Beerbohm Collection, Merton College Library, Oxford University, Oxford, UK.

Papers of Althea Gyles, University of Reading Special Collections, Reading, UK.

University of Delaware Special Collections, Newark, DE.

Vernon Lee Collection, British Institute of Florence, Florence, Italy.

William Andrews Clark Memorial Library, University of California, Los Angeles.

Printed Sources

Alcock, Caterina Bower. "A Satirist among Us." *Arts and Crafts* 2.2 (1928): 67–69.

Anonymous. "The Decay of Satire." *Times Literary Supplement*, June 24, 1920, 389–90.

———. "New Books." *Manchester Guardian*, June 23, 1920, 7.

———. "Review of 'A Survey' and 'Rossetti and His Circle' by Max Beerbohm." *The Connoisseur: An Illustrated Magazine for Collectors* 64 (1922): 254–55.

———. "Review of *Proteus, or the Future of Intelligence* by Vernon Lee." *The Living Age* 326.4232 (1925): 386.

———. "Review of *Satan the Waster* by Vernon Lee." *Spectator*, May 9, 1930, 26.

______. "Rossetti, Laszlo, Zorn, and Sargent: Four Great Names." *Christian Science Monitor*, April 28, 1916, 8.

______. "Wilde Centenary Tribute." *The Stage*, October 21, 1954, 1, 11.

Beerbohm, Max. *A Christmas Garland*. London: William Heinemann, 1912.

______. "A Defence of Cosmetics." *The Yellow Book* I (1894): 65–82.

______. "A Letter to the Editor." *The Yellow Book* II (1894): 281–84.

______. *And Even Now*. London: William Heinemann, 1920.

______. *A Peep into the Past*. New York: M. Harzof, 1923.

______. *A Survey*. London: William Heinemann, 1921.

______. *Letters of Max Beerbohm, 1892–1956*. Edited by Rupert Hart-Davis. New York: W. W. Norton, 1989.

______. *Letters to Reggie Turner*. Edited by Rupert Hart-Davis. London: R. Hart-Davis, 1964.

______. *Lytton Strachey*. New York: Alfred A. Knopf, 1943.

______. *Mainly on the Air*. New York: Alfred A. Knopf, 1946.

______. *Observations*. London: William Heinemann, 1925.

______. *The Poets' Corner*. London: William Heinemann, 1904.

______. *Rossetti and His Circle*. London: William Heinemann, 1922.

______. *The Second Childhood of John Bull*. London: Stephen Swift, 1911.

______. *Seven Men*. London: William Heinemann, 1919.

______. *The Works of Max Beerbohm*. London: John Lane, The Bodley Head, 1896.

Bennett, Arnold. *Letters of Arnold Bennett*. Vol. III. Edited by James Hepburn. New York: Oxford University Press, 1970.

Bernard, L. L. "Review of *The Biology of War*." *The American Journal of Sociology* 25, no. 1 (1919): 96–97.

Bridges, Robert. "Thou Careless Awake." In *Lord God of Battles: A War Anthology*, edited by A. E. Manning Foster, 7–8. London: Cope, 1914.

Burdett, Osbert. *The Beardsley Period: An Essay in Perspective*. London: John Lane, 1925.

Butts, Mary. "Baron Corvo." *London Mercury* 30 no. 175 (1934): 619–24.

______. *Catalogue of an Exhibition Entitled "Ghosts."* London: E. Brown and Phillips, the Leicester Galleries, 1928.

Cloud, Yvonne. "Max Beerbohm." *The Graphic*, April 18, 1925, 610.

Cookman, Anthony Victor. "Max: An Enduring Cult." *Times Literary Supplement*, September 7, 1946, 426.

Country Life. "South African Tourism Board, Advertisement." October 6, 1928, xxxiii.

Corvine Society. "A True Recital of the Procedure of the First Banquet Held by the Corvine Society." 1929.

______. "A True Recital of the Procedure of the Second Banquet Held by the Corvine Society." 1929.

Corvo, Baron [Frederick Rolfe]. "About Beata Beatrice and the Mamma of San Pietro." *The Yellow Book* IX (1896): 93–101.

______. "About San Pietro and San Paolo." *The Yellow Book* VII (1895): 209–14.

———. "About the Lilies of San Luigi." *The Yellow Book* VII (1895): 214–24.
———. "A Caprice of the Cherubim." *The Yellow Book* IX (1896): 86–92.
———. *In His Own Image*. London: John Lane, The Bodley Head, 1901.
Crowley, Aleister. "At the Fork of the Roads." *Equinox* 1, no. 1 (1909): 101–8.
Douglas, James. "A Book That Must Be Suppressed." *Sunday Express*, August 19, 1928, 10.
Egan, Beresford. *But the Sinners Triumph: A Drypoint*. London: Fortune Press, 1934.
———. *Epilogue*. London: Fortune Press, 1946.
———. *Epitaph*. London: Fortune Press, 1943.
———. *Pollen: A Novel in Black and White*. London: Denis Archer, 1933.
Egan, Beresford, and C. Bower Alcock. *Baudelaire: Fleurs Du Mal in Pattern and Prose*. London: Sophistocles Press, 1929.
Egan, Beresford, and Brian DeShane [Caterina Bower Alcock]. *De Sade: Being a Series of Wounds Inflicted with Brush and Pen, upon Sadistic Wolves Garbed in Masochists' Wool*. London: Fortune Press, 1929.
Egan, Beresford, and P. R. Stephensen. *The Policeman of the Lord*. London: Sophistocles Press, 1929.
———. *The Sink of Solitude*. London: Hermes Press, 1928.
F., R. E. "Lady Lilith by Dante Gabriel Rossetti." *Bulletin of the Metropolitan Museum of Art* 3, no. 7 (1908): 144–45.
Farjeon, Eleanor. *Edward Thomas: The Last Four Years*. London: Oxford University Press, 1979.
Forster, Edward Morgan. *Abinger Harvest*. New York: Harcourt, Brace, 1936.
Foster, A. E. Manning, ed. *Lord God of Battles: A War Anthology*. London: Cope, 1914.
Fry, Roger. *Letters of Roger Fry*. Vol. II. Edited by Denys Sutton. London: Chattoand Windus, 1972.
———. "Rossetti's Water Colours of 1857." *The Burlington Magazine for Connoisseurs* 29, no. 159 (1916): 100–109.
Gagel, Mandy. "Selected Letters of Vernon Lee (1856–1935)." PhD diss., Boston University, 2008.
Goodrich, Lloyd. "*Rossetti and His Circle* by Max Beerbohm." *The Arts* 5 (1924): 293–94.
Grande, Constance, and Julian Grande. "Translator's Preface." In *The Biology of War*, by G. F. Nicolai, v–viii. London: J. M. Dent, 1919.
Gwynn, Stephen Lucius. *Experiences of a Literary Man*. London: Thornton Butterworth, 1926.
Gyles, Althea. "The Farm-Hand." In *Lord God of Battles: A War Anthology*, edited by A. E. Manning Foster, 32. London: Cope, 1914.
———. "From Rosamor Dead to Favonius for Whom She Died." *Academy* 71 (1906): 549.
———. "The Holy War." In *Lord God of Battles: A War Anthology*, edited by A. E. Manning Foster, 46. London: Cope, 1914.
———. "The Love-Child." *Kensington* 1, no. 5 (1901): 174.
———. "Mary Magdalen." *New Age* 1, no. 18 (1907): 281.

______. "The Song of the Seine: To the Court of Kings." *Candid Friend* 1, no. 1 (1901): 13.

Hobson, Harold. *The Devil in Woodford Wells: A Fantastic Novel.* London: Longmans, 1946.

Holland, Vyvyan. "Ronald Firbank." In *Ronald Firbank: A Memoir*, edited by Ifan Kyrle Fletcher, 101–12. New York: Brentano's, 1932.

Hollinghurst, Alan. *The Swimming-Pool Library.* New York: Random House, 1989.

House, Floyd N. "Review of the Today and Tomorrow Series." *The American Journal of Sociology* 31, no. 2 (1925): 271.

J., E. H. "A Posy for Rapallo." *Christian World*, August 28, 1952, 4.

Jackson, Holbrook. *The Eighteen Nineties: A Review of Art and Ideas at the Close of the Nineteenth Century.* London: G. Richards, 1913.

Kronenberger, Louis. "The Perfect Trifler." *The Saturday Review of Literature*, June 21, 1947, 9–10.

Le Gallienne, Richard. *The Romantic Nineties.* New York: Doubleday, 1925.

Lee, Vernon. "Bach's Christmas Music in England and Germany." *Jus Suffragii*, 1915, 218.

______. *Belcaro: Being Essays on Sundry Aesthetical Questions.* London: T. Fisher Unwin, 1887.

______. "Bismarck Towers." *New Statesman*, 1915, 481–83.

______. "Deterioration of the Soul." *Fortnightly Review* 59 (1896): 928–43.

______. *For Maurice.* London: The Bodley Head, 1927.

______. *The Golden Keys and Other Essays on the Genius Loci.* London: John Lane, The Bodley Head, 1925.

______. *Gospels of Anarchy and Other Contemporary Studies.* London: T. Fisher Unwin, 1908.

______. "The Heart of a Neutral." *Atlantic Monthly* 116 (1915): 687.

______. *Laurus Nobilis: Chapters on Art and Life.* London: John Lane, The Bodley Head, 1909.

______. *Miss Brown.* London: William Blackwood, 1884.

______. *Music and Its Lovers: An Empirical Study of Emotion and Imaginative Response to Music.* London: George Allen and Unwin, 1932.

______. *Peace with Honour.* London: Union of Democratic Control, 1915.

______. *The Poet's Eye.* London: Hogarth, 1926.

______. *Proteus, or the Future or Intelligence.* London: Kegan Paul, 1925.

______. *Renaissance Fancies and Studies.* London: Smith, Elder, 1895.

______. *Satan the Waster: A Philosophic War Trilogy.* London: The Bodley Head, 1920.

______. "The Sense of Nationality." *The Nation*, 1912, 96–98.

______. "Varieties of Musical Experience." *North American* 207 (1918): 748–57.

Lee, Vernon, and Clementina Anstruther-Thomson. "Beauty and Ugliness, I." *Contemporary Review* 72 (1897): 544–69.

______. "Beauty and Ugliness, II." *Contemporary Review* 72 (1897): 669–88.

Leverson, Ada. *Love at Second Sight.* London: Grant Richards, 1916.

______. *Tenterhooks.* New York: Mitchell Kennerley, 1912.

Louÿs, Pierre. *Aphrodite: A Novel of Ancient Morals.* London: The Fortune Press, 1928.

Lucian and Pierre Louÿs. *Cyprian Masques.* London: The Fortune Press, 1929.

Lynch, Bohun. *Max Beerbohm in Perspective.* London: William Heinemann, 1921.

Mackenzie, Compton. *My Life and Times: Octave Four, 1907–1915.* London: Chattoand Windus, 1965.

———. *My Life and Times: Octave Five.* London: Chatto and Windus, 1971.

———. *Sinister Street.* London: M. Secker, 1913–14.

Mackenzie, Faith Compton. *Always Afternoon.* London: Collins, 1943.

———. *As Much as I Dare.* London: Collins, 1938.

———. *Tatting: A Novel.* London: Jonathan Cape, 1957.

McBride, Henry. "Max Beerbohm's Rossetti." *Dial* 74 (1923): 206–8.

Meade, John [Althea Gyles]. *Letters to Children about Drawing, Painting, and Something More.* London: Mills and Boon, 1914.

Muddiman, Bernard. *The Men of the Nineties.* London: Henry Danielson, 1920.

New York Evening Post. "Today and Tomorrow Series, Advertisement." November 16, 1925, 11.

Nicolai, G. F. *The Biology of War.* London: J. M. Dent, 1919.

Nordau, Max. *Degeneration.* London: William Heinemann, 1895.

Pater, Walter. *Marius the Epicurean.* London: Macmillan, 1885.

———. "The School of Giorgione." *The Fortnightly Review* 22 (1877): 526–38.

———. *Studies in the History of the Renaissance.* London: Macmillan, 1873.

Playne, Caroline E. *The Neuroses of the Nations.* London: G. Allen and Unwin, 1925.

Rolfe, Frederick. "An Unforgettable Experience." *To-day*, April 21, 1894, 324–26.

———. *The Desire and Pursuit of the Whole: A Romance of Modern Venice.* London: Cassell, 1934.

———. *Hadrian the Seventh.* London: Chatto and Windus, 1904.

———. *Hubert's Arthur.* London: Cassel, 1935.

———. *Letters to James Walsh.* Edited by Donald Weeks. London: Bertram Rota, 1972.

———. *Nicholas Crabbe; or the One and the Many: A Romance.* London: Chatto and Windus, 1958.

———. *The Venice Letters.* Edited by Cecil Woolf. London: Cecil and Amelia Woolf, 1974.

Russell, Bertrand. "The Faultless Max at 80." *New York Times Magazine*, August 24, 1952, 18–19, 41.

Sassoon, Siegfried. *Siegfried Sassoon: Letters to Max Beerbohm with a Few Answers.* Edited by Rupert Hart-Davis. London: Faber and Faber, 1986.

Saturday Review of Literature. "Today and Tomorrow Series, Advertisement." April 14, 1928, 766.

Shaw, George Bernard. "A Political Contrast." *The Nation*, September 18, 1920, 758–60.

———. *Intelligent Woman's Guide to Socialism and Capitalism.* London: Constable, 1928.

Sherard, Robert. *The Real Oscar Wilde*. London: T. Werner Laurie, 1916.
Sparrow, Carroll Mason. "Phoebus, or the Future of Prophecy." *The Virginia Quarterly Review* 2, no. 2 (1926): 275–84.
Strunsky, Simeon. "About Books, More or Less: Here Are Babies." *New York Times*, January 25, 1925, BR4.
Symons, A. J. A. *A. J. A. Symons to Wyndham Lewis: Twenty-Four Letters.* Edited by Julian Symons. Edinburgh: Tragara Press, 1982.
______. ed. *An Anthology of "Nineties" Verse*. London: E. Matthews and Marrot, 1928.
______. "Editorial Notes." *The Book Collector's Quarterly* I (1930): v–viii.
______. *Frederick Baron Corvo*. London: Curwen Press, 1927.
______. *The Quest for Corvo: An Experiment in Biography*. New York: Macmillan, 1934.
Symons, Arthur. "The Decadent Movement in Literature." *Harper's New Monthly* 87 (1893): 858–68.
Trotter, Wilfred. *Instincts of the Herd in Peace and War*. London: T. Fisher Unwin, 1917.
Van Vechten, Carl. *Excavations*. New York: Knopf, 1926.
Waugh, Evelyn. "Lesson of the Master." *The Sunday Times*, May 27, 1956, 8.
Wilde, Oscar. *The Complete Letters of Oscar Wilde*. Edited by Merlin Holland and Rupert Hart-Davis. New York: Henry Holt, 2000.
______. *The Complete Works of Oscar Wilde*. Vol. IX. Edited by Josephine Guy. New York: Oxford University Press, 2007.
______. *The Harlot's House: A Poem by Oscar Wilde with Five Illustrations by Althea Gyles*. London: Mathurin, 1904.
______. *The Picture of Dorian Gray*. London: Ward, Lock, 1891.
______. "The Soul of Man under Socialism." *Fortnightly Review* XLIX (1891): 292–319.
Wilson, Edmund. *Classics and Commercials: A Literary Chronicle of the Forties*. New York: Farrar, Strauss, 1948.
Winwar, Frances. "Max Beerbohm at the Microphone." *New York Times*, January 26, 1947, BR4.
Woolf, Virginia. "The Modern Essay." In *The Common Reader*, 267–81. London: Hogarth, 1925.
Yeats, W. B. "A Symbolic Artist and the Coming of Symbolic Art." *The Dome* 1 (1898): 232–37.
______. *The Autobiography of William Butler Yeats*. New York: Collier Books, 1965.
______. *The Collected Letters of W. B. Yeats, 1896–1900*. Vol. II. Edited by Warwick Gould, John Kelly, and Deirdre Toomey. New York: Oxford University Press, 1997.
______. *The Letters of W. B. Yeats*. Edited by Allan Wade. New York: Macmillan, 1955.

———. *The Speckled Bird.* Edited by William H. O'Donnell. Toronto: McClelland and Stewart, 1976.

SECONDARY SOURCES

Adams, Jad. *Madder Music, Stronger Wine: The Life of Ernest Dowson, Poet and Decadent.* New York: I. B. Tauris, 2001.

Adorno, Theodor. *Aesthetic Theory.* Minneapolis: University of Minnesota Press, 1997.

Agathocleous, Tanya. "London Mysteries and International Conspiracies: James, Doyle, and the Aesthetics of Cosmopolitanism." *Nineteenth-Century Contexts* 26, no. 2 (2004): 125–48.

Alford, Norman. *The Rhymers' Club: Poets of the Tragic Generation.* New York: St. Martin's, 1996.

Allen, Paul. *Beresford Egan: An Introduction to His Work.* Lowestoft, UK: Scorpion Press, 1966.

Allison, Jonathan. "Yeats and Politics." In *The Cambridge Companion to W. B. Yeats,* edited by Marjorie Howes and John Kelly, 185–205. New York: Cambridge University Press, 2006.

Anderson, Amanda. *The Powers of Distance: Cosmopolitanism and the Cultivation of Detachment.* Princeton, NJ: Princeton University Press, 2001.

Antonielli, Arianna. "Althea Gyles's Symbolic (De)Codification of William Butler Yeats's Rose and Wind Poetry." *Studi Irlandesi: A Journal of Irish Studies* 1, no. 1 (2011): 217–47.

Baker, Michael. *Our Three Selves: The Life of Radclyffe Hall.* New York: Morrow, 1985.

Beaumont, Matthew. "Socialism and Occultism at the Fin De Siècle: Elective Affinities." *Victorian Review* 36, no. 1 (2010): 217–32.

Beer, Gillian. "The Dissidence of Vernon Lee: *Satan the Waster* and the Will to Believe." In *Women's Fiction and the Great War,* edited by Suzanne Raitt and Trudi Tate, 107–31. New York: Oxford University Press, 1997.

Behling, Laura L. *The Masculine Woman in America, 1890–1935.* Urbana: University of Illinois Press, 2001.

Behrman, S. N. *Portrait of Max.* New York: Random House, 1960.

Benkovitz, Miriam J. *Frederick Rolfe, Baron Corvo: A Biography.* London: Hamilton, 1977.

Billiani, Francesca, and Stefano Evangelista. "Carlo Placci and Vernon Lee: The Aesthetics and Ethics of Cosmopolitanism in Fin-De-Siècle Florence." *Comparative Critical Studies* 10, no. 2 (2013): 141–61.

Binnie, Eric. *The Theatrical Designs of Charles Ricketts.* Ann Arbor, MI: UMI Research Press, 1985.

Breen, Margaret. "Narrative Inversion: The Biblical Heritage of *The Well of Loneliness* and *Desert of the Heart.*" In *Reclaiming the Sacred: The Bible in Gay and Lesbian Culture,* edited by Raymond-Jean Frontain, 187–206. New York: Harrington Park Press, 1997.

Bristow, Joseph. "Being Gay: Politics, Identity, Pleasure." *New Formations* 9 (1989): 61–81.

———. *Effeminate England: Homoerotic Writing after 1885*. New York: Columbia University Press, 1995.

———, ed. Introduction to *Oscar Wilde and Modern Culture: The Making of a Legend*, 1–45. Athens: Ohio University Press, 2008.

Brittain, Vera. *Radclyffe Hall: A Case of Obscenity*. South Brunswick, NJ: A. S. Barnes, 1969.

Brockington, Grace. "Performing Pacifism: The Battle between Artist and Author in *The Ballet of the Nations*." In *Vernon Lee: Decadence, Ethics, Aesthetics*, edited by Catherine Maxwell and Patricia Pulham, 143–59. New York: Palgrave Macmillan, 2006.

Brophy, Brigid. *Prancing Novelist: A Defense of Fiction in the Form of a Critical Biography in Praise of Ronald Firbank*. New York: Macmillan, 1973.

Brosman, Catharine Savage. "Pierre Louÿs." In *Nineteenth-Century French Fiction Writers: Naturalism and Beyond, 1860–1900*, 173–87. Detroit, MI: Gale Research Incorporated, 1992.

Bürger, Peter. *Theory of the Avant-Garde*. Minneapolis: University of Minnesota Press, 1984.

Canning, Richard, ed. Introduction to *Vainglory: With Inclinations and Caprice*, xiii–vliv. London: Penguin, 2012.

Cary, Richard. "Shaw Reviews *Satan the Waster*." *Colby Quarterly* 9, no. 6 (1971): 335–47.

Cecil, David. *Max: A Biography*. London: Constable, 1964.

Clive, H. P. "Pierre Louÿs and Oscar Wilde: A Chronicle of Their Friendship." *Revue de Littérature Comparée* 43 (1969): 353–84.

Cohen, Ed. *Talk on the Wilde Side: Towards a Genealogy of a Discourse on Male Sexualities*. New York: Routledge, 1993.

Colby, Vineta. *Vernon Lee: A Literary Biography*. Charlottesville: University of Virginia Press, 2003.

Constable, Liz, Dennis Denisoff, and Matthew Potolsky, eds. Introduction to *Perennial Decay: On the Aesthetics and Politics of Decadence*, 1–32. Philadelphia: University of Pennsylvania Press, 1999.

Crook, Paul. *Darwinism, War and History: The Debate over the Biology of War from the "Origin of Species" to the First World War*. Cambridge: Cambridge University Press, 1994.

———. "Nature's Pruning Hook? War and Evolution, 1890–1918." *Australian Journal of Politics and History* 33, no. 3 (1987): 237–52.

Crowell, Ellen. "Mr. Gielgud Regrets: Panic at the Wilde Centenary." *The Center and Clark Newsletter* 50 (2009): 12–15.

———. "'We Are Odd!': Ye Archive of Ye Sette of Odd Volumes." *The Center and Clark Newsletter* 54 (2011): 9–10.

Cullen, Tom A. *A Playful Panther: The Story of J. Maundy Gregory, Con-Man*. Boston: Houghton Mifflin, 1975.

Danson, Lawrence. *Max Beerbohm and the Act of Writing.* New York: Oxford University Press, 1989.

———. "Max Beerbohm and the Mirror of the Past." *Princeton University Library Chronicle* 43, no. 2 (1982): 77–111.

Deane, Seamus. "Yeats, Ireland and Revolution." *The Crane Bag* 1, no. 2 (1977): 56–64.

Debelius, Margaret. "Countering a Counterpoetics." In *Women and British Aestheticism*, edited by Talia Schaffer and Kathy Psomiades, 192–210. Charlottesville: University of Virginia Press, 1999.

Deer, Patrick. *Culture in Camouflage: War, Empire, and Modern British Literature.* Oxford: Oxford University Press, 2009.

Dellamora, Richard. *Apocalyptic Overtures.* New Brunswick, NJ: Rutgers University Press, 1994.

———. *Friendship's Bonds: Democracy and the Novel in Victorian England.* Philadelphia: University of Pennsylvania Press, 2004.

———. "Productive Decadence: 'The Queer Comradeship of Outlawed Thought': Vernon Lee, Max Nordau, and Oscar Wilde." *New Literary History* 35 (2005): 529–46.

———. *Radclyffe Hall: A Life in the Writing.* Philadelphia: University of Pennsylvania Press, 2011.

———. "Vernon Lee's Moment." *Nineteenth-Century Gender Studies* 2, no. 2 (2006), http://www.ncgsjournal.com/issue22/dellamora.htm.

Denisoff, Dennis. *Aestheticism and Sexual Parody 1840–1940.* New York: Cambridge University Press, 2006.

———. "Decadence and Aestheticism." In *The Cambridge Companion to the Fin De Siècle*, edited by Gail Marshall, 31–52. New York: Cambridge University Press, 2007.

Dierkes-Thrun, Petra. *Salome's Modernity: Oscar Wilde and the Aesthetics of Transgression.* Ann Arbor: University of Michigan Press, 2011.

Dixon, Joy. *Divine Feminine: Theosophy and Feminism in England.* Baltimore: Johns Hopkins University Press, 2001.

Doan, Laura. "Sappho's Apotheosis? Radclyffe Hall's Queer Kinship with the Watchdogs of the Lord." *Sexuality and Culture* 8, no. 2 (2004): 80–106.

Dollimore, Jonathan. *Sexual Dissidence: Augustine to Wilde, Freud to Foucault.* New York: Oxford University Press, 1991.

Dowling, Linda C. *Language and Decadence in the Victorian Fin De Siècle.* Princeton, NJ: Princeton University Press, 1986.

Eagleton, Terry. "History and Myth in 'Easter 1916.'" *Essays in Criticism* 21, no. 3 (1971): 248–60.

Earle, David M. *Re-Covering Modernism: Pulps, Paperbacks, and the Prejudice of Form.* Burlington, VT: Ashgate, 2009.

Eastham, Andrew. *Aesthetic Afterlives: Irony, Literary Modernity and the Ends of Beauty.* New York: Continuum, 2011.

Feldman, Jessica. "Modernism's Victorian Bric-a-Brac." *Modernism/Modernity* 8, no. 3 (2001): 453–70.
______. *Victorian Modernism: Pragmatism and the Varieties of Aesthetic Experience.* New York: Cambridge University Press, 2002.
Fennelly, L. W. "W. B. Yeats and S. L. Macgregor Mathers." In *Yeats and the Occult,* edited by George Hills Harper, 285–306. New York: Macmillan, 1975.
Fletcher, Ian. "Poet and Designer: W. B. Yeats and Althea Gyles." *Yeats Studies* 1 (1971): 42–79.
Foster, John Wilson. *Fictions of the Irish Literary Revival: A Changeling Art.* Syracuse, NY: Syracuse University Press, 1987.
Franke, Damon. *Modernist Heresies: British Literary History, 1883–1924.* Columbus: Ohio State University Press, 2008.
Fraser, Hilary. "Writing in the Margins and Reading between the Lines in Vernon Lee's Library." In *Dalla Stanza Accanto: Vernon Lee E Firenze Settant'anni Dopo: Atti Del Convegno Internazionale Di Studi Firenze 26–27–28 Maggio 2005,* edited by Serena Cenni and Elisa Bizzotto, 231–41. Florence: University of Florence, British Institute and RegioneToscana, 2006.
Freedman, Jonathan. *Professions of Taste: Henry James, British Aestheticism and Commodity Culture.* Stanford, CA: Stanford University Press, 1990.
Gagnier, Regenia. "The Global Circulation of the Literatures of Decadence." *Literature Compass* 10, no. 1 (2013): 70–81.
______. *Individualism, Decadence and Globalization: On the Relationship of Part to Whole, 1859–1920.* New York: Palgrave Macmillan, 2010.
______. *The Insatiability of Human Wants: Economics and Aesthetics in Market Society.* Chicago: University of Chicago Press, 2000.
Gould, Warwick. "The Crucifixion of the Outcasts: Yeats and Wilde in the Nineties." In *Rediscovering Oscar Wilde,* edited by C. George Sandulescu, 167–92. Gerrards Cross, UK: C. Smythe, 1994.
______. "Margaret Alethea Gyles [Known as Althea Gyles] (1868–1949), Artist and Poet." In *Oxford Dictionary of National Biography,* online ed., ed. Lawrence Goldman. Oxford: Oxford University Press, 2004. http://www.oxforddnb.com/view/article/59193.
Green, Martin Burgess. *Children of the Sun.* New York: Basic Books, 1976.
Grossman, A. R. *Poetic Knowledge in the Early Yeats: A Study of the Wind among the Reeds.* Charlottesville: University Press of Virginia, 1969.
Halberstam, Judith. *Female Masculinity.* Durham, NC: Duke University Press Books, 1998.
Hall, N. John. "A Genre of His Own: Max Beerbohm's Title-Page Caricatures." *English Literature in Transition* 27, no. 4 (1984): 270–88.
______. *Max Beerbohm: A Kind of Life.* New Haven, CT: Yale University Press, 2002.
______. *Max Beerbohm Caricatures.* New Haven, CT: Yale University Press, 1997.
Harding, Alan. *England in the Thirteenth Century.* New York: Cambridge University Press, 1993.

Harris, Susan. *Gender and Modern Irish Drama*. Bloomington: Indiana University Press, 2002.

Hekma, Gert. "'A Female Soul in a Male Body': Sexual Inversion as Gender Inversion in Nineteenth-Century Sexology." In *Third Sex, Third Gender: Beyond Sexual Dimorphism in Culture and History*, edited by Gilbert Herdt, 213–39. New York: Zone Books, 1994.

Hoffer, Sheryl Denise. "The Savoy Poems of William Butler Yeats." *Language and Literature* 16 (1991): 75–126.

Holdstock, Douglas. "Wilfred Trotter and the Biosociology of Peace and War." *Medicine and War* 2 (1986): 43–50.

Hollinghurst, Alan. "Alan Hollinghurst, the Art of Fiction No. 214." Interview by Peter Terzian. *The Paris Review* 199 (Winter 2011), http://www.theparisreview.org/interviews/6116/the-art-of-fiction-no-214-alan-hollinghurst.

Hutcheon, L. "Irony, Nostalgia, and the Postmodern." In *Methods for the Study of Literature as Cultural Memory*, edited by Raymond Vervliet and Annemarie Estor, 189–207. Amsterdam: Rodopi, 1998.

———. *A Poetics of Postmodernism*. London: Routledge, 1988.

Ike, Ben. "On 'The Biology of War': The Work of the German Cardiologist G. F. Nicolai, a Herald of Modern Peace Research." *Medicine and War* 3 (1987): 33–42.

Jackson, H. J. "Writing in Books and Other Marginal Activities." *University of Toronto Quarterly* 62, no. 2 (1993): 217–31.

Jamison, Anne Elizabeth. *Poetics en Passant: Redefining the Relationship between Victorian and Modern Poetry*. New York: Palgrave Macmillan, 2009.

Johnson, Pamela. "The Fascination of the Paranoid Personality: Baron Corvo." *Essays and Studies* 16 (1963): 12–15.

Joyce, Simon. *The Victorians in the Rearview Mirror*. Athens: Ohio University Press, 2007.

Kandola, Sondeep. *Vernon Lee*. Devon, UK: Northcote House, 2008.

Kaye, Richard. "Oscar Wilde and the Politics of Posthumous Sainthood: Hofmannsthal, Mirbeau, Proust." In *Oscar Wilde and Modern Culture: The Making of a Legend*, edited by Joseph Bristow, 110–32. Athens: Ohio University Press, 2008.

Kearney, Richard. *Myth and Motherland*. Derry, UK: Field Day Theatre, 1984.

Khan, Noshee. *Women's Poetry of the First World War*. Lexington: University Press of Kentucky, 1988.

Kiely, Declan. "Partnerships in Symbolic Book Craft: W. B. Yeats and His Cover Designers." *Biblion: The Bulletin of the New York Public Library* 8, no. 2 (2000): 45–80.

Kirchknopf, Andrea. *Rewriting the Victorians: Modes of Literary Engagement with the 19th Century*. Jefferson, NC: McFarland, 2013.

Kohlke, Marie-Luise. "Introduction: Speculations in and on the Neo-Victorian Encounter." *Neo-Victorian Studies* 1, no. 1 (2008): 1–18.

Kucich, John, and Dianne F. Sadoff. *Victorian Afterlife: Postmodern Culture Rewrites the Nineteenth Century*. Minneapolis: University of Minnesota Press, 2000.

Laity, Cassandra. *H.D. and the Victorian Fin de Siècle: Gender, Modernism, Decadence*. New York: Cambridge University Press, 1996.

Lane, Christopher. *The Ruling Passion: British Colonial Allegory and the Paradox of Homosexual Desire*. Durham, NC: Duke University Press, 1995.

Letissier, Georges. 2013. "Alan Hollinghurst/Ronald Firbank: Camp Filiation as an Aesthetic of the Outrageous." *Études britanniques contemporaines* 45 (2013), http://ebc.revues.org/742.

Linklater, Andro. *Compton Mackenzie: A Life*. London: Chatto and Windus, 1987.

Livesey, Ruth. *Socialism, Sex, and the Culture of Aestheticism in Britain, 1880–1914*. New York: Oxford University Press for the British Academy, 2007.

Llewellyn, Mark. "What Is Neo-Victorian Studies?" *Neo-Victorian Studies* 1, no. 1 (2008): 164–85.

Love, Heather. *Feeling Backward: Loss and the Politics of Queer History*. Boston: Harvard University Press, 2007.

Luckhurst, Roger. "Queer Theory (and Oscar Wilde)." *Journal of Gender Studies* 4, no. 3 (1995): 333–40.

Mahoney, Kristin. "Haunted Collections: Vernon Lee and Ethical Consumption." *Criticism* 48, no. 1 (2006): 39–67.

Maltz, Diana. *British Aestheticism and the Urban Working Classes, 1870–1900: Beauty for the People*. New York: Palgrave Macmillan, 2005.

______. "Engaging 'Delicate Brains': From Working-Class Enculturation to Upper-Class Lesbian Liberation in Vernon Lee and Kit Anstruther-Thomson's Psychological Aesthetics." In *Women and British Aestheticism*, edited by Talia Schaffer and Kathy Psomiades, 211–29. Charlottesville: University of Virginia Press, 1999.

Mao, Douglas, and Rebecca Walkowitz. "The New Modernist Studies." *PMLA* 123, no. 3 (2008): 737–48.

Marcus, Laura. "The Newness of the 'New Biography': Biographical Theory and Practice in the Early Twentieth Century." In *Mapping Lives: The Uses of Biography*, edited by Peter France and William St. Clair, 193–218. New York: Oxford University Press, 2002.

Marshik, Celia. "History's 'Abrupt Revenges': Censoring War's Perversions in *The Well of Loneliness* and *Sleeveless Errand*." *Journal of Modern Literature* 26, no. 2 (2002): 145–59.

Martin, Augustine. "Apocalyptic Structure in Yeats's *Secret Rose*." *Studies: An Irish Quarterly Review* 64, no. 253 (1975): 24–34.

Maxwell, Catherine, and Patricia Pulham. *Vernon Lee: Decadence, Ethics, Aesthetics*. New York: Palgrave Macmillan, 2006.

McLeod, Kirsten. "Making It New, Old School: Carl Van Vechten and Decadent Modernism." *Symbiosis* 16, no. 2 (2012): 209–24.

McMahon, Gary. *Camp in Literature*. Jefferson, NC: McFarland, 2006.

McWilliam, Rohan. "Victorian Sensations, Neo-Victorian Romances: Response." *Victorian Studies* 52, no. 1 (2009): 106–13.

Medd, Jodie. "'The Cult of the Clitoris': Anatomy of a National Scandal." *Modernism/Modernity* 9, no. 1 (2002): 21–49.

Miller, Jonathan. “Crowds and Power: Some English Ideas on the Status of Primitive Personality.” *The International Review of Psychoanalysis* 10 (1983): 253–64.

Mills, Stephen. Introduction to *Victorianism in the United States: Its Era and Its Legacy*, edited by Steve Ickingrill and Stephen Mills, ix–xxi. Amsterdam: VU University Press, 1992.

Moore, Doris Langley-Levy. *E. Nesbit: A Biography*. Philadelphia: Chilton, 1966.

Munro, Craig. *Inky Stephensen: Wild Man of Letters*. St. Lucia, Australia: University of Queensland Press, 1992.

Murphy, J. Stephen. “Past Irony: Trauma and the Historical Turn in *Fragments* and *The Swimming-Pool Library*.” *Literature and History* 13, no. 1 (2004): 58–75.

Murray, Alex. “Decadence Revisited: Evelyn Waugh and the Afterlife of the 1890s.” *Modernism/Modernity* (forthcoming).

Musser, Charles. “The Hidden and the Unspeakable: On Theatrical Culture, Oscar Wilde and Ernst Lubitsch’s Lady Windermere’s Fan.” *Film Studies* 4 (2004): 12–47.

Nelson, J. G. *Publisher to the Decadents: Leonard Smithers in the Careers of Beardsley, Wilde, Dowson*. State College: Pennsylvania State University Press, 2000.

Nowell-Smith, Simon. “The Turn of the Century.” *The Saturday Book* 25 (1965): 9–17.

O’Brien, Conor Cruise. *Ancestral Voices: Religion and Nationalism in Ireland*. Chicago: University of Chicago Press, 1994.

O’Donnell, W. H. “Yeats as Adept and Artist.” In *Yeats and the Occult*, edited by George Mills Harper, 55–79. Toronto: Macmillan, 1975.

Owen, A. *The Place of Enchantment: British Occultism and the Culture of the Modern*. Chicago: University of Chicago Press, 2007.

Pelling, Henry. “Baron Corvo and Labour.” *Labour Review* V (1960): 35–36.

———. “Corvo and Labour Politics.” *Times Literary Supplement*, February 6, 1969, 137.

Potolsky, Matthew. “Decadence, Nationalism, and the Logic of Canon Formation.” *Modern Language Quarterly* 67, no. 2 (2006): 213–44.

———. *The Decadent Republic of Letters: Taste, Politics, and Cosmopolitan Community from Baudelaire to Beardsley*. Philadelphia: University of Pennsylvania Press, 2012.

Praz, Mario. *The Romantic Agony*. Translated by Angus Davidson. New York: Oxford University Press, 1985.

Prettejohn, Elizabeth. *Art for Art’s Sake: Aestheticism in Victorian Painting*. New Haven, CT: Yale University Press, 2008.

Price, Claire. “The Last of the Exquisites.” *New York Times Magazine*, September 10, 1939, 14.

Propriety and Honours: Interim Findings, Fourth Report of Session 2005–06. London: Stationery Office, 2006.

Psomiades, Kathy Alexis. "'Still Burning from This Strangling Embrace': Vernon Lee on Desire and Aesthetics." In *Victorian Sexual Dissidence*, edited by Richard Dellamora, 21–41. Chicago: University of Chicago Press, 1999.

Pulham, Patricia. "Violence and the Pacifist Body in Vernon Lee's *The Ballet of the Nations*." In *Conflict, Nationhood and Corporeality in Modern Literature: Bodies-at-War*, edited by Petra Rau, 46–63. New York: Palgrave Macmillan, 2010.

Robbins, Ruth. "Vernon Lee: Decadent Woman?" In *Fin de Siècle/Fin du Globe*, edited by John Stokes, 139–61. New York: St. Martin's, 1992.

Robinson, Bonnie. "Althea Gyles: A Black and White Artist." *Turn-of-the-Century Women* 5 (1990): 18–25.

Rosenman, Ellen Bayuk. "Sexual Identity and *A Room of One's Own*: 'Secret Economies' in Virginia Woolf's Feminist Discourse." *Signs* 14, no. 3 (1989): 634–50.

Rosenthal, Donald. *The Photographs of Frederick Rolfe*. Hanover, NH: Elysium Press, 2008.

Ross, Margery. *Robert Ross: Friend of Friends*. London: Jonathan Cape, 1952.

Roth, David. "A Corvo Collection." *Desiderata* 4 (February 1955): 1–4.

Ruehl, Sonja. "Inverts and Experts: Radclyffe Hall and the Lesbian Identity." In *Feminist Criticism and Social Change: Sex, Class and Race in Literature*, edited by Judith Newton and Deborah Rosenfelt, 165–80. New York: Methuen, 1985.

Sadoff, Dianne F. *Victorian Vogue: British Novels on Screen*. Minneapolis: University of Minnesota Press, 2010.

Schaffer, Talia. *The Forgotten Female Aesthetes: Literary Culture in Late-Victorian England*. Charlottesville: University of Virginia Press, 2000.

Schoonraad, Murray, and Elzabé Schoonraad. *Companion to South African Cartoonists*. Houghton: A. D. Donker, 1989.

Schultz, Gretchen. "Terms of Estrangement: Renée Vivien's Construction of the Lesbian Subject." In *The Rhetoric of the Other: Lesbian and Gay Strategies of Resistance in French and Francophone Contexts*, 79–100. New Orleans, LA: University Press of the South, 2002.

Scoble, Robert. "The Corvine Banquets of 1929." *The Book Collector* 56, no. 1 (2007): 66–74.

———. *Raven: The Turbulent World of Baron Corvo*. London: Strange Attractor, 2013.

Sedgwick, Eve Kosofsky. *Between Men: English Literature and Male Homosocial Desire*. New York: Columbia University Press, 1985.

———. *Epistemology of the Closet*. Berkeley: University of California Press, 1990.

Sherry, Vincent. *Modernism and the Reinvention of Decadence*. New York: Cambridge University Press, 2014.

Showalter, Elaine, ed. *Daughters of Decadence: Women Writers of the Fin-de-Siècle*. New Brunswick, NJ: Rutgers University Press, 1993.

Sinfield, Alan. *The Wilde Century: Oscar Wilde, Effeminacy and the Queer Moment*. London: Cassell, 1994.

Snodgrass, Chris. *Aubrey Beardsley: Dandy of the Grotesque*. Oxford: Oxford University Press, 1995.

Sontag, Susan. "Notes on Camp." In *A Susan Sontag Reader*, 115–19. New York: Farrar, Straus, Giroux, 1982.

Stepan, Nancy Leys. "'Nature's Pruning Hook': War, Race, and Evolution, 1914–18." In *The Political Culture of Modern Britain*, edited by J. M. W. Bean, 129–48. New York: Columbia University Press, 1987.

Stetz, Margaret. "The Afterlives of Aestheticism and Decadence in the Twenty-First Century." *Victorian Literature and Culture* 38, no. 1 (2010): 306–11.

Suess, Barbara A. *Progress and Identity in the Plays of W. B. Yeats, 1892–1907*. New York: Routledge, 2003.

Symons, Julian. *A. J. A. Symons: His Life and Speculations*. London: Eyre and Spottiswoode, 1950.

Teukolsky, Rachel. *The Literate Eye: Victorian Art Writing and Modernist Aesthetics*. New York: Oxford University Press, 2009.

Tibballs, Geoff. *The World's Greatest Hoaxes*. New York: Barnes and Noble, 2006.

Tontiplaphol, Betsy Winakur. *Poetics of Luxury in the Nineteenth Century: Keats, Tennyson, and Hopkins*. Burlington, VT: Ashgate, 2011.

Troubridge, Una. *The Life and Death of Radclyffe Hall*. London: Hammond, Hammond, 1961.

Vicinus, Martha. *Intimate Friends: Women Who Loved Women, 1778–1928*. Chicago: University of Chicago Press, 2004.

Vogeler, Martha S. *Austin Harrison and the English Review*. Columbia: University of Missouri Press, 2008.

Walkowitz, Judith R. *City of Dreadful Delight: Narratives of Sexual Danger in Late-Victorian London*. Chicago: University of Chicago Press, 1992.

Walkowitz, Rebecca. *Cosmopolitan Style: Modernism beyond the Nation*. New York: Columbia University Press, 2006.

Waugh, Thomas. *Hard to Imagine: Gay Male Eroticism in Photography and Film from Their Beginnings to Stonewall*. New York: Columbia University Press, 1996.

Weeks, Donald. *Corvo*. London: Michael Joseph, 1971.

———. *Frederick William Rolfe and Artists' Models*. Edinburgh: Tragara Press, 1981.

Weir, David. *Decadence and the Making of Modernism*. Amherst: University of Massachusetts Press, 1995.

———. *Decadent Culture in the United States: Art and Literature against the American Grain, 1890–1926*. Albany: State University of New York Press, 2007.

White, Patricia. "Nazimova's Veils: Salome at the Intersections of Film History." In *A Feminist Reader in Early Cinema*, edited by Jennifer Bean and Diane Negra, 60–87. Durham, NC: Duke University Press, 2002.

Woodhouse, Adrian. *Beresford Egan*. Leyburn, UK: Tartarus Press, 2005.

Wright, Patrick. *Iron Curtain: From Stage to Cold War*. New York: Oxford University Press, 2007.

Zorn, Christa. *Vernon Lee: Aesthetics, History, and the Victorian Female Intellectual*. Athens: Ohio University Press, 2003.

Index